So
What?

So What?

THE
Writer's
Argument

Second Edition

Kurt Schick
Laura Schubert
both of
James Madison University

New York   Oxford
Oxford University Press

Oxford University Press is a department of the University of Oxford.
It furthers the University's objective of excellence in research,
scholarship, and education by publishing worldwide. Oxford is a
registered trade mark of Oxford University Press in the UK and certain
other countries.

Published in the United States of America by Oxford University Press
198 Madison Avenue, New York, NY 10016, United States of America.

© 2017 by Oxford University Press

Library of Congress Cataloging-in-Publication Data
Names: Schick, Kurt, 1964- author. | Schubert, Laura, author.
Title: So what? : the writer's argument / Kurt Schick, Laura Schubert.
Description: Second edition. | New York ; Oxford : Oxford University Press,
    [2017] | Includes index.
Identifiers: LCCN 2016015624| ISBN 9780190297404 | ISBN 9780190297411
Subjects: LCSH: English language--Rhetoric--Study and teaching. | Report
    writing--Study and teaching (Higher)
Classification: LCC PE1404 .S337 2017 | DDC 808/.0071/1--dc23 LC record
available at https://lccn.loc.gov/2016015624

9 8 7 6 5 4 3 2 1

Printed by LSC Communications, United States of America

contents

Contents

preface

ACADEMIC WRITING confounds many college students—not because they lack sophistication, but because of the natural expertise that they already possess. Decades of real-world language use have taught them that authentic writing involves a genuine audience, purpose, and context—all of which school writing seems to lack.

So What? The Writer's Argument approaches college reading, writing, and argument as scholarly activities and treats students as apprentice scholars. *So What?* gives writing a real audience, purpose, and context by teaching apprentice scholars authentic styles, organizing structures, and persuasive moves that they can use in writing classes and beyond. This book introduces students to many of the thought processes, motivations, and strategies that scholars use to answer questions, to solve problems, and to defend their ideas.

To the Instructor

Professors, employers, and politicians agree that college students should learn to write well, but not everyone agrees how or why. Should writing classes prepare students to write in their majors? Should we teach writing skills for the workplace, or for citizenship? Should we focus on the processes of writing or critical thinking, or on various types and technologies of writing? Which approach will have the greatest impact?

Learning how to write arguments accomplishes many of these outcomes at once. By blending communication with problem solving, argumentation prepares students to use language and thinking so they can participate effectively in their academic, civic, and professional communities. As writing scholar David Fleming explains, arguing teaches a process of "reasoning with others."

Still, teaching argument doesn't magically solve a challenge that writing teachers and students inevitably face: motivation. What kinds of authentic arguments can students make while in school? How can they discover something interesting to argue about when academic writing often seems like regurgitating the words and thoughts of others? Too often, students cannot imagine significant reasons for writing other than for a grade and some blurry sense of audience and purpose. Left without reasons to care about their writing, students (and their readers) are often left wondering, *so what?* Students and faculty need an approach that teaches argument as useful and meaningful.

The Scholarly Apprentice Model

Our solution is not to separate academic writing from the "real" world but to teach it as an authentic activity. We invite students to participate in scholarly argument, to apprentice alongside their scholarly mentors (professors) who use writing to understand the world and engage others. Our apprentice model elevates students by treating them as colleagues. Redefining students as scholarly apprentices invites them to become active citizens of the scholarly community from which they often feel disconnected or even alienated.

This book seeks to open students' eyes to the notion of the academy—a place where scholars debate, create, and communicate knowledge. *So What?* treats students as apprentices with less experience and knowledge but with equal potential to contribute to the vibrant conversations that characterize higher education. Given the opportunity to create knowledge—for themselves and sometimes for others—students are more likely to make what they're doing matter.

The apprentice–scholar framework in *So What?* gives students a meaningful way to view academic writing, one that they can use to understand the technical moves of argumentation. Rather than defining argument only as persuasion, designed primarily to change people's minds, we teach students how to use argumentation to create knowledge, promote understanding, and bridge differences—the way experienced scholars do. Scholarly argument seeks to enlighten, to open new areas of discussion, and to advance society, not primarily to convert or persuade.

In addition to motivating students and legitimizing their work as apprentices, by training them to think like scholars, *So What?* teaches students habits of mind that will benefit them personally and professionally. While we champion the vision of the classical liberal arts, we also recognize students' and society's desire for practical education that prepares graduates to transition quickly and smoothly into the workforce and civic life. Rather than focusing on specific genres or technical knowledge, we believe the most transferable skills that students can learn through argument are scholarly habits of mind that writing teachers can model and teach.

Transferability

Recent studies indicate that introductory writing classes may not bring as many long-term benefits as we once imagined. Students do not automatically "transfer" what they learn into their major studies ("near" transfer), and they don't always apply the skills and understanding to new contexts outside of school ("far" transfer).

To improve transfer, we must imagine learning outcomes that can be woven through the curriculum—skills, habits, and knowledge that will be relevant in many different situations. Recently, organizations of writing teachers and professors (the Council of Writing Program Administrators, the National Council of Teachers of English, and the National Writing Project) developed an inventory of "intellectual and practical" habits of mind that "will support students' success in a variety of fields and disciplines" (http://wpacouncil.org/framework). *So What?* reinforces these habits through each chapter:

- **Engagement**—"a sense of investment and involvement in learning." We introduce scholarly argument as a means of engagement and the writing process as an investment worth students' time and effort. We present argument as a tool to discover, communicate, and revise what we know, think, and believe.
- **Curiosity**—"the desire to know more about the world." We encourage students to follow an inquiry-based writing process, inspired by questions, careful reading, and analysis. Apprentice scholars learn how to discover compelling questions and problems and situate their arguments within scholarly conversations.
- **Creativity**—"the ability to use novel approaches for generating, investigating, and representing ideas." Our chapter on creating a compelling thesis explains that behind every relevant, significant, and original thesis is a compelling, challenging, and controversial question or problem awaiting a creative response. Descriptions of stylistic choices throughout the book encourage students to approach writing creatively.
- **Openness**—"the willingness to consider new ways of being and thinking in the world." Our chapter on supporting arguments helps students effectively choose and evaluate evidence and other sources. Arguing in conversation with sources helps students understand the value of enlarging their perspectives.
- **Metacognition**—"the ability to reflect on one's own thinking as well as on the individual and cultural processes used to structure knowledge." A chapter on organization and development shows students how to structure arguments to meet their audience's needs, and another chapter on finding faults provides practice in scrutinizing reasoning. Many of the exercises throughout the book stimulate students' metacognitive thinking skills.

- **Persistence**—"the ability to sustain interest in and attention to short- and long-term projects." Several of the chapters encourage students to investigate issues exhaustively and to defer conclusions until weighing all evidence and assumptions. Practicing scholarly argument as case building helps students see knowledge building as an iterative process.

- **Responsibility**—"the ability to take ownership of one's actions and understand the consequences of those actions for oneself and others." A chapter on using sources models how to design arguments by responsibly borrowing and building on the words and thoughts of others. Responsibility can also be developed by collaborating with others, as writers often do in a classroom that focuses on argument.

- **Flexibility**—"the ability to adapt to situations, expectations, or demands." The introductory chapters on rhetoric and scholarly processes—along with our attention to style throughout the book—maintain students' focus on the craft of writing, developing a tool kit of options that can be adapted for various audiences, purposes, genres, and contexts.

Contents

We have arranged the book's contents in the order that makes most sense to us and to our reviewers. However, writing and research processes are neither neat nor linear, so you may find it useful to assign chapters in whatever sequence works best for your class. *So What?* begins by explaining how a scholarly apprenticeship can build skills, knowledge, and habits that students can use throughout college and in their personal and professional lives. Chapters 2 and 3 focus on college-level literacy, guiding students toward a more sophisticated, adaptive process of reading, writing, and using sources. Chapters 4 and 5 teach students how arguments work and how to analyze them effectively. From Chapter 6 onward, we explain how to create and develop arguments for various purposes and audiences, explaining how to support, organize, and troubleshoot arguments. The final chapter—along with exercises throughout the book—focuses on developing a more flexible, deliberate writing style. Appendices provide techniques for peer review and collaboration, along with common layouts for various argument genres.

Our approach to argumentation continues the classical and modern rhetorical tradition, owing heavily to Aristotle, Cicero, and Stephen Toulmin. Although we do introduce some fundamentals of rhetoric (stasis questions, appeals, fallacies, genre, and style), we do not overwhelm students with unnecessary technical jargon or theory. We also do not attempt to introduce every scholarly style or genre, or even specific disciplinary research techniques; rather, we attempt to teach students how to learn these things for themselves by providing them with heuristics and tools that help them think like writers and scholars.

We have attempted to write in a style that would be straightforward and engaging. In doing so, we risk oversimplifying complex theories and practices of argument that scholars have been developing and debating for the past 2,000 years. As a selection and interpretation of that tradition, the book is itself a kind of argument. We anticipate that both students and instructors will find points of clarification and points of disagreement with our work. Indeed, we hope that readers will use the book to generate discussion, debate, and inspiration for further investigation.

Features

- CHAPTER CHECKLISTS present the key topics included in each chapter.
- CONSIDER THIS activities embedded in each chapter provide opportunities for students to reflect on the book's content and style and on their own writing. These exercises maintain a focus on the craft of writing throughout the book.

- TRY THIS exercises allow students to practice or investigate what they learn immediately via short exercises that can be used in class or as homework.
- WHAT'S NEXT features conclude each chapter with activities and assignments that help students transfer and apply what they've learned into other classes and beyond school.

In addition:

- APPENDICES at the end of the book provide quick guides for peer review and collaboration, and for organizing arguments. Students can refer to these guides to complement their writing and reading process.
- READINGS include a brief scholarly article; a student essay; an annotated magazine article; and a sample, draft rhetorical analysis with peer review comments.

To the Student

Many new college students either think that they already know how to write well (because teachers told them so and they believed it) or they cannot write well (because teachers told them so and they believed it). Both perspectives contradict the idea that writers can always improve their craft. Probably the most important factor for learning to write, or do most anything else, is to embrace a "growth mindset"—a belief that practice pays off. After all, none of us were born knowing how to speak or walk or drive a car, either. **Thinking that your writing ability is "fixed" or biologically predetermined nearly guarantees that you won't improve.**

Most students who saw themselves as "good writers" before college eventually discover that whatever formulas they mastered previously cannot guarantee their success in college or beyond. For example, knowing how to write research reports or five-paragraph themes with correct grammar and citations will not necessarily enable you to perform the following tasks:

- For your environmental science class: Write a public policy recommendation on hydraulic fracturing ("fracking") for natural gas based on current laws, economic factors, and scientific research.
- For your boss: Write a memo justifying why your team cannot complete a project on time in accordance with your client's contract.
- For your local planning commission: Write a letter requesting a zoning exception so you can build an addition to your house that violates existing code.

Each of these tasks would require you to adapt your message for a different audience, purpose, topic, and type of writing. The good news is that you can learn to be a more adaptable writer by studying and practicing the kind of arguments that scholars use to discover, improve, and communicate ideas.

Similarly, learning more about argument can help if you've struggled with writing in the past. The most important challenges of writing in college or in the workplace are not grammar and punctuation (although those are also important for many readers). Good writing is not just pretty words and sentences but carefully crafted ideas. **The most difficult part of producing good writing is finding something significant and compelling to write about.**

So What? will teach you how to invent and present significant, compelling arguments. The core lessons will teach you how to discover controversies or public problems to argue about, plus patterns of organizing and supporting arguments that address those controversies. Mastering these techniques will help you find something substantial to write about in almost any situation.

Creating arguments to solve problems that matter to others is a powerful and valued skill in college and in the workplace. Why not seize the opportunity to learn these essential habits of mind now? Your professors, through years of study and practice, have mastered the arts of argument in the subjects they teach. Take advantage of your apprenticeship with these master scholars. As you learn their craft, you can build the kind of expertise that makes college worth your investment.

Changes to the Second Edition

In response to feedback from faculty and students who used the first edition, this edition features the following revisions:

- Simplified terminology and expanded explanations for elements of rhetoric and argumentation and incorporated more examples and exercises to illustrate and explain concepts
- Substantially reorganized content to frame scholarly argument within college and everyday literacy practices
- Added an annotated reading and sample rhetorical analysis with peer review commentary
- Added original illustrations, created by an undergraduate writing tutor

acknowledgments

THE AUTHORS WISH TO THANK many colleagues for their excellent contributions, including Emiline Buhler, Kathy Clarke, Jared Featherstone, Kevin Jefferson, Lucy Malenke, Karen McDonnell, Paige Normand, Justin Thurston, and Jim Zimmerman. Thanks to Garon Scott and the team at Oxford University Press for their support in publishing this second edition—and to Maya Chandler for creating original drawings to illustrate our ideas. We are indebted to Frederick Speers, development editor for the first edition, who first imagined this book and who provided wisdom and generous guidance to see it through.

We appreciate the help of many outside reviewers in strengthening the first edition manuscript, including Clark Draney, College of Southern Idaho; Christopher Ervin, Western Kentucky University; Jeff Pruchnic, Wayne State University; Brooke Champagne, University of Alabama; Greg Hagan, Madisonville Community College; Danielle Zawodny Wetzel, Carnegie-Mellon University; Megan Swihart Jewell, Case Western Reserve University; Cheryl Edelson, Chaminade University; Dave Badtke, Solano Community College; Andrew Higl, Winona State University; George Cusack, University of Oklahoma; Gina Weaver, Southern Nazarene University; Susie Crowson, Del Mar College; Anthony Cavaluzzi, SUNY Adirondack; Joe Musser, Ohio Wesleyan University; Tisha Turk, University of Minnesota-Morris; Brian Walter, St. Louis College of Pharmacy; Michael Morgan, Bemidji State University; Jessica Gravely, Prairie State College; Eileen Abrahams, Schenectady County Community

College; Eleanor Welsh, Chesapeake College; Andrew Scott, Ball State University; and Stephanie Mood, Grossmont College. Thank you as well to those reviewers who helped with reviews for the second edition: Rebecca Addy, University of Nebraska at Kearney; Jill Anderson, Tennessee State University; Diann Baecker, Virginia State University; Joshua Borgmann, Southwestern Community College; Kristi Costello, Arkansas State University; Vanessa Cozza, Washington State University; Joshua Dickinson, Jefferson Community College; Michael Donnelly, Ball State University; Marjorie Ellenwood, La Sierra University; Tyler Fleming, University of Louisville; Amanda Freeman, James Madison University; Mary Beth Kwenda, Black Hills State University; Jennifer Marlow, The College of Saint Rose; Bonnie Markowski, University of Scranton; Mark Meritt, University of San Francisco; Christine Murray, Texas A&M University–College Station; Jun Okada, SUNY Geneseo; Kelly Rivers, Pellissippi State Technical Community College; Leslie Roberts, Oakland Community College; Keaghan Turner, Coastal Carolina University; Paul Walker, Murray State University; Gina Weaver Yount, Southern Nazarene University; Eloise Whisenhunt, Young Harris College; Julia Whyde, Casper College; Gregory Winston, Husson University; and Susan Wright, William Paterson University.

We received invaluable feedback from many students in our first-year writing classes, especially Nathan Boone, Taylor Coats, Danielle Camiso, Erin Dooley, Kaitlyn Keyser, Jordan Lewis, Nick Love, Liz Mott, Will Mullery, Laura Nettuno, Trygve Rorvig, Jessie Seymour, Olivia Smithey, Tyler Young, Cameron Yudkin, and also outstanding suggestions from tutors in our University Writing Center.

We are also indebted to our past teachers and mentors who instructed and inspired us, particularly Jim Corder, Becky Howard, Bob Jacobs, Robert Keys, Joseph Petraglia, Gary Tate, Robert Carballo,

Patricia King, Jay B. Landis, Janet Martin, Gretchen McTavish, Kenneth Morefield, Virginia Schlabach, and Beverly Schneller.

Finally, we want to thank our families for their encouragement, patience, and wisdom. We are especially grateful for their support and care—and for cheering us on.

So
What?

CHAPTER one

What's the Purpose of Scholarly Writing

chapter checklist

- What does scholarly writing achieve?
- How can we use writing to improve our lives?
- What distinguishes scholarly writing?
- How can rhetoric deepen our understanding of communication?

For many students, academic writing seems awkward or pointless. Even if you've been a successful writer in school, you've probably encountered some assignments that ask you to do things that don't make much sense. What's the point, for example, of endlessly practicing five-paragraph essays? Why, you might wonder, must I use MLA citation format for my bibliography? Why does my teacher demand six sources (only two of which can be from the Internet)? And *so what* if I use Wikipedia?

We wrote this book to reveal the motivations behind academic writing and to help you understand how creating arguments, in particular, can teach you things that will be useful to you in college, in work, and in life. Writing can be empowering: it gives us a voice and an opportunity to say something meaningful and significant. When we write about something, we stretch our minds and we learn more deeply. When faced with a writing task, we have the potential to change the world in some small way—even if it's just to inspire or pester or provoke one reader—and to change our own minds about something. Writing and arguing are *active*, and they can even be fun.

So, What's the Point of Scholarly Writing?

You may not realize this, but you're already an expert communicator. You were using language before you could walk. And despite criticisms that "people don't read or write enough these days," we actually do so more than our ancestors ever did. With Google, Facebook, Wikipedia, Twitter, and text messaging at our fingertips, many of us consume and produce writing constantly, with sophistication that we're still trying to understand. So, although we might not read books the way our grandparents did, we may very well be the best information foragers and social networkers who ever walked this planet.

Our natural expertise may also be the reason why academic writing seems so baffling at times. Decades of real-world language use have taught us that authentic communication involves a genuine audience, purpose, and context—all of which academic writing seems to lack. What's the point, for example, of writing a paper about the deeper meanings of Shakespeare for your English teacher, who likely knows and cares more about literature than his students probably do? Or, why should a teacher really care about students' opinions on, say, legalizing marijuana? In either case, the reader or writer may be left wondering: *so what?*

A Scholar's Work—in College and Beyond

The *so what?* question can only be answered if you understand how and why scholarly writing works as a genuine form of communication, with real audiences and purposes. To begin, you should know that higher education has two interrelated functions:

- To *communicate* knowledge
- To *create* knowledge

Professors not only teach; many are also professional scholars who, in various ways, work to investigate humanity's endless supply of unanswered questions and unsolved problems. In fact, human progress depends on posing and answering such questions, from the most broad and consequential ("How might humans live together peacefully?") to the specific and seemingly obscure ("How does climate change affect the migration patterns of ruby-throated hummingbirds?"). Scholars, such as professors and other researchers, are experts at advancing what we know by investigating such questions. What's potentially exciting about college is that you might have an opportunity to learn from professors who literally "wrote the book" on the subjects you're studying.

College will provide you with an opportunity to *apprentice* as a scholar. Just as an artist, mechanic, or teacher might practice under the mentorship of an expert, you will learn how master scholars discover and communicate knowledge. As an apprentice, you can begin making sense of how and why scholars use writing and argument to expand the bounds of human understanding.

Why Bother?

By now, you might be wondering how you might reasonably be expected to "expand the bounds of human understanding." After all, aren't you mostly in college to learn what others have been discovering for the last few thousand years—or simply to get a good job? Who ever said that you wanted to become a professional scholar, anyway? How will all this make you a better citizen, professional, or worker?

Our answer: **You'll use the skills, knowledge, and habits that you learn as an apprentice scholar throughout college and in your personal and professional life.** As an undergraduate student, you won't really be expected to cure cancer, end world hunger, or design an income tax system that actually makes sense but rather to *practice* some of the skills that are necessary to do such things.

TRY THIS ➤   Set Some Goals for Yourself

TRY THIS exercises will give you an opportunity to practice or investigate chapter content.

For this exercise, seek outside expertise to help you set some goals for developing as a writer. Chances are good that you have friends or relatives who are established in the workplace (or maybe you have extensive work experience yourself). Whether or not they attended college, working professionals know something about what characteristics contribute to a successful career. They might even be in a position to hire new employees. Call or e-mail a few of them and ask the following questions:

- What skills would you look for when screening applicants?
- What do you think are the most important things for me to learn in college?
- What's the role of writing and continued learning in your work?

Scholarly Habits of Mind

Whether or not you plan to become a professional scholar, developing the skills and habits that scholars use can help you succeed in college and beyond. For example, you'll be more likely to notice what others overlook, to solve problems creatively, and to make decisions independently. People who are well educated, either by schooling or by years of life experience, exhibit habits of mind that others can learn.

Your apprenticeship will teach you how to think like a well-educated person. How, you might ask, do well-educated people think?

- Well-educated people **make decisions carefully and take their time**. They appreciate that the world is complicated, that there's more to most issues than meets the eye, so they understand the importance of studying an issue from multiple viewpoints, gathering as much information as possible before rushing to judgment.
- By practicing scholarly argument, well-educated people learn that they must **carefully explain and support their conclusions for others to scrutinize**. They understand that their readers won't let them off the hook with half-baked assertions, judgments, or decisions.
- Well-educated people know that **everyone's perspective, including their own, is limited**. That's why educated people practice critical thinking, which involves looking carefully for errors in reasoning.

Learning how scholars think and write is one of the best ways to develop these educated habits of mind. People who are well educated about how arguments work can craft logically sound, persuasive cases that benefit them personally and professionally. For example, citizens rely on their critical thinking skills when they spot the tricks that politicians use to get their vote or that advertisers use to entice consumers to buy things they don't really need. A company's chief executive officer, or CEO, thinks like a scholar when she compares competing business proposals and selects the most viable and profitable option. A physical therapist thinks like a scholar when he develops an evidence-based treatment plan that will withstand the scrutiny of a health insurance company. An entry-level worker thinks like a scholar when she builds a bulletproof case for a pay raise. And so forth. The point is that whether or not you see yourself as a scholar, thinking like one can make you more successful in college and beyond.

CONSIDER THIS ➤ Nonsexist Language

Occasionally, we'll pause so can you reflect on the content of the chapter, your own writing, or the stylistic choices we've made while writing. These mini-lessons should remind you that whenever you read, you should pay close attention not just to what you're reading about but also to how it's written. Even if you disagree with the decisions a writer makes, it's worth your time to stop, study, and collect a few more techniques for your writing tool kit.

For this reflection, consider why we alternate between using "he" and "she." Most academic disciplines now advocate or require that scholars use nonsexist language. A common but confusing question is how to use third-person pronouns. Decades ago, writers would always use masculine pronouns (he, him, his) unless referring to a specific female person. To support equality, scholarly writers eventually adopted *gender-neutral* language by using "he/she" or sometimes "s/he." Because these versions seemed clunky, many writers now alternate between "she" and "he," as we have chosen to do in this book.

What do you think of our decision? Can you think of better ways to be gender neutral? Do you think this really matters? Why or why not?

The Rhetorical Situation

This book carries on an educational tradition that's more than 2,000 years old, a tradition in which you've participated all your life, whether you've known it or not. That tradition is the study of *rhetoric*: the investigation of how communication works, with particular emphasis on argument and persuasion. Studying and practicing rhetoric was important as far back as the early democracies of Greece and Rome, whose citizens used various kinds of argument to solve problems, settle disputes, and build consensus. Throughout this book, you'll learn elements of rhetoric that will help you ask compelling questions, select reliable sources, dig for better data, and recognize weak or deceptive arguments—all of which will make you a better reader and writer.

We've already been building up to the first lesson about rhetoric: To be an effective communicator, you should always **pay careful attention not just to the contents of your message but also to your intended audience and purpose.** These elements—audience, purpose, and message—are the main components of what we call the *rhetorical situation.* Rather than seeing writing simply as lifeless words and ideas on a page (or on a computer or mobile screen), scholars think of reading and writing as social activities—a conversation that involves real people and human motivations.

Analyzing Rhetorical Elements

Understanding rhetorical elements will help you become a more deliberate, adaptable communicator. Think of rhetoric as a flexible tool for problem solving: **These rhetorical principles will help you figure out how to proceed when you don't already know what to do in a communication situation.** They will help you read and write more effectively by helping you orient yourself in situations that you've never encountered before—and they will reveal things you probably never noticed about already familiar situations.

Begin by thinking of communication as an interconnected framework involving an author (writer or speaker), an audience (reader or listener), and a message (written text, speech, or image)—all interacting for some purpose within a specific social context or setting.

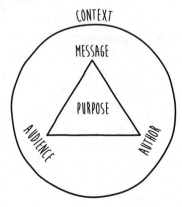

7

This rhetorical triangle helps us understand that meaning is not simply the contents or subject matter of a message. Authors and audiences *create* meaning by writing and reading messages, and they do so within contexts that shape that meaning.

An easy way to remember these rhetorical elements is to ask yourself the investigative questions that reporters and detectives use: *who?*, *what?*, *when?*, *where?*, *why?*, and *how?* Whenever you read or write, ask yourself questions related to these primary categories. To emphasize our attention to the *so what?* question, we begin with *why*.

Why? (*So What?*)

- *Inspiration* of the writer: What is the author's motivation? What question, problem, or other inspiration prompted him to write?
- *Purpose* of the message: How is the message supposed to affect the audience? What function does the message serve?
- *Implications* for the reader: Why is this a significant topic for the audience? What are the larger consequences and applications?

Who? (*Author, Audience*)

- *Author*: How does the author establish his credibility? What might readers already know about the author that could influence how they interpret the message?
- *Audience(s)*: Who is the intended audience? Are there other readers? What is the audience's background (age, gender, income, education, values)? What assumptions or biases might readers have about the topic?
- *Roles*: What "role" is the writer playing? For example, is he playing the part of an anxious parent? Frustrated customer? Concerned physician? Passionate volunteer? What's the audience's role? Jury? Boss? Teacher? Peer reviewer?

When and Where? (*Context*)

- *Timing*: When was the message published? Is there something about the timing that might be significant to an audience?
- *Publication*: Where was the message published? For example, did it appear in a scholarly journal, a popular magazine, or on the Internet? What does the publication venue suggest about the text's audience, purpose, and credibility?
- *Place*: In what setting and culture was the message published?

What and How? (*Message*)

- *Thesis*: Does the message contain an explicit or implied thesis, or main point?
- *Supports*: How much (and what kind of) background information does the author present? What kinds of evidence or examples does the message use?
- *Genre*: Does the message follow a recognizable genre, such as a business proposal, newspaper editorial, or research article?
- *Style*: What kind of tone do you notice? Is it serious, funny, sarcastic, scholarly, arrogant, immature, or what? Which words stick out? What hints do they give you about the author's purpose and audience?
- *Design*: What design elements are used? Does the design seem informal, playful, ordinary, formal, technical, or what? How does the message use charts, images, or other visual elements?

If you read only for content—as students often do with assigned readings—you may overlook the bigger picture and deeper meaning of what you read. You will miss the opportunity to develop more quickly as a reader, writer, and scholar if you don't slow down to examine communication as a complex social interaction.

Let's consider an example to illustrate our point: the rhetorical situation of this book. We, the coauthors, are experienced college writing teachers. We also tutor writers from all over campus, so we've helped thousands of students with all kinds of writing in many different subjects. Knowing that about us can help you understand where we're coming from and maybe even trust us more than, say, your friends or relatives, to give good advice about college writing. Wherever you, our intended audience, are right now, we are thinking about you as we write, trying to explain ideas in ways that will make sense, seem interesting, and be most useful to you.

You should also try to imagine our motivations and context. Why did we choose to write this book? On the one hand, writing is part of our occupation. To be successful in a college like ours, professors must publish. For us, though, writing this book is more than just a job. We're especially interested in the *problems* that this book attempts to solve:

- What are the most important things that students should know about writing in college and in life?
- How can we present those topics in fresh and interesting ways?
- How can we translate our expertise in writing and rhetoric into something that's useful for students who may not like to write and probably have never formally studied rhetoric?

Knowing our motivations for writing this book can help you comprehend and even evaluate our message, including our stylistic choices. If, for instance, our purposes were different—such as to provide a comprehensive description of Western rhetorical theory or to explain the advanced intricacies of argumentation—this book would read very differently. We would likely have used a more formal style and included more technical details. A change in purpose has a ripple effect on content, style, organization, and so forth.

Our point is that if any of the rhetorical variables in a situation change (such as the audience or context), so does the meaning. Failing to consider the rhetorical situation—whenever you read, whatever you're reading—means that you're missing parts of the message, and you may even misunderstand the message completely.

Scholarly Writing as a Rhetorical Activity

Examining scholarly writing through a rhetorical lens can reveal how it is similar to and different from other kinds of communication.

- **Scholarly writing has real *purposes* based in problems that interest the participants.** In Chapter 5, we discuss common categories of problems, for example: "How should we interpret X?" "What caused Y?" "What should we do about Z?" Each of these questions prompts a different kind of scholarly investigation and a distinct kind of writing designed to answer the question.
- **Scholarly writing addresses specific *audiences*.** Unlike some school writing that seems to be intended for no particular reader, scholarly arguments always address a specific group of people, often defined as a specialized academic *discipline*—for example, chemical engineers or US Civil War historians.
- **Scholarly writing belongs to larger conversations, histories, and *contexts* that determine the rules for what counts as good communication.** Lawyers use established courtroom procedures, rules of evidence, and precedents to build a case. Similarly, to establish new knowledge in a discipline, scholars must know what methods of reasoning are typical, what kinds of evidence are acceptable, and what other scholars have already said about the subject.

Along with the similarities between scholarly and everyday arguments, there are also some important distinctions to keep in mind:

- **Scholarly writing addresses sophisticated, *demanding audiences*.** Scholars will expect that you examine your subject from different angles, that you anticipate other perspectives or counterarguments, that you validate your evidence, and so on.
- **Scholarly writing pursues *knowledge, not victory*.** Unlike advertising or political campaigns, scholars use writing to communicate

and create knowledge, rather than merely to persuade their audience. Because winning isn't the ultimate goal, *how* we communicate is just as important as *what* we communicate about. In fact, in college you will often be judged more on how you develop and defend your ideas than on the ideas themselves. For instance, in a literature class, your professor will evaluate your interpretation of a poem based on the evidence you provide to support your thinking, rather than whether you arrived at a single "right" answer. Remember, your goal in college is to apprentice as a knowledge-maker. The "product" of this learning is not so much *what* you make as learning *how to make*.

Understanding these characteristics can help you make sense of why scholars make specific stylistic moves and rhetorical choices. For instance, the point of following MLA citation practices or addressing readers' counterarguments makes more sense when you remember that scholars typically write for specific, demanding audiences. The technical details of scholarly writing become much more meaningful within this framework.

So What?

Scholars read and write to answer three basic questions:

1. How do we know what we know?
2. Why do we believe what we believe?
3. How can we improve what we know and believe?

Remember throughout your scholarly apprenticeship that most professors want to hear what *you* think. They will encourage and expect you to demonstrate your knowledge, to exercise your critical thinking skills, and to take some intellectual risks. Typically, they don't want you to regurgitate old knowledge and reuse familiar formulas. We hope you'll take them up on the challenge, using writing as a tool to discover, communicate, and revise what you know, think, and believe.

In the next chapter, we will explain how you can use the rhetorical principles we've described so far to develop a more flexible, sophisticated process for reading and writing. This foundation will prepare you to read, analyze, and write in a variety of rhetorical situations. In Chapter 3, we'll describe how to select and incorporate sources that will help you engage in scholarly discussions. After that, we will begin to explore one of the main tools that scholars use to communicate and solve problems—*argument*, which happens to be a crucial but often confusing feature of scholarly writing, and is therefore the focus of the rest of this book.

What's Next

WHAT'S NEXT features will help you transfer and apply what you've learned into other classes and beyond school. Take what you've learned in this chapter and respond to the following prompts.

1. **Seeing yourself as a scholar.** Write a 1,000-word essay that introduces your intellectual interests and motivations to your instructor and your classmates. Use the following questions to get you started:
   - Think back on previous writing assignments and try to remember one that you liked the most and one that you liked the least. What inspired or discouraged you? What motivates you—or *might* motivate you—to write?
   - What do you want to know more about? What questions inspire you most? What beliefs do you want to interrogate and understand? Identify some significant questions—related to your major or to your life—that spark your curiosity.

2. **Analyzing audiences.** College classes often assign readings that were not originally intended for a student audience. To get the most out of such readings, it's helpful to imagine how the original readers might have responded to a message. We can begin by looking for

clues about those primary audience members. One kind of clue is called a *paratext*, which includes textual elements that originally accompanied the reading, for example, a book cover or other articles published within a magazine, newspaper, or website. Advertisements yield especially useful clues about intended audiences.

For this activity, select three different communication media (such as a commercial website, a television news program, and a popular print magazine). Scrutinize several of the advertisements and analyze what they indicate about the identity of the intended audience members (for example, their age, political affiliations, level of education, interests, values). Then, share your notes with a classmate, present your findings to the class, or write about your analysis for an outside audience.

3. **Writing and researching in your discipline.** Interview a professor in your discipline to learn about writing and research practices in your field. Then, write a two-page summary of your professor's comments. Some sample questions that you might consider asking are as follows:
   - What is the purpose of research?
   - How do scholars think and analyze in this discipline?
   - What "moves" (such as explicitly stating the thesis early in an argument or using personal opinion to support a claim) do you expect students to make in their papers? What features do you value most in student writing?
   - How do scholars in our discipline write? What does their writing process look like?

If you were to present this interview to an audience, you could add a photograph of the person being interviewed or a video or audio clip. Can you think of ways that this might make your presentation more persuasive? Do you think this would add something substantive or just add unnecessary ornamentation?

CHAPTER two

How Do Scholars Read and Write

chapter checklist

- When, why, and how do we read sources?
- How do experienced writers structure their writing processes?
- How can we improve our writing processes?

Scholarly writing is a conversation. By publishing their views, findings, and arguments, scholars build on each other's work. However, before beginning a project, scholars typically review what others have said before. They "listen" awhile to get their bearings and to ensure they know what's already been established. Although scholars frequently conduct research to update or corroborate previous work, topics lose their compelling luster if others have already covered the subject sufficiently. Just as jokes become less funny when heard over and over, scholars lose interest in rehashing questions that have already been settled. That's why, **for scholars, the writing process usually begins with reading.** Reviewing the work of current and previous scholars gives us a sense of what topics interest our scholarly community, what gaps or questions still need investigation, and where we might contribute to the ongoing conversation. Therefore, scholars usually begin the writing process by reading sources (journal articles, books, and other scholarly references), which can help us:

- Verify whether our work will yield fresh understanding
- Begin collecting information to answer our research questions
- Provide context for our investigation by relating our study to other scholars' work
- Borrow methods of investigation or theories that worked for other scholars
- Identify views, assumptions, or conclusions to build on or diverge from

Starting the writing process by reading other scholars' work helps us learn what has already been said and explain how our contribution or approach is different. Ideally, then, we'll be able to offer readers some *news*.

Read Like a Scholar

In their daily routines, scholars read much more than they write. As an apprentice, your primary means of learning will be reading other scholars' work. Of course, you'll spend plenty of time listening to lectures or participating in class discussions, but much of your learning will be on your own, reading books or articles assigned by your professors. Reading is more difficult than many students realize or care to admit. Although reading for comprehension may seem simple when the content is familiar, the kind of reading required for analyzing ideas and arguments can be quite challenging. Fully comprehending scholarly writing requires careful, thoughtful, and analytical reading.

Challenges to Effective Reading

You may already think you are a good reader. These days, we seem to be reading all the time, but we read differently than our parents or grandparents did. Immersed in electronic texts, most of us have become good (although we could always become better) at "surfing," or literally, skimming along the surface of the Web. With some tweaking, the skills you use to quickly browse websites or Wikipedia will also help you handle the reading that you will likely encounter in college.

However, success at surfing may also conceal a weakness. Have you ever been reading for a long time and then suddenly realized that you can't remember what you just read? Have you ever been overwhelmed by trying to make sense of a long, complicated article or book that you were assigned? While you may excel at skimming, you may not be as good at remembering, comprehending, and analyzing what you've read.

Reading requires concentration, engagement, and a quiet mind—all of which are difficult to maintain in our highly distracting society that values technology, multitasking, and immediacy. These priorities potentially overload our attention, as Nicholas Carr argues in his provocative article "Is Google Making Us Stupid? What the Internet Is Doing to Our Brains" (*The Atlantic*, July/August 2008). Carr summarizes the views of neuroscientists, psychologists, sociologists, and writers who believe that the Internet's scattered, fast pace threatens our ability to concentrate and think deeply. We all can relate to Carr's distracted reading experience. For many of us, if something isn't highly captivating with flashy graphics, bright colors, short snippets of text, and lots of pictures, it won't hold our attention for very long. This is unsettling, given the fact that complex problems and grueling tasks require deep concentration. If Carr is correct, then we need to think carefully about how the Internet affects how we process information.

By practicing reading, you can train your brain to slow down, to focus, and to move beyond surface-level thinking. These habits of mind are essential for us to be productive members of society. We need doctors who can think through a diagnosis carefully and deliberately, without losing concentration at the drop of a hat. We need senators who can debate an issue at length, without succumbing to distraction. Furthermore, we want these habits of mind to come naturally, which requires practice. Reading is like a fitness class for your brain.

> **TRY THIS ➤**   Reflect on Your Reading Process
>
> To begin this exercise, find and read Nicholas Carr's article, "Is Google Making Us Stupid?" on *The Atlantic* magazine's website. Briefly summarize why Carr thinks online reading is "making us stupid" and what he thinks we should do about it. Then, reflect in writing on how technology has shaped your reading process—in positive and negative ways. Compare your responses with those of your classmates.

Reading Strategically

The first lesson in strategic reading is to **have a clear, specific purpose in mind every time you read**. Are you reading to understand new concepts for a class? Are you trying to collect background information or to answer a specific question? Or are you examining models of writing that you want to imitate?

Your answers should determine your reading pace, place, and approach. For example, if you're searching through the library or Internet databases to find sources for a paper, you might only need to scan them to decide whether you should invest more time in reading. When you find sections of a book or article to be useful, then you can layer on deeper reading and analysis techniques. The bottom line is that you shouldn't read everything the same way.

To get the most out of your reading, you'll need reading techniques that focus on concentration and repetition. If your mind is not actively engaged and you don't review what you've read, you won't re-member it, let alone be able to comprehend or analyze new informa-tion and difficult arguments. Brain research indicates that **repetition enhances memory**. The more times you think about information or ideas, the better they stick. Also, repeating the information in a slightly different way each time increases your level of comprehension. So, in order to enhance and monitor your concentration, reading ex-perts advocate a reading process that involves three different phases: previewing, reading, and reviewing.

Previewing

Before you read something, scan the table of contents, headings, tables, images, and key words to get some sense of the main ideas and organization. Think about how the reading connects to what you al-ready know and want to learn. Also, consider the rhetorical elements we discussed in the previous chapter: author, purpose, context, and so forth.

Reading

Once you've previewed the text, you're ready to begin reading as you normally would, except now you can read much more quickly (proba-bly twice as fast) with greater comprehension because you already know most of what the text is about. As you're reading, take notes about important concepts, along with any questions and reactions to the reading. Speed up when reading information you already know, and slow down for new or complicated material.

Reviewing

Lost concentration presents the biggest obstacle to remembering and comprehending what you read. Whenever you forget what you just read, you've lost concentration. That's why we suggest reading and re-viewing in a continuous loop. Whether you pause every few minutes, every page, or every paragraph, **stop reading and recall what you**

just read. If you can accurately recall what you just read, then continue. If not, you've only wasted a few minutes of effort, so go back and read and review again.

You can also **improve concentration by limiting distractions**. Every time you stop reading to answer a text message, to check social media, or to have a conversation with a friend, you break concentration. Consider finding a quiet place and turning off your cell phone while you study—or better yet, disconnect from your wireless network. You'll end up getting better results in less time than if you allow yourself constant interruptions. You might even discover what reading was like before Google.

Write Like a Scholar

Just as scholars adapt their reading process for different situations, experienced writers customize how they write for specific purposes, audiences, and occasions. Learning a flexible writing process can be especially useful for writing outside of school where, instead of having a structured rhetorical situation (assignment guidelines), you encounter unfamiliar kinds of writing, in different contexts, for new audiences.

In the past, you may not have needed such a sophisticated writing process. Inexperienced writers use a simplified process for good reasons. Remember, when you first started driving, how difficult it was to think about turning; accelerating; braking; and navigating roads, signs, and traffic all at the same time? To avoid information overload and to simplify the writing process for students, teachers often require a formula that looks something like this. First, pick a topic. Then, research the topic, as needed. After reading enough sources, create an outline and write a first draft. Finally, revise, edit, and submit the paper. In theory, this process works reasonably well because it forces students not to skip steps and because it's easier to learn a complicated process by concentrating on one part at a time.

However, **experienced writers usually don't write in such a formulaic, straight line**. Scholars typically follow a more *recursive* process—that is, they move back and forth among the stages, often repeating steps multiple times and at different points in their process. Although they typically create a plan before they begin, scholars also allow drafting, revision, and peer feedback to reshape their ideas. Throughout the writing process, they improve and focus their ideas by imagining different audiences and purposes and by finding potential gaps in their arguments.

Learning to use a more complex writing process might seem overwhelming, but scholarly writing takes practice and persistence. Inexperienced writers sometimes have an unrealistic and unattainable view of writing—that good writing happens magically for the lucky few, with little effort, as though you're either born a good writer or not. Here's the good news: **Effective writing is not a magical or natural talent**. It can be explained and learned. In fact, research about learning indicates that people who have a "growth

---

CONSIDER THIS ➤ Habits and History

For this reflection, use the following questions to help you think through how you typically write for school assignments. Be honest.

1. What, if anything, do you do before you start to write a draft? Do you freewrite or use an outline? How do you generate ideas?
2. What conditions do you prefer while writing? Do you like to write at a desk—or maybe in bed? By hand or on a laptop? What time of day do you do your best writing? Do you need quiet, or does background noise or music help you focus?
3. What do you do with your first draft? What kinds of changes do you typically make before handing it in?
4. How did you learn these strategies and habits? Why do you write this way?

---

mindset"—meaning they believe that they can improve their abilities and increase their intelligence—are more successful at learning new things. To develop your writing ability, you only need four things: knowledge; practice; feedback; and, most important, motivation. These key ingredients can help you become a more effective writer in college and beyond.

Remember, too, that college professors expect you to *apprentice* as a scholar, not to become professors or professional writers. Keep your goals within reason, and don't let scholarly writing intimidate you. Like learning to drive, it might seem awkward and frustrating at first, but becoming proficient may be easier than you think.

The One-Draft Wonder

Despite how much teachers try to improve students' writing process, research indicates that most new college students write one draft and make few changes before submitting their writing for a grade. For practical purposes, novice scholars often hand in their rough drafts.

Why do so many students still trust their one-draft wonders? Efficiency.

If, based on your own experiences, a single draft and some light proofreading have given you the results you want (an acceptable grade or a completed assignment), then why would you expect big rewards from multiple drafts? And if no one has ever taught you how to draft and revise effectively, how could you be expected to do so?

Most writers can achieve *some* success without much planning or revising. As long as investing the bulk of your time and energy in drafting yields the results you want, that's okay for now. But if you're like us, when you encounter difficult writing projects (like a 20-page research paper, or a short but complex argumentative essay), you'll need a process that includes careful planning and lots of revision.

So our first writing process lesson is this: Adapt your writing process to fit the particular writing situation. **Experienced writers don't write the same way every time, and neither should you.**

If your teacher assigns a short argument and you can effectively organize your ideas in your head without making an outline beforehand, then go ahead. If you can write an effective short-response paper in one draft the night before it's due, that's okay. But before you think your one-draft wonders will always work in college, think back to when you first learned algebra. You probably thought "showing your work" was pointless, at least at the beginning. When the problems became more difficult, however, you learned that you could no longer solve them in your head. You needed a more complex process to solve more complex problems. The same is true in writing.

A Better Writing Process

So, what does a more complex writing process look like? We'll begin by breaking the writing process down into four parts: discovery, drafting, revision, and editing.

- *Discovery* includes tasks such as choosing a topic, identifying the right questions to ask, finding and processing outside sources, organizing ideas, and so forth.
- *Drafting* generates the first version of a complete draft.
- *Revision* involves significantly adding, deleting, or rearranging chunks of text or content.
- *Editing* polishes paragraphs and sentences for style, formatting, grammar, and so forth.

Note carefully how we distinguish between revision and editing. Think of revising as major surgery and editing as cosmetic surgery. Major surgery repairs vital organs, whereas cosmetic surgery changes a person's appearance. Good writing requires both.

We assume that since you're in college, you're willing to invest serious time and energy into your studies. Still, you can only afford to spend a certain amount of time and effort on a given assignment. Thus, the four parts of the writing process are inversely proportional to each other: **The more time and effort you spend drafting, for example, the less time you have to invest in discovery or revision.** To illustrate these proportionalities vividly, we might use a pie chart like this.

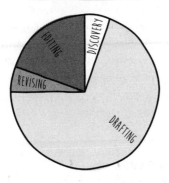

INEXPERIENCED WRITING PROCESS

Of course, these portions are not scientifically precise, but the pie chart can help us imagine the typical writing process of one-draft wonder writers who spend most of their time drafting and editing, leaving little to invest in discovery or revision.

How might the one-draft process hinder your development as a writer? What are its potential costs? First, if you love your draft too much, you won't want to change it. After all, if the majority of your investment is drafting, then you probably won't want to redo that work, even when it's not very good. More important, **if you only write one draft, you lose the opportunity to revise and expand your thinking**—to reenvision your message, to understand your subject matter more deeply, and to discover new insights and better ways to present your ideas. Again, a simple writing process might work fine if you want a simple written product, but if you want something more substantial and sophisticated, you'll need to use a better writing process.

Rather than relying so much on a single-draft process, you might find it useful to experiment with other economical ways to invest your time and energy. For example, if you begin thinking about an assignment as soon as you get it, maybe even jot down ideas as they occur to you, then you can add discovery time with little cost. Similarly, a 15-minute visit to your instructor's office to talk about plans for the paper can pay big dividends. If you change your topic or misread the assignment at that early stage, then you haven't already "wasted" time drafting, right? Scholars do this, too, when they discuss an idea for a research article or a conference paper with a colleague who can help them brainstorm and develop a research plan. Another good time investment is using your campus writing center, where you should be able to obtain help during any stage of the writing process. All of these discovery strategies save drafting time by helping you to organize and avoid later problems. In fact, for some scholars, drafting takes the least amount of time because they do most of the hard thinking and problem solving before they compose their first paragraph and after their first draft is complete.

Experienced Writers' Processes

For complex tasks, experienced writers try to balance the elements of the process, spending more time before and after drafting to develop and refine their writing. In fact, experienced writers often spend more time thinking (discovery) and rethinking (revising)

their writing than they do creating their first draft because they realize how much these activities can expand and deepen their understanding.

Researchers have also discovered that experienced writers customize their writing process to the task at hand. For example, a research-based project written for scholarly publication requires a significant investment of discovery

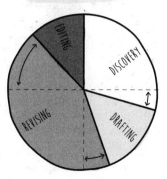

EXPERIENCED WRITING PROCESS

and revision, whereas creating a resume may require more time drafting and editing.

TRY THIS ➤ Adapt Your Writing Process

For this exercise, consider how you would customize your writing process for different situations. Create a pie chart to illustrate how you would invest your time in discovery, drafting, revising, and editing for the following tasks:

- A resume for your dream job
- An in-class essay exam
- A group research assignment
- A science lab report

Compare your pie charts with classmates and discuss differences and similarities among your writing processes.

Set Priorities and Adapt Your Process

Experienced writers don't feel locked into a linear process, but they do set priorities. Following writing experts Paula Gillespie and Neal Lerner, we divide these priorities into higher order/global drafting and revising concerns and later order/local editing issues.

Table 2.1   DRAFTING VERSUS EDITING

DRAFTING & REVISING CONCERNS	EDITING CONCERNS
Higher order: first priority, major	Later order: later priority, minor
Global: essay or paragraph-level	Local: sentence-level
Examples: content, focus, organization	Examples: style, grammar, formatting

How can these distinctions help you adapt your writing process?

Experienced writers address higher order concerns first, not just because they're more important. **Prioritizing increases the effectiveness and efficiency of your writing process.** Trying to address everything at once is overwhelming, even for expert writers. Focusing your attention on a few issues at a time will decrease your cognitive load, which increases the effectiveness of finding and fixing problems in your writing. Prioritizing also increases efficiency. For example, before you edit a paragraph to make sure your writing is clear and correct, you should make sure that the paragraph effectively develops necessary content. If a paragraph presents information that is off topic or restates information that you already covered, then you may need to revise it. Why waste time tweaking sentences that might later be removed or substantially changed?

Another way to save time is to think carefully about your audience and purpose so you can adapt your writing process according to the needs of each particular situation. You will be frustrated if you assume that chemists write the same as economists, that every professor in your major will follow the exact same grading criteria for every

---

CONSIDER THIS ➤ Introducing Sources

For this reflection, examine how we introduced Gillespie and Lerner's idea of "higher" and "later" order writing issues above. We called them "writing experts" and used an "attributive tag" to introduce their terminology. Attributive tags such as these help us clearly delineate between our ideas and other scholars' thoughts:

- "According to the author, _____"
- "The text states _____"
- "The writer makes the point that _____"

You might also point out your sources' credentials (area of expertise, level of education, relevant accomplishments) like a lawyer would do for an expert witness. In this instance, did the amount of information we provided about Gillespie and Lerner help you trust them?

---

assignment, or that every job will require the same kind of writing tasks. By experimenting with different strategies, you can assemble a writing tool kit to use when you encounter new or difficult writing situations. Throughout this book, we'll present many ways of interpreting, handling, and excelling at various writing tasks.

Manage the Writing Process

Experienced writers organize their efforts to improve effectiveness and efficiency. To be successful—and to reduce unnecessary stress—we don't recommend tackling a large writing task at once, in one sitting, the night before the assignment is due. The level of thinking and writing expected in college requires us to work in stages. Remember, writing is a process. We need time for our ideas to "marinate," time to find sources, time to get feedback on drafts, and time to revise and edit. To reserve time for all of these things, try to manage writing tasks sensibly:

- **Break the assignment into a series of manageable tasks, and then assign a deadline for each task.** For example, set a deadline for completing your research and another deadline for the first draft. If you create a timeline that organizes your tasks, you can hold yourself accountable. You might use a daily planner for this, install scheduling apps on your smartphone or tablet, or find resources available online.
- **Break a long assignment into chunks.** For example, you could think of a 20-page paper as 4 shorter papers, each with its own purpose. Thinking about the assignment in this way can make a daunting task more manageable. Focusing on smaller objectives, in stages, helps us be more productive and feel less overwhelmed. Consult the Scholarly Model on pp. 177–178 for ideas on how to divide large assignments into segments.
- **Take good notes throughout the research process.** The process of sifting through sources can be overwhelming, and it's easy to

mix up your sources. That's why it's imperative to take careful notes along the way. Some writers keep all of their notes in one place, like a notebook or online research folder. Other writers like to record information about each source on separate note cards or files. When you find a particularly useful quotation, write it down in your research notebook or on a note card or type it into a document. That way, you can cut and paste quotations, along with their citations, into your paper easily and efficiently.

- **Keep meticulous records.** As you conduct your research, invest time in recording bibliographic information for all your sources: author, title, publication information, and page numbers for any quotations or paraphrases. If you keep meticulous records, you won't waste time shuffling through files or papers, trying to remember where you found a memorable phrase. Online reference management systems can help you track, organize, and format citations while you conduct your research.

- **Get feedback along the way.** Assuming it's okay with your instructor, always have someone you trust read and respond to an early draft. Your professor might be willing to do this during office hours. If you have access to a writing center, try working with a tutor who can help you think through an assignment's various parts, brainstorm ideas, develop a plan, and revise your drafts. Tutors typically see many different kinds of assignments, so they can teach you strategies and give you a different perspective than you may have considered.

- **Don't insist on following a fixed or linear plan.** Just because your paper begins with an abstract or an introduction doesn't mean you have to start on that section first. If you don't know where to begin—if you feel stuck or overwhelmed—start with something straightforward: for instance, begin with your Works Cited page. Type up quotations that you might include in the paper. Format your document. All of these simpler tasks can get you started and alleviate some fear of the blank page. Remember, writing is difficult for everyone, and just because you're stuck doesn't mean that you can't find your way. Sometimes, in order to make progress, you have to jump around and then go back to reorganize or fill in the gaps.

Interpreting Assignments

Because scholars in most disciplines use writing to communicate their discoveries, another challenge of college writing is that it comes in many forms or genres—from scientific research articles to business case studies to artistic analysis papers. You probably won't write in every class, but you may very well write more often than you have before in classes other than English. These writing tasks will have different purposes, audiences, and writing styles, so there are no clear-cut rules or go-to formulas for every scenario. Instead, you'll need to make informed decisions by interpreting your professors' assignments thoughtfully and looking for clues in the assignment that suggest its rhetorical situation and a smart approach to take. The sections that follow provide some features to consider.

Writing with Purpose

As an apprentice, you can assume that most writing assignments will ask you to showcase your knowledge and understanding of subject matter while also using critical and creative thinking to develop some fresh understanding. Your professor might provide clues for the assignment's purpose by using specific terms to focus your attention, such as:

- *Analyze*—to take something apart to see how it works
- *Interpret*—to examine something's meaning, implications, or significance
- *Evaluate* or *critique*—to judge something according to established criteria

Whenever professors use less specific terms such as "discuss" or "examine," ask them to clarify or provide some strategies for how to meet their expectations. Think carefully about your audience and purpose, and ask yourself, should the writing:

- Persuade the audience to adopt a new position?
- Enlighten readers and give them new ideas to think about?
- Defend a controversial interpretation?

Regardless of your writing task's central aim, professors usually expect you to demonstrate what you're learning in class. Here's where you'll need to use a little gamesmanship, because you'll often find yourself explaining something to someone who already knows more than you do about a subject, or arguing a point to demonstrate that you know how to build an argument. Keep in mind that you're *practicing* scholarly writing—just as you would a sport—so your professor wants to see you make specific moves. Like a coach watching a football team run a new play, your professor is observing from the sidelines, expecting to see you demonstrate the strategies and skills you've been learning. Knowing this makes clear why you should elaborate your ideas and explain concepts, even ones your professor already understands. You need to convince your professor that *you* grasp the concept, and explaining it allows you to display the intricacies of your understanding. Think of it this way: **The paper that best demonstrates learning is the one that you could not have written before taking a course**. Write that paper.

To demonstrate learning successfully, try to exaggerate your new knowledge: refer to key terms in the textbook or mention important theories or topics covered in class. We don't mean that you should regurgitate information to the point where you dilute your own voice and thoughts. You can connect your ideas to concepts you've been studying in ways that display your new knowledge. Scholars must also "overexplain" what they're talking about sometimes because their subject matter is often so specialized and their discoveries are so original that even their expert peers need extra help to understand. Connecting prior knowledge to new ideas helps audiences understand messages more easily.

Even when it's "just practice," writing for your professor provides an opportunity for you to engage with a real audience and to get more immediate and helpful feedback than professional scholars typically receive. Seize opportunities to interact with your scholarly mentors by asking questions in class, visiting during office hours, and paying careful attention to written feedback. This experience conversing with professors and interpreting and meeting their demands can prepare you to impress future employers who might not clarify their expectations so explicitly and give feedback so generously.

Writing for Multiple Audiences

When interpreting assignments, you also need to identify the intended audience, so it's important to decipher readers' dispositions and their needs. You can imagine your audience metaphorically as a dartboard, with the bulls-eye representing your target audience and the surrounding rings signifying secondary and tertiary audiences (other readers who could also benefit from your work). Apprentice scholars usually aim for professors as their primary target audience. Professors can stand in as a proxy for the scholarly community by identifying credible sources, asking relevant research questions, and suggesting an appropriate style and format for a specific community of scholars.

Alternatively, some professors will ask you to consider your classmates as your audience, in which case you can write for peers who have a similar level of expertise and experience as you. Just as scholars use peer review to improve and validate their work, you may have the opportunity to give and receive feedback from fellow apprentices.

Sometimes, professors will ask you to imagine addressing "real" secondary audiences. For example, you might investigate tax reform and write an evaluation or proposal argument in the form of a blog post, a letter to your legislator, or an op-ed piece for your local newspaper. Each of these assignments should prompt you to consider distinct audiences, purposes, and styles. Even if you don't actually publish your work for an outside audience, such writing can be fun and useful practice—and you can still look for places to publish your work (for example, in your student newspaper or an undergraduate research journal).

Undergraduate and even graduate students often write for an audience of "no one in particular," which can leave their prose flat and uninteresting. When experienced scholars have something important to say, they try to imagine specific audiences early and often during the writing process by asking themselves:

- Who would care about my topic and findings? Who needs to know what I've learned? Who can act on what I've found?
- What writing styles will those readers expect and find persuasive?
- What publications does that audience read?

Make It Matter: The *So What?* Factor

Experienced scholars not only consider who would care about their message but also **why their message matters to them and to their readers in the first place**. Thinking carefully about the larger implications of your writing task—how it relates to your course's learning objectives, your personal goals, and other classes—can give you a clearer rationale for doing the work. Having a sense of the *so what?* question can also help you make smart decisions. For example, ask yourself:

- Why might my professor have assigned this?
- What does she hope I'll learn from doing this?
- How does this assignment relate to the readings we've discussed in class or other course material?
- What skills or habits of mind might this assignment help me practice, and how could these help me later?

Identifying the purpose, audience, and larger significance of a writing task can help you make decisions about content, length, organization, and writing style, among other things. Plus, you'll gain greater insight into the authentic reasons for writing, which can increase your motivation.

CONSIDER THIS ➤ Using First Person

For this reflection, consider the appropriateness of using the first person in scholarly writing. We argue that professors really want to hear what you think. However, teachers have probably warned you not to use "I" in formal academic writing. So, you might be wondering,

- How am I supposed to express my thoughts without using the first person?
- Can I ever use "I" in college writing? If so, when?
- When might it be inappropriate to use "I"? Why?

Considering what we've said so far, how do you think we'd answer these questions? What have you been taught before, and what do you *really* think?

(Note: We continue discussing the use of first person in Chapter 10.)

So What?

Adopting some of the reading and writing practices that scholars use can make your processes more efficient and effective. Equipped with these practices and a broad understanding of scholarly writing's unique purposes and features, you are ready to dig deeper into how we integrate sources effectively and responsibly into your own writing. Scholars are expected to write with integrity, so we explain how to borrow from sources and intertwine your ideas with those of others. We show you how to create a conversation with sources by summarizing, paraphrasing, quoting, interpreting, and elaborating on source material. We also explain some of the fundamentals of citation to help you decide when and how to cite sources in your writing.

What's Next

Take what you've learned in this chapter and respond to the following prompts.

1. **Categorize characteristics of good writing.** For this exercise, identify the distinguishing features of "good" writing, and then sort them as either global/higher order or local/later order concerns, using the following steps:
   - As a class, discuss the following question: "What are some defining qualities of 'good' writing?" List the characteristics on the board.
   - Assign each of the characteristics into one of two categories: higher order concerns and later order concerns. For example, if you decide that clarity is an important feature, which category does that fall under?
   - Discuss what you observe about labeling writing characteristics this way. Do any of the features fall into both categories? Which characteristics seem most important? What does this exercise teach you about writing?

2. **Online reading guide.** Reading on-screen is increasingly common. You might already use e-textbooks or do the majority of your reading on a laptop or tablet. Given what we've said about the importance of careful and critical reading, along with the

35

challenges of reading online, what problems might you encounter when reading electronic texts? Do you think e-readers help or hinder reading? What strategies could you use to combat any ill effects of reading online? What apps or resources might help you? Develop a list of strategies and resources for reading online that you can share with your classmates.

CHAPTER three

How Do We Select and Use Sources Responsibly

chapter checklist

- How can we find the best sources?
- What are effective strategies for summarizing, paraphrasing, quoting, and citing sources?
- How—and why—do we write with integrity?
- How do we avoid plagiarizing?

You might wonder why we're talking about sources before we've developed an argument to write about. After all, scholars use sources to back up their arguments, so we need a thesis *before* we know which sources we need, right?

Not exactly. As we've said, scholars rarely begin writing an argument before they've reviewed the work of current and previous scholars. In fact, scholars almost always contextualize their own arguments in light of what others are saying or have said in the past. So, **for scholars, nearly every paper is a research paper**. Or at least every paper presents an opportunity to conduct some kind of research, because for scholars, every paper attempts to answer a question through investigation. That's why professors care so much (sometimes it might seem like a little too much) about finding good sources and "documenting" or citing those sources in elaborate bibliographies or lists of "works cited." As scholars, we value each other's contributions and we leave a paper trail to prove it.

Sifting Through Sources

In college, most professors will expect you to include sources—at least your class readings, if not "outside" library sources—every time you write. But how do we know which sources are best? Let's begin by considering our trusty Internet pal, Wikipedia.

As you've probably noticed, many teachers dislike or distrust Wikipedia. Why do they discount "the free encyclopedia that anyone can edit" as a credible source for scholarly writing? There are several reasons:

1. **Stability.** Wikipedia content changes all the time, and therefore your readers may not be able to go back and find the same information that was there when you accessed it. Although folks are getting more used to the idea of dynamic, electronic publications, many readers still trust printed text more (although this may change with time).

2. **Credibility.** Anyone can write Wikipedia entries, and contributors often do so anonymously (known as "crowdsourcing"). Scholars care about credentials, which is why they place more trust in authors with proven expertise. If they don't know you, they don't (yet) trust you. That's why apprentices must earn credibility by borrowing it from more established sources. By selecting sources that have been peer-reviewed, apprentice scholars can appear even more credible. Scholarly publications undergo a rigorous review process through which experts scrutinize quality. Wikipedia does

have an editorial review process, but it's more organic and egalitarian. Contributors edit each other's entries and make decisions through consensus. Scholars generally don't trust unstable sources written and reviewed by anonymous crowds. So, if you're trying to impress a scholar, citing Wikipedia probably won't work (unless, of course, you're writing a paper *about* Wikipedia).

3. **Bias.** Although Wikipedia urges contributors to maintain a "neutral point of view," some articles show bias, especially when the author is motivated by his own self-interest or when he seems closed-minded or prejudiced. Keep in mind, though, that just because an author presents an argument (or "opinion") doesn't make something "biased." Bias has more to do with whether a source examines a controversy from multiple perspectives or is one-sided, or whether the investigator is open-minded or approaches a topic with a predetermined answer, regardless of what the evidence suggests. A biased scholar discovers what she wants to find, rather than letting the investigation lead toward whatever truth unfolds. Intentionally presenting inaccurate information or misrepresenting sources isn't so much biased as it is manipulative. All writers are biased to some extent because our perspectives are colored by previous experiences. However, we can limit the extent to which our bias influences our investigation by remaining informed, open-minded, and devoted to accuracy.

Despite objections about its stability, credibility, and bias, Wikipedia provides a vast, easily accessible, and *relatively* accurate storehouse of information about almost anything. In fact, here's a little secret: most of us use Wikipedia anyway—experts and apprentices alike. That's because it's a useful reference for gathering background information—a good place to get a general sense about a topic, then dig deeper into other, more credible sources. Notice that Wikipedia entries often contain extensive references and suggestions for "further reading," many of which might be trustworthy enough to use as scholarly sources.

So What's a Better Source?

As we say throughout this book, when it comes to what works in writing, everything depends on the particular audience, purpose, and context. For an audience of scholars, the most trustworthy sources are those written by other scholars in reputable publications that use a rigorous review process, such as scholarly journals. Other situations call for different sources, but generally you can follow our trusty "credibilimeter" when deciding what sources carry the most scholarly credibility.

Notice that we haven't claimed that any of these sources are necessarily invalid or incorrect. Entertainment media, for example, are sometimes true and often believable. That's just our point: **Credibility**

depends on the particular audience and situation. If you're arguing with a friend about sports, you probably don't need a scholarly source to seem convincing. *SportsCenter* will probably do.

Even if they may not be the most credible scholarly sources, social media, Wikipedia, newspapers, and other popular sites can be good places to start searching for background information or interesting topics to write about. Scholarly print publications lag behind popular and electronic media because it takes so long for scholars to complete their research and have it reviewed and revised for publication. So Wikipedia isn't necessarily a bad place to start.

Just don't stop searching after skimming the first few paragraphs on Wikipedia or the first page of Google hits, and remember to think carefully about what sources and evidence your audience will trust. Experienced scholars mistrust sources that haven't been scrutinized by experts, so if you want to communicate or argue with scholars, you need to be able to find, understand, and use academically credible references.

> **CONSIDER THIS ➤** Appropriate Sources
>
> For this reflection, describe some different situations when non-scholarly sources would be effective. When might scholarly sources be ineffective?

How Do We Find Credible Scholarly Sources?

Ask other scholars. When we're initially investigating a topic and looking for the best sources, we often start by asking other scholars to identify journals, books, or articles that experts in the field know well. These books and journal articles may even be on our colleagues' shelves. From these, we find a clearer starting point, which can save us lots of time. Also, when other scholars read our work, they will expect us to reference these key sources to prove that we know what we're talking about, or at least that we've done our homework.

You should do the same.

Instructors hold office hours for a reason: to help students. Take advantage of this time and meet with a professor who is an expert in the field that you're studying. For example, if you're writing a paper on alienation and the effects of social media on teenage girls, an English professor specializing in feminist literature or a sociologist who studies gender could probably recommend some reliable and useful sources. This might seem intimidating and time consuming, but beginning your research in the right place can save you many hours of frustration.

Plus, most professors will be thrilled to help. Imagine how you'd feel if you spent years studying something like the feeding habits of Amazonian frogs, waiting patiently for that one student who showed genuine interest in your expertise.

We also consult reference librarians who can help us identify research techniques that will yield better results. Librarians work with research databases more often than we do, so they can share lots of techniques and shortcuts. For example, librarians can help you select appropriate databases for your topic or narrow your database search terms. They can also show you how to locate sources by proximity, because libraries and databases cluster sources by subject headings.

If we already have a handle on search techniques and want to work independently, we'll **explore a research database**, like Academic Search Complete. (If you don't have easy access to library databases, Google Scholar can help find scholarly articles in a pinch.) Online journals allow us to access full-text versions of most articles. Many databases only include material that has been peer-reviewed, so we can usually be confident that the articles are accurate and well researched, although they could still be biased or controversial. In addition to being credible, many articles are searchable, so we can move through them quickly using our computer's *find* function to search for relevant sections of an article.

If we're looking for more general sources, such as magazine articles or newspaper editorials, we'll **search online**. We might look at company websites, blog posts, or personal Web pages, depending on our purpose. But whenever we're viewing public sites like these, we shift our rhetorical thinking into overdrive. We ask ourselves:

- Who wrote this? What makes the authors credible?
- What are they trying to achieve? For example, is anyone profiting from this? Who? How might money-making efforts influence the content?
- How do they support their claims?
- When was this written? Will this still be here next month?

Sources need to convince us that they deserve a place in our writing. Thoughtful investigation helps us determine whether an online source is credible and worth using. We expect to do a lot of hunting around, so we don't just settle with the first hits that our search engine picks. Settling is a rookie mistake. Unlike most online navigation that is quick and easy, searching for good sources takes time and patience. To find the prize, we must wade through forests of dense material, trek across mountains of reading, and trudge through deserts with no relevant sources in sight. Remember, the buried treasure might not appear until the final leg of the journey—or the third page of search results.

TRY THIS ➤ Practice Sifting Through Sources

For this exercise, practice searching for credible sources. As a class or in small groups, select a research topic that interests you—any topic that you're truly curious about. Then, search online for three to four credible sources.

1. If your library has access to research databases online, begin by entering search terms in a scholarly database, such as Academic Search Complete.
2. Select the full-text version of an article that seems promising and use your computer's *find* function to search for terms that will lead you to the article's most relevant sections. For example, if you find a long scientific article on the health benefits of meditation, you might search for words such as "stress" or "relationships" to quickly find the sections of the article that you're most curious about. Jot down notes on the most interesting information and points you find.
3. Search online for high-quality public sources, such as articles from a reputable newspaper, magazine, or organization's website. Use the questions above to evaluate these sources' credibility.
4. Skim each of the source's Works Cited or References page for other articles and books that are worth checking out. Once you've found some promising leads, try following that "paper trail" or at least make a list of additional sources to consult.
5. Wow your classmates by sharing your fascinating discoveries.

What's the Best Research Container?

Another criterion that you should consider when sifting through sources is *scope*. Look for the right-sized research container for the scope (the breadth and depth) of your argument. If your topic is broad, begin with a source that has enough room to meet your needs. **Big topics need big research containers.**

Here we're not talking about *Encyclopedia Britannica* or Wikipedia, either. If your topic has been studied extensively, you might find a more exhaustive and credible reference book on the subject in your school library. For example, for a topic as broad as World War II, our school's library holds several scholarly encyclopedias (including the five-volume *The Encyclopedia of World War II*) that could help you discover exactly what you want to write about.

BROAD SUBJECT ⟶

NARROWED TOPIC ⟶

RESEARCH QUESTION ⟶

Once you narrow your topic a bit, you might search your library for more manageable, medium-sized sources. Scholarly books, which are often 200 to 400 pages, focus more narrowly than most novice scholars might think. Our library has hundreds of books on narrower World War II topics, including *The African American Experience in World War II* or *London at War, 1939–45*.

Scholarly journals publish cutting-edge research, so they usually present specialized topics for subject matter experts. Most journal articles are about 20 to 30 pages in length, with an appropriately narrow scope that "fits" into that page count. For example, a journal article about World War II would have a very specific focus, like "Replacing Battleships with Aircraft Carriers in the Pacific in World War II," published in a discipline-specific journal, *Naval War College Review*. One advantage of a recently published journal article—as opposed to a book or an encyclopedia—is that it reflects the most current debates in a field.

Novice scholars sometimes think that journal articles are the quickest to read because they are the shortest. Wrong. They might be short, but because of their specificity, they often require prior knowledge about a subject before they can be useful. That's why it's usually smart to educate yourself with a "bigger" source before diving into a specialized journal article.

If you want to write about a contemporary controversy, you might also consider starting with online sources that examine topics from multiple angles, such as *Issues and Controversies* or *Opposing Viewpoints in Context*. Much like encyclopedias for a big topic, these sources can help you narrow a broad topic. Say, for example, you're interested in comparing educational standards in public versus private schools. You might begin with *Issues and Controversies* and from there, find a book like *Keeping Them out of the Hands of Satan: Evangelical Schooling in America* or an even more specific journal article, such as "School Vouchers and Student Attainment: Evidence from a State-Mandated Study of Milwaukee's Parental Choice Program," from *Policy Studies Journal*. Following a research process like this one, which moves from "large" research containers to "smaller" ones, can help you narrow your scope, minimize frustration, and learn a lot more.

And that's the whole point. For apprentice scholars, "research" typically means learning from more experienced scholars, borrowing from the established credibility of their investigations, and using their writing as models for making arguments. "Library research" may not enable you to expand the bounds of human understanding, but it will initiate you into the habits and practices of a community that does.

Summarizing, Paraphrasing, and Quoting Sources

As we collect credible sources, we begin choosing how we want to integrate them into our writing through summary, paraphrase, and quotation (see Figure 3.1). Working closely with sources will help you better understand other people's ideas and build on them in your own writing. Often, after you read an essay or scholarly article, you'll be asked to write about it. But before you can fairly evaluate the argument or respond to it with your own ideas, you'll need to be sure that you understand the source's message.

Summary is the most important and common technique when writing about sources, and it incorporates paraphrasing and sometimes quotation. Scholars use summaries to *distill* a source—either all or part

Summarize
- To capture the whole text in a smaller amount of space
- To identify the most important parts of a larger text
- To condense

Paraphrase
- To represent a portion of the text in your own words
- To restate an idea in a different style but maintain the original length
- To translate someone else's words into your own phrasing
- To avoid quoting too frequently, in order to maintain a consistent tone

Quote
- To express a specific idea verbatim
- To credit an author's original term, phrase, or controversial statement
- To boost your credibility

Figure 3.1
The Rationale for Summary, Paraphrase, and Quotation

How would you decide when to use each of these techniques?

of a text—into a more condensed, selective version. In practice, scholars typically summarize just the parts they need, such as a source's findings or the methodology. While a summary is a scaled-down version, a paraphrase is typically about the same length as the original passage.

Why is it important to understand this distinction? Because you'll need to use the technique that best suits your purpose.

In many classes, you'll need to report on your library research by summing up major theories and significant previous research on your topic. Scholars also regularly summarize, paraphrase, and quote other scholars when they write "literature reviews" or "research reviews," which they publish with their findings to help their readers enter the conversation and share background information. When we're describing something long and complicated, a summary allows us to *select* main points and *condense* the original. However, if we're restating just a paragraph or a sentence, a paraphrase allows us to *translate* the original into our own words—not just do a synonym swap—while maintaining a similar length.

Generally, scholars prefer summarizing and paraphrasing over quoting. That's because both of these techniques allow the writer to maintain his voice and display his grasp of the material. Think about it. We can't condense or translate something unless we really know what it says, so when we summarize and paraphrase, we demonstrate that we understand the source. Simply quoting doesn't give us the opportunity to display this depth of understanding.

Quoting less also makes your writing smoother because readers don't need to transition repeatedly from your style to other writers' styles. Quoting is more acceptable or even necessary in literature or writing classes because those disciplines care most about language. On the other hand, scholars writing in the sciences or business may quote rarely, if at all. Still, you can bet that in most scholarly writing you'll be doing a lot more summarizing and paraphrasing than quoting. These techniques leave a lot more room for your own ideas and arguments than if you overwhelm your writing with quotations.

But summarizing a source can be difficult.

How Do We Summarize?

Summarizing requires us not only to understand *what* the text says but also *how* it says—how it's structured, how it builds its argument, how it achieves its purpose, and so on. After we understand the original in its entirety, we can select the most relevant details. We focus on main claims and don't get bogged down in the details. Just like someone who builds model cars or airplanes, we construct a scaled-down version of the original that will fit the size of our paper. We also have to consider the proportions of the original; if the original is 20 pages long, we can't spend one-third of our summary on the first 2 pages. We don't have room for every detail, but we can't leave out any major parts, either. So we look carefully at the original and how all of the parts fit together before we decide what to include and what to leave out.

To select the right parts, it's helpful to get in the "believing" mindset: give the author the benefit of the doubt and try to understand exactly what he is trying to accomplish. Imagine how all of the parts could possibly fit together (even if they seem unrelated). Assume that the author's intentions are logical. Withhold evaluation and see the absolute best in the text so that you can write fair and nonevaluative summaries. There's plenty of time to discount ideas, reject messages, and tear apart evidence in assignments that call for analysis or response. But, when summarizing, we try to be nonjudgmental and play the role of an objective reporter. To do that successfully, we follow these steps:

1. **Read the text** carefully, paying attention to the genre of the original and how it's organized. For example, if you're summarizing a research article and you know how that genre is typically organized (described in Appendix B), you know where to find the main claims and support. Reading is the most important step because if we don't understand what we read, we can't summarize it well.

2. **Create a "reverse outline," or schematic, of the text's layout.**
   This technique comes in handy whenever you're reading complicated arguments, and even when you're revising your own writing.
   To compose a reverse outline, first write down the main claim of
   each paragraph, either in the margins of the text or on a separate
   sheet of paper. You might be able to find a topic sentence, or you
   might need to express the main ideas in your own words; aim for
   one phrase or short sentence per paragraph. Forcing yourself to
   identify each paragraph's main idea helps you break down a complex argument and recognize its many parts. Then, write those
   points in outline form so that you can see the progression of the
   ideas on a single page, if possible.

3. **Select the most relevant points.** Study the reverse outline to
   identify the most central ideas—the blueprint of the text—which
   someone who hasn't read the source would need to know in order
   to grasp the overall argument. Don't get bogged down in the supporting details, examples, and evidence. Also, briefly **include
   other rhetorical elements that would help your reader understand your source's rhetorical situation**, such as the author,
   intended audience, purpose, genre, and publication context. (Use
   the first paragraph of our sample rhetorical analysis on pp. 267–273
   as a guide.)

4. **Write a summary** that aims to be unbiased, clear, and proportionally accurate but shorter than the actual text. The first time you
   write the summary, it might still be pretty long. Don't worry about
   that; you can condense it further later. Just try to clearly convey all
   of the text's main points.

5. **Revise the summary** to make it even shorter. Now's the time to
   make the most brutal cuts. Figure out what deserves to be there
   and what can be left out. Beware also of any inaccuracies or judg-
   mental language, and note any paraphrases or quotations that
   need citations.

> **TRY THIS ➤** Practice Summarizing
>
> For this exercise, practice reading and summarizing the scholarly article "A Wandering Mind Is an Unhappy Mind" by Matthew A. Killingsworth and Daniel T. Gilbert (printed on pp. 243–247). The essay contains approximately 900 words. Use the techniques we've covered so far, and track your word count. Maximum words = 150, or about 15% of the original. Then, in class, compare your summaries with your peers: How similar are they? Which parts are different? How did you decide which details to include and which ones to omit? If you included any paraphrases or quotations, how did you decide which ones to use?
>
> After comparing your notes with classmates, condense your summary even further. Try summarizing the essential contents of the article in 100 words or less.

Paraphrasing

Paraphrasing is a difficult skill for apprentice scholars to master. To paraphrase effectively, you must closely read and fully understand your source, and you must practice, using the techniques we outline in this chapter. Before we describe techniques for paraphrasing, let's look at some examples of inappropriate paraphrases and then more sufficient changes. Here's an example of paraphrases using an excerpt from later in this chapter. Compare the original text with the inappropriate paraphrase, noticing the similar—and even exact—phrasing and syntax (word order).

- **Original quotation:** "This may seem odd, but schools typically do not allow students to recycle papers. For example, you probably cannot dust off a paper you wrote in high school—however long ago that was—for use in a college class."

- **Inappropriate paraphrase:** It might seem weird, but schools typically prohibit students from reusing papers. You cannot hand in an old paper from high school in your college class.

Notice how the inappropriate paraphrase changes a few words but retains nearly the same sentence structure as the original? Simply exchanging synonyms does not make the paraphrase appropriate. The writer has just replaced a few terms and copied the syntax. Even with an accompanying citation, most colleges consider this a kind of plagiarism. Writing scholar Rebecca Moore Howard coined the term "patch-writing" to describe this "failed" paraphrasing, or what many honor codes call insufficient paraphrasing—source material that is neither quoted nor adequately rephrased. Regardless of what an honor code says, patch-writing is a poor use of source text because it does not indicate that the writer has deeply processed or even understands the source. Students use patch-writing more often when they are not familiar with the content or language of a source, so be sure to invest adequate time practicing the reading strategies from Chapter 2.

Now compare the inappropriate paraphrasing with the following two examples of proper paraphrases:

- **Proper paraphrase:** According to Schick and Schubert, colleges may consider resubmitting old assignments to be a kind of plagiarism (65).
- **Proper paraphrase with quotation:** Writing scholars Schick and Schubert warn students not to "recycle papers" from high school for college classes (65).

Notice how these versions are significantly different from the original? They reframe the original, using both different words and different sentence structure to express the same idea. They also contain needed citations, which we'll explain later.

How Do We Paraphrase?

How do we paraphrase appropriately, without running the risk of plagiarism (stealing another person's words or ideas)? The key is to represent the source closely without using the author's style or phrasing. To do so, follow these steps:

1. **Read carefully** the paragraph or sentence that you want to paraphrase.
2. **Think about what it's saying**. Mull it over. Chat with yourself about the ideas. (Experienced scholars talk to themselves all the time.)
3. **Rewrite the gist of what the source says**, without looking at the original paragraph or sentence. Resist the temptation to glance at the author's exact wording; otherwise, you might be influenced by the author's style and find it difficult to rephrase. The only reason to return to the original is to get a clearer grasp of the content. If you review the original, then repeat Step 2 before trying to write again.
4. **Double-check the original** to ensure your paraphrase is accurate but significantly different from the original—in terms of sentence structure, word choice, tone, and possibly even length.
5. **Cite the author** with an in-text citation or use an attributive tag (see p. 27). We will talk more about citation styles and practices, along with quotation techniques, later in this chapter.

Following these steps should help you maintain integrity when incorporating other people's words and ideas into your own writing, which is the focus of the next section.

TRY THIS ➤ Evaluate Paraphrases

For this exercise, compare the original quotations from "A Wandering Mind Is an Unhappy Mind" with the accompanying, attempted paraphrases. Are the paraphrases appropriate or not? Why?

1. **Original quotation:** "Many philosophical and religious traditions teach that happiness is to be found by living in the moment, and practitioners are trained to resist mind wandering and 'to be here now.' These traditions suggest that a wandering mind is an unhappy mind. Are they right?"

   Attempted paraphrase: Killingsworth and Gilbert question whether people should limit their tendency to daydream. They suggest mind-wandering may be harmful if scholars are correct that people are most content when they are fully present, living one moment at a time.

2. **Original quotation:** "In conclusion, a human mind is a wandering mind, and a wandering mind is an unhappy mind. The ability to think about what is not happening is a cognitive achievement that comes at an emotional cost."

   Attempted paraphrase: Killingsworth and Gilbert conclude by saying that a wandering mind is an unhappy mind. Although humans have a natural ability to think about the future, this ability may come at a high price.

3. **Original quotation:** "We solved this problem by developing a Web application for the iPhone (Apple Incorporated, Cupertino, California), which we used to create an unusually large database of real-time reports of thoughts, feelings, and actions of a broad range of people as they went about their daily activities."

   Attempted paraphrase: Killingsworth and Gilbert rectified this issue by creating an iPhone app, which they utilized to compile an uncommonly huge database of live reports of people's ideas, sentiments, and behaviors as they experienced their daily lives.

Revise any of the above paraphrases that are inappropriate, and then compare versions with a classmate.

Quoting and Integrating Sources

Most scholarly writing, including the kinds of assignments you're likely to encounter in college, uses published sources to support arguments.

Every time you include a summary or paraphrase or quotation, you might think of that source as an expert witness in a trial. As the trial lawyer, you might borrow the expertise and credibility of a scientist, for example, to validate or refute DNA evidence. Then you'll have a conversation with that source—and with your audience—about what that evidence means.

Unless your readers, the "jury," already know your source (if he's Einstein or Shakespeare, they might know him already), then they'll expect you to introduce your "expert witness" and explain why we should trust him. One of the best places to learn how to do this in nonscholarly writing is to study newspaper reporting.

Newspaper reporters seamlessly integrate other people's words into their articles, as Alan Schwarz does in his *New York Times* article "Attention Disorder or Not, Pills to Help in School" (Oct. 9, 2012):

> [S]ome experts note that as wealthy students abuse stimulants to raise already-good grades in colleges and high schools, the medications are being used on low-income elementary school children with faltering grades and parents eager to see them succeed.

> "We as a society have been unwilling to invest in very effective nonpharmaceutical interventions for these children and their families," said Dr. Ramesh Raghavan, a child mental-health services researcher at Washington University in St. Louis and an expert in prescription drug use among low-income children. "We are effectively forcing local community psychiatrists to use the only tool at their disposal, which is psychotropic medications."

> Dr. Nancy Rappaport, a child psychiatrist in Cambridge, Mass., who works primarily with lower-income children and their schools,

added: "We are seeing this more and more. We are using a chemical straitjacket instead of doing things that are just as important to also do, sometimes more."

Reporters don't just assume that readers intuitively know who their sources are, so they don't just insert a quote without any warning or description of the source's identity. Otherwise, readers might be confused. They need to know the identity of the source and how the source will contribute to the reporter's story. So it's important for writers to *frame* their quotations with:

1. **An introduction:** usually an "attributive tag" (what some scholars call a "signal phrase") that clarifies who's speaking, such as "According to . . ." or "The author states . . ."
2. **An explanation** of why the source is relevant to the story

Newspaper reporters can model the basics of creating attributive tags, but they don't show us how to *converse with* sources as deeply as scholars do. As you notice in the example above, the reporter relies more heavily on the source to present information than is typical in scholarly writing. If you deleted the quotations from this excerpt, there would hardly be any content left. You can't really get away with that as a student because, as we keep saying, professors are typically more interested to hear what *you* think than what your sources say. Write like an apprentice scholar, not a reporter. In the next section, we'll describe how to create a conversation with your sources.

TRY THIS ➤ Study How Popular Publications Introduce Sources

For this exercise, collect several examples of popular sources (newspapers, magazines, etc.) and study how the authors introduce their sources. Create a list of rules or techniques that authors use.

How to Create a Conversation

When we build sources into arguments, we not only clarify who our sources are, but we also tell readers:

- Why a quotation is there
- What it means
- How it's related to, or supports, our argument

We don't expect our readers to figure this stuff out through ESP. For one thing, readers could misunderstand or misinterpret quotations. More important, readers wouldn't know what *we thought about* the quotation. We want to involve our sources and our readers in a conversation. When we introduce and elaborate on sources, we help readers clearly "hear" our sources' messages. These techniques amplify and connect sources to our argument, like plugging an electric guitar into a 50-watt amplifier. Without such wired connection, our source may be muffled or inaudible.

Instead of quoting a source and immediately moving on, we elaborate on sources in the following ways:

- **Interpret the source.** Unless a quotation's message is blatantly obvious, we typically offer some kind of explanation. Readers usually need help interpreting a quotation because we've taken it out of its original context. Especially when there's unfamiliar vocabulary or dense information, we translate the source's ideas into more accessible language. We add explanations directly after each quotation, such as:
  - "This passage suggests that . . ."
  - "In other words, . . ."
  - "Here, the writer explains that . . ."
- **Explain how the quotation relates to our argument.** Although the relationship between a quotation and our ideas might seem clear, readers often need us to highlight that

57

connection. We link a quotation to our paragraph's central point by telling readers exactly *why* and *how* the source is relevant. Quotations can serve as evidence that supports our point when we add commentary like:

- ° "Dr. X illustrates my point exactly: . . ."
- ° "The author's views are relevant because they show that . . ."
- ° "All of this relates to my point that . . ."

- **Tell readers what makes the quotation significant.** Because we only quote a source when it's necessary, we should know why a quotation is important. But readers need to understand the implications, too. They need to know what is meaningful about a quotation—why it matters—and what the consequences of its ideas are. To shed light on a quotation's implications, we say:
  - ° "The author's ideas have important consequences, mainly that . . ."
  - ° "If we extend the scholar's argument, we can see that . . ."
  - ° "What makes this point particularly _____ (urgent, puzzling, thought provoking, valid, etc.) is . . ."

- **Consider ways to make a source our own.** Link a source to our argument by providing our own unique example, analogy, or related experience to illustrate the idea, like this:
  - ° "My own learning process matches the theories proposed by John Dewey in his book, *Experience and Education*. For example . . ."
  - ° "Nancy Sommers says that the writing process is like a 'seed' (384). A more fitting metaphor to describe my writing process would be . . ."

These strategies allow us to talk alongside our sources, rather than expecting them to speak *for* us. We can maintain ownership of the argument by preventing our sources from overpowering our own voice. We also gain some points with our readers—especially with professors—when we show off our analytical abilities and critical thinking skills.

> **TRY THIS ➤** Integrate Sources More Fully
>
> For this exercise, review a manuscript that you're currently drafting or that you recently composed and look for places where you can introduce and elaborate on your sources more fully. Use the model phrases you learned to introduce quotations and explain, interpret, and/or contextualize your sources' arguments.

Citing Sources

While integrating other writers' words and ideas into our own writing, we are careful to mark those contributions and leave a trail back to our sources. That's what citation is all about: **Scholars value accurate citations because they illuminate the genealogy of our work.** Missing or incorrect citations can hinder other scholars' efforts to evaluate the credibility of an argument or to relocate a source.

However, as important as citations may be for scholars who publish their research, experienced writers treat citations like they treat grammar and punctuation—as local, later order concerns that we described on p. 26—and you should, too. As an apprentice scholar, your writing will develop more quickly if you concentrate *first* on selecting good sources, analyzing and evaluating their content, and responsibly integrating their words and ideas into your own writing.

How Do We Know When We Need to Cite Something?

Here's the easy answer:

- **Always cite quotations and paraphrases,** and include the page number, if available.

- **Cite summaries, too.** If you're summarizing part of a source, include the appropriate page numbers. When summarizing an entire source, page numbers are not necessary.
- **Cite statistics, dates, and other details** that are not common knowledge.

Now, here's where it gets more complex: what exactly *is* "common knowledge"? We don't need to cite things that everyone already knows, right? As with most things in writing, that depends.

Before the Internet, teachers often told students that if you could find the same information in some arbitrary number of sources (three or five or however many different places), then you could consider that information "common knowledge," so you wouldn't need a citation. This general rule doesn't work so well anymore for two reasons.

First, the number of times information gets published may or may not indicate anything about it being commonly known. Websites often "borrow" information and text from each other without attribution. (Please don't follow their example.) Finding an urban legend repeated on 15 different websites doesn't make it true *or* common knowledge. Just because the Internet operates as a public domain for everyone's benefit does not exempt scholars from citing what we find there, either.

Secondly, while the five-sources-equals-common-knowledge rule may have helped students before the Internet, the rule doesn't really get at the heart of the matter, which isn't really whether we need a citation but rather *When do we need to use a source to verify information in our arguments?*

The answer, of course, depends on your topic and audience: *How confident are you that your audience already knows what you're talking about?* For example, you can probably be confident that an audience educated in a US high school already knows what happened on July 4, 1776. But even a college-educated US audience would expect a citation if you were discussing the events of October 29, 1923 (the date when, according to Wikipedia, the modern Republic of Turkey was established). You can probably find the details of Turkey's history in hundreds of books, articles, and websites, but if your audience doesn't already know it—and *you* didn't before reading your sources—then they'll expect to see where you got your information. Otherwise, they just might not believe you.

Citation Fundamentals

Many academic disciplines (such as history, engineering, or sociology) or clusters of disciplines (such as humanities, sciences, or social sciences) have created consistent guidelines for how to cite sources. Disciplines publish their "citation styles" so that everyone in their field can use a consistent, recognizable citation format. For example, humanities scholars such as literary and language specialists often use Modern Language Association's (MLA) *Handbook for Writers of Research Papers.* Social scientists (including psychology, business, education, and health sciences) typically use the *Publication Manual of the American Psychological Association* (APA). As an apprentice scholar, you will most commonly use MLA and APA styles. However, you may also encounter more specialized citation styles used by historians, journalists, lawyers, mathematicians, engineers, or other professionals.

Because there are so many different citation styles, we recommend consulting handbooks and online resources when formatting citations. However, before consulting these resources, it's helpful to know about the two main ways that scholars cite or "document" their sources: bibliographic and in-text citations.

Bibliographic citations appear at the end of a scholarly article or paper as a list of "References" or "Works Cited" or as a "Bibliography." A bibliographic citation includes everything that a reader would need to know to find the exact source that you used. Creating this list of bibliographic citations will be much easier if you collect the basic information you need whenever you encounter a new source: author, title, and publication information (when, where, and who published the source). If you remember to collect these basic elements as you conduct your research, you'll have whatever information you need to create your bibliography later. Bottom line: **Keep track of whatever details you or your reader would need to retrace your steps to find each source again**.

Brief in-text citations appear right next to where you summarize, paraphrase, or quote from your source. In-text citations point readers toward a specific source and, when needed, a specific place (page or pages) in that source.

So Many Styles . . .

Try to remember the main elements of a citation, but don't try to memorize the finer points of citation formatting. If you need to collect many sources, you might consider using an automatic formatting tool like RefWorks or EndNote. When you need to verify accuracy or format your citations manually, consult library resources, such as the MLA and APA style manuals, or a reputable writing center website, like the Purdue University Online Writing Lab (OWL).

Write with Integrity

Anyone who's been interviewed by a newspaper or television reporter knows what it's like to have his words taken out of context or used to prove a point that he really didn't intend to make. Even if reporters try to use their sources responsibly, when they distill a long interview down to a pithy sound bite, the person being interviewed can feel cheated.

Scholars maintain their integrity by making a good faith effort not to "cheat" the authors whose words and ideas they borrow. That's why we work so diligently—using the techniques for careful reading and analysis that we've discussed in this book—to fully understand our sources' content, intended purpose, and persuasive strategies *before* we critique them, disagree with them, or use them to support our own arguments.

As a community of scholars, we must be able to trust each other's work and trust that our colleagues will use our work responsibly. That's where the idea of plagiarism comes from. Yes, plagiarism is a kind of stealing (in fact, the word "plagiarism" comes from the Latin term for "kidnapping"). But more important, plagiarism violates the trust of the scholarly community. How can we build on each other's discoveries if we cannot trust the integrity of the work done to produce and communicate those discoveries?

Because we never know how our work will influence others, we take scholarly integrity very seriously. The results of "cheating" sometimes have obvious and immediate consequences. Imagine, for example, the potential health and safety risks caused by a medical researcher who takes shortcuts in testing a new drug. And think of all the previous research on which that medical innovation depended. Faulty research by a previous biologist or chemist or physicist might also have indirectly tainted the development of the new drug.

The credibility and integrity of our scholarly work is therefore *networked* and *interdependent*, which is why we cite our sources. We didn't design citation styles just to torture scholarly apprentices. Our specialized referencing systems (MLA and APA, for example) enable us to exhibit scholarly genealogies for our discoveries. Scholars who review our work can judge its credibility, in part, by scrutinizing the lineage of our work, which we present to readers through citations and bibliographies. So even though we don't expect you, as a scholarly apprentice, to begin "expanding the bounds of human understanding" just yet, we do expect you to acknowledge your sources from the beginning.

So far, we've been justifying why scholars cite their sources. The last, and perhaps most obvious rule of writing with integrity is simply that you do the work yourself and don't copy from other writers. Learning requires practice. **Copying from others denies you the opportunity to learn.**

Plagiarism

Most schools have formal honor codes that define various kinds of cheating. The term "plagiarism" typically means copying someone else's words or ideas without giving attribution, or explicit acknowledgment. Buying a paper off the Web or copying someone else's writing is deemed the most serious of offenses and often carries the strictest penalties, such as failing the assignment or the course, or even expulsion from school.

You will also get into trouble for copying a passage from a source without quoting it. Remember to mark all quotations and provide proper citations as we described earlier.

Students are often less familiar with other kinds of honor code violations, which may include unauthorized collaboration and recycled writing.

Unauthorized Collaboration

Scholars rarely write alone. They usually discuss their ideas with others and ask colleagues to critique their writing. You should do the same whenever possible, with one caveat. **Always ask your instructor, in advance, about what kinds of collaboration she allows.**

Most professors, most of the time, will appreciate that you're using every available (ethical) means to improve your writing. However, there may be occasions when you'll be expected to complete your work alone to demonstrate your own, individual learning. Seeking help from writing center tutors is usually acceptable, but to be safe, consider asking your professor first.

Recycled Writing

This may seem odd, but schools typically do not allow students to recycle papers. For example, you probably cannot dust off a paper you wrote in high school—however long ago that was—for use in a college class. This rule may not seem fair (after all, the paper is your intellectual "property," so you're not really stealing someone else's work), but handing in the same paper twice violates the primary purpose of academic integrity policies: **You can't learn something new if you don't do the work**.

If you want to reuse some words or ideas from a previous paper, ask your professor for guidance. He can probably help you think of ways to expand on your previous work. Scholars do this all the time as part of an evolving "research agenda," when they develop ideas over a series of research projects and publications. Tough questions and problems often take years to resolve.

Tips for Avoiding Plagiarism

- **As you read, pay careful attention to how writers use their sources.** Practice by imitating various styles. More skill with using sources will increase your confidence and lower the risk of plagiarism.
- **Maintain careful notes as you read and conduct research.** When taking notes, mark quotations with quotation marks, and keep track of page numbers and which material comes from which source.
- **Don't be tempted to write your paper and *then* go back to fill in the citations.** Doing so will only generate more work

(retracing your research steps) and increase the risk of inadvertent plagiarism.

- **Don't procrastinate.** Looming deadlines cause anxiety that can cloud judgment. Don't be tempted to take shortcuts, and don't fool yourself into thinking that you write best under pressure. If, for some reason, you cannot complete your work on time, discuss your situation with your professor. Be honest, don't make excuses, and know that the sun will rise again tomorrow.

- **Get to know your honor code** so you'll know how your school handles academic integrity. Ask questions when in doubt. Ignorance of the rules is typically not an excuse for breaking them.

TRY THIS ➤   Investigate the Honor Code

For this exercise, find and review your school's policies for academic integrity. Then, answer the following questions:

- How does your school's policy compare to the honor codes you encountered in schools you attended previously?
- Are there any inconsistencies between your honor code and the guidelines we provided in this chapter?
- What are the implications or applications of academic integrity policies outside of school?

So What?

We create arguments from sources by responsibly borrowing and building on the words and thoughts of other scholars. When in doubt, cite what's not already in your head. You won't be accused of plagiarism for citing too much. And remember, your writing should demonstrate *your* thinking. Use sources to support your ideas; don't let them dominate your writing.

Now that you know something about how scholars read, write, and use sources, you're ready to learn more about *argument*: the essential tool that scholars use to explain their ideas. In the next chapter, we introduce the ways that arguments work in college and in life. We explain how arguments grow out of problems and controversies, and how they use research and evidence to answer significant questions. We describe how to locate weak spots and assumptions in arguments in order to make a compelling case. And we reveal how effective arguments are built on a strong basis of agreement with shared knowledge, values, and beliefs. This overview will give you a strong foundation for creating arguments that matter—those that answer the important *so what?* question, connect with audiences, and improve our understanding of the world.

What's Next

Take what you've learned in this chapter and respond to the following prompts.

1. **Using sources in scholarly and nonacademic work.** Find a scholarly journal article in your field on a subject that interests you, and investigate how the author uses sources. In three different colors, highlight quotations, paraphrases, and summaries. Then, find a magazine or newspaper article that also uses outside sources. Use the same colors to highlight the different ways the author uses sources. After you finish color-coding the articles, estimate the percentages and create a pie chart or other graphic to show your results. Compare your results with a classmate and reflect on the following:
   - How much does each author use each technique?
   - How much of the article is the author's argument?
   - How do the scholarly arguments use sources differently than the nonacademic ones?

2. **Citation systems.** Look up the citation system that your discipline uses and practice formatting a few different bibliographic citations.

For variety, format a book, a scholarly article, and a credible website. Then, compare your citations with a few classmates:

- What differences do you notice among styles?
- What disciplinary values might influence these different details, such as the date placement?

3. **Trace a scholarly genealogy.** Killingsworth and Gilbert credit a number of sources in their bibliography on which they built their research—their scholarly ancestors, so to speak. If you can access the online version of the article via your library's website, their citations are hyperlinked to the sources. Also on the website is a listing of subsequent research that grew out of Killingsworth and Gilbert's research—their scholarly descendants.

Read one of the subsequent articles (scholarly descendants) listed on the website under the heading "This Article Has Been Cited by Other Articles." (If you can't access their article online, you can search Google Scholar for links to sources that cite the article.) Consider how the article builds off of Killingsworth and Gilbert's research, and reflect on the following:

- Where in the article do the authors cite Killingsworth and Gilbert?
- How is the article related to "A Wandering Mind Is an Unhappy Mind"?
- Can you imagine how Killingsworth and Gilbert's article might have been an inspiration for this article?

Then, write a one-page summary of the article, describing how it continues the scholarly conversation. Share your summaries in class to discuss the different threads that Killingsworth and Gilbert's "scholarly descendants" take up. If you're interested in pursuing this further, read one of Killingsworth and Gilbert's "scholarly ancestors" to see how their work influenced "A Wandering Mind Is an Unhappy Mind."

CHAPTER four

How Do Arguments Work

chapter checklist

- How do people use arguments in school and beyond?
- What are the elements of arguments, and how do we build them?
- How do we locate underlying assumptions, gaps, and weak spots?
- How does investigation inspire arguments?

When you hear the term "argument," you might first think about kids squabbling over whose turn it is to sit in the front seat of the car, or you might imagine you and your parents fighting over how late you can stay out. "Argument" may also conjure visions of television lawyers presenting their case before a jury, or senators debating over the particulars of a new energy regulation. For us, the term "argument" signifies a tool that helps us explain *what* we think and *why* we think so. A thesis states what we think, and the rest of the argument shows why. Arguments influence our audiences' knowledge, beliefs, or actions, and they can also clarify or enhance our own thinking. Scholars use argument to justify their discoveries.

Effective arguments enact significant purposes. They are a means of doing work in the world, not a process of fighting or persuading others that we're right. Compelling arguments respond to questions or problems that seem urgent, controversial, or significant to writers and their audiences. They help us create and communicate answers and solutions, and they influence us to modify what (or how) we know, believe, think, or act.

Arguments use different structures, depending on their purposes, but they typically include four main elements: a claim, support, rationale, and some explanation of why the argument matters. Some forms of argument are easy to spot, such as editorials, proposals, and advertisements. However, other forms may not appear argumentative, even though they contain common elements of argument. Let's look at some examples in different situations that you might not immediately recognize as arguments.

What Does Argument Look Like in Different Contexts?

Arguments originate from a gap or imperfection, an unknown answer, or an unsolved problem—an inspiration that matters to the writer. The problem could be as simple as an employee facing financial difficulty or as complicated as the federal deficit. We design arguments that respond to these practical or theoretical controversies.

Let's consider some examples from school and the world beyond that illustrate how arguments can be used to achieve various purposes.

- **Scholars** use arguments to explain and improve our world. In recent years, for example, increased occurrences of school shootings in the United States have led us to ask why these tragedies *occur*, what *causes* people to do such terrible things, and what might be *done* to prevent future violence. Researchers in psychology, sociology, criminal justice, and other disciplines conduct investigations and build arguments to help us understand and address problems like these.

- **Government and military intelligence experts** use arguments to inform politicians. Analysts piece together information from limited or incomplete sources, compare different versions of what might be happening, make judgments, and draw conclusions about what they think. Their answers help justify foreign policy actions of all kinds.

- **Criminal trial lawyers** use arguments to establish guilt or innocence. Juries decide questions of guilt or innocence based on the cases presented by prosecution and defense attorneys in the courtroom. The justice system seeks the truth about the case, but regardless of what actually happened, the verdict determines a defendant's fate.

- **Scientists** discover evidence through research, which others use to build compelling cases for new laws or regulations. For instance, in the 1920s, a German scientist posed the research question: What diseases might be linked to cigarette smoking? Other scientists conducted follow-up research and gathered mounting evidence about the dangers of smoking, which eventually led governments to require health warnings on cigarette packaging.

These examples illustrate a defining feature of arguments: All arguments—whether they intend to solve practical problems or simply deepen our understanding of an issue—**begin with a question or uncertainty and use some method of investigation and case building to arrive at a conclusion**. That is, honest jurors, politicians, and scholars examine the evidence *before* drawing conclusions.

Creating strong arguments requires careful thinking and consideration of others. Arguments have serious implications when they influence decisions that affect people. In government, arguments can determine whether programs receive funding or soldiers go to war. A trial can determine a defendant's freedom or death. Jumping to conclusions can lead to bad decisions that harm others, which is why ethical writers and readers don't take shortcuts.

CONSIDER THIS ➤ Starting with Questions

For this reflection, consider the following: we believe the scholarly approach of case building increases the chances of finding the truth or the best decision/answer possible. However, this process (starting with a question and withholding judgment until investigation is complete) might be different from how you have been taught to develop arguments:

- When you write, when do you come up with a thesis?
- When were you taught to consult sources?
- How do you think the writing process might affect scholars' ability to discover accurate information, to think objectively, and to build ethical arguments?

Thinking through these questions can make you more aware of your writing habits and can help you develop new and better practices. Reflecting on your writing process can also give you insight into potential problems in your approach. For instance, if you always look for sources after you develop a thesis, you might overlook compelling evidence that contradicts your argument.

What about Specialized Scholarly Arguments?

Right about now, you might be thinking that some scholarly arguments you've read or heard about don't seem to have purposes that are obviously significant, practical, or urgent. In the examples we listed earlier, the issues are clearly important to the world. In contrast, scholars often work in such narrow specializations that their arguments may seem insignificant or impractical to people outside their scholarly community. However, such work is significant and compelling to those writers and their audiences. In fact, a scholarly community signals the importance of such work by publishing arguments for everyone to hear.

Of course, scholars don't always address problems of great urgency or practical significance, but even when their work is theoretical or esoteric, their arguments respond to questions or problems that matter to them and to their audience. For example, scholars might:

- Discover a disciplinary question that puzzles them
- Feel aggravated by a problem in their teaching
- Vehemently disagree with another scholar's findings
- Notice something new that contradicts previous experience

Such topics compel scholars to investigate and to write arguments for others in their field to consider and build on. Some of these arguments may ultimately influence people outside of academia, while others might more immediately affect specific disciplinary fields.

Here are some specific examples of arguments that scholars make to each other:

- A literary scholar, on the basis of textual evidence, biographical information about an author, and historical information about the time and place of a publication, argues for a new interpretation of a famous novel.
- An education scholar, using theories about learning and results of experimental teaching, argues for a new method of effective instruction.
- A nursing scholar synthesizes previous studies to argue for standardizing a "best practice" medical technique.

Apprentice scholars can feel more motivated and be more successful when they identify similar gaps and imperfections. If you can find a question or problem that really interests you—something you want to figure out—you can get a taste for what it's like to solve a scholarly puzzle. The next few chapters explain how to discover arguments that ignite your curiosity. Finding a *purpose* to write (beyond completing the assignment) will help you develop as a scholar. It might even feel less like practice and more like something that matters.

How Do Scholars Create Arguments?

Now that you know what scholarly arguments are, you might be wondering how scholars develop an idea. Experienced scholars tend to follow a process that looks like this:

1. **Begin with a very specific problem or question** within your discipline that interests you.
2. **Review scholarly publications** to make sure that your question is worth asking or that your problem still needs solving, so that fellow scholars won't be wondering *so what?*
3. **Design and conduct some kind of investigation** to solve the problem or answer the question, such as conducting an interview or distributing surveys. Chapter 6 includes additional guidelines for conducting original research.
4. **Report results of the research**, in the form of an argument, to colleagues in your discipline via a scholarly conference presentation and/or publication.

Because scholars create arguments *from* previous scholarship, original data, practical experience, and other inspirations, **writing typically follows research** for experienced scholars. However, here's a little secret: experienced scholars often dread writing as much as students do. Most scholars find answering questions and solving problems more stimulating than writing papers about what they discover. Once they've answered their question, scholars can get bored and just want to move on to the next problem. The last thing they want to do is worry about APA citation styles and manuscript formatting, but they know they have to publish their work so others can use it—and they understand that they must present their work in certain established forms (genres and styles) that their readers recognize and value.

Apprentices can begin to practice scholarly writing by investigating problems and questions through the work that others have done. Often the problems will be assigned by instructors who (a) already know the key issues and background well and (b) can provide relevant sources through course readings.

Other times, you can choose your own questions and engage in what we call "library research." Rather than collecting and analyzing raw data (a "primary" source), scholarly apprentices mostly use information that has already been examined and reported by others ("secondary" or "library" sources). As you mature as a scholar, you might even conduct original experiments or study historical artifacts or archives as primary source materials.

Argument as Investigation and Case Building

As you may recall from the first chapter, scholars use arguments to seek truth and justify discoveries that result from careful investigation. This means that scholars often don't know their thesis when they begin but rather *discover* it through investigation and research.

Imagine an archaeologist who unearths some petrified bones. She might suspect that the bones belong to a dinosaur, but she must continue digging, analyzing, and assembling the skeleton to discover the animal's identity. If you've seen a dinosaur skeleton in a museum, you probably noticed plastic "bones" and wires that the archaeologists added to complete the puzzle and hold everything together. Writing an argument requires a similar process of finding sources and evidence and assembling them to create a coherent message.

Sometimes, this process takes decades. Consider, for example, the smoking example that we cite earlier in the chapter. When scientists initially questioned the health effects of cigarette smoking, they began their research process with a question or a hypothesis; they suspected that smoking might not be good for us. *After all,* they thought, *you're inhaling smoke.*

By investigating piles of medical records and discovering that many people suffering from lung cancer were, indeed, heavy smokers, scientists began to assemble compelling evidence to build a case against smoking. As evidence of cigarettes' danger mounted, the US government's warnings (or arguments) grew proportionally stronger, from a statement in 1966 that sounded more like opinion ("Cigarette smoking may be hazardous to your health") to statements of fact like ones we see now ("Smoking causes lung cancer, heart disease, emphysema, and may complicate pregnancy").

In other words, the thesis intensified as the evidence became stronger: "We *suspect* this might be hazardous," then "We *think* this is dangerous," and finally "We *know* that cigarettes can kill you!" The thesis, which originated in a question, became more "certain" and convincing as the support accumulated.

Implications and Applications

The smoking example demonstrates how arguments can gradually change the way we think about issues over time. Much of what we know, think, and believe evolves through investigation, new experiences, and persuasive arguments.

If you don't think that arguments can influence what we know, think, and believe, consider the effects of:

- Arguments made by civil rights leaders who changed how we think about equality
- Arguments made by feminists who influenced the way American families function
- Arguments made by activists who demanded health care reform
- Arguments made by respected mentors who inspired you to question a previously held opinion

These examples illustrate how arguments can have tangible effects on our daily lives. Can you think of more examples of arguments that have influenced what you know and how you live?

Indeed, the best arguments are the ones that have important *implications* and *applications*—consequences or effects that answer the *so what?* question. For instance, arguments can inspire readers to reconsider their position, to modify their behavior, or to open themselves up to another possibility. Or arguments can evoke a change in the writer himself: for example, when he develops a deeper understanding of an issue or

77

problem, when he encounters new viewpoints, or when he experiences the peace of mind that comes from validating his beliefs and values.

As with the writer's purpose or inspiration, implications can be stated explicitly or inferred by the reader. Sometimes we tell audiences how and why our arguments matter so they won't miss the impact. Research articles often begin with a section that contextualizes the study's significance (called a Research or Literature Review) and conclude with a section that discusses the larger implications of the research findings. Whether or not we tell our readers outright how and why our arguments matter, we at least hint at some implications so they're not left to wonder, *so what?*

Compelling arguments have significant implications that not only change what audiences think but also inspire follow-up questions and arguments. In this way, the process is circular. For example, we might read a *Science* magazine article that concludes that we are less happy when our minds wander. One implication of this argument might be that we should pay more attention to what we're doing while we're doing it. Discovering this might lead us to ask, "What techniques can we use to quiet our minds?" Now, we have some inspiration for research that might ultimately lead to an argument about the benefits of meditation. See how the process works?

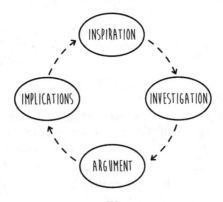

TRY THIS ➤ Use Precise Vocabulary

For this exercise, take a break from the chapter's content to examine and experiment with some language choices that writers make.

We have attempted to write this book in an engaging, straightforward, and informal style. That includes not overwhelming readers with technical jargon or unnecessarily complicated words. However, you'll notice that we occasionally choose less familiar terms to express precise meaning. (On p. 73, for example, we described some scholarly work as "esoteric.")

Part of what makes language marvelous—and writing potentially fun—is gathering a deep pool of available vocabulary. Whenever you read, keep a dictionary or smart phone app handy so you can acquire new words for your own use.

Beware, though. Scholars who use big words just to sound smart do no favors for themselves or their readers. If we need a complex word to convey a complex idea, that's fine, but often we don't.

Effective writing is deliberate and precise—not overcomplicated.

What do you think of our choice to use "esoteric"? What other words or ways of expressing this idea would work as well or better? To reflect on the effects of using sophisticated vocabulary, experiment with the following:

1. Write a simple sentence.
2. Consult the thesaurus to rewrite the sentence with more sophisticated words.
3. Revise the sentence to strike a tasteful balance between sophistication and clarity. Then, compare with a peer and explain your word choices.

How Do We Build Arguments?

Imagine an argument as a bridge between a writer and reader. The **thesis** is the roadway, built by investigation and thinking. The road will not stand alone without displaying our investigation and thinking for readers to scrutinize. We must build **supports** to hold the road up and **rationales** to link everything together.

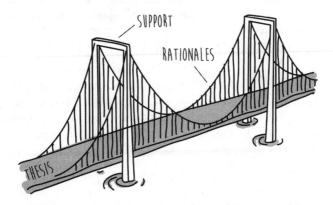

The thesis is our argument's central **claim**, a debatable or controversial idea that we're proposing to our audience. A thesis can be stated explicitly or implied. Although it often appears in the beginning of an argument, sometimes we state our thesis most clearly in the conclusion, because that's what it really is: the conclusion or result of our investigation and thinking. Sometimes the thesis can be more like a hypothesis (used in experimental or scientific method), when it's a tentative thesis that needs to be tested and validated through investigation and argumentation.

Supporting Claims

Because claims are controversial or open to question, we pair them with some kind of support that our audience will trust. The basic structure looks like this: [Claim] because [support]. For example,

Claim: You should keep reading BECAUSE
Support: this chapter will be really useful.

In everyday arguments, we call this kind of support a "reason," but a reason is actually another kind of claim that our audience might question (like "this chapter will be really useful"). Rather than relying only on reasons, scholars seek the firmest, most well-developed supports they can find, ones that critical audiences will trust. The three most common categories of support used by scholars are evidence, verification, and illustration (see Table 4.1).

Evidence includes anything we can observe. During an experiment, for example, we might observe a chemical reaction or response from a plant that we're studying. We can also use evidence acquired through personal experience, as when we witness an event or observe a film or work of art. When writing a literary analysis, we can use quotations from a poem or novel as evidence for our interpretation. As we discuss in Chapter 6, we typically use evidence to activate our audience's sense of logic or reasoning.

Verification includes things we can look up. Students often support arguments by summarizing, paraphrasing, and quoting from scholarly articles or books to corroborate their claims. Lawyers refer to laws and legal precedents as verification. Scholars rely on

Table 4.1   KINDS OF SUPPORT

EVIDENCE Something you can observe	VERIFICATION Something you can look up	ILLUSTRATION Something you can imagine
• Empirical data • Personal experience • Textual evidence	• Previous research • Law or precedence • Established theory	• Fictional narrative • Hypothetical example • Analogy or metaphor

When might these different kinds of support activate reasoning, build credibility, or evoke emotion?

established theories and previous research to verify their work. Verification often determines the credibility of an argument.

Illustrations involve things we imagine. For example, we might offer a hypothetical example or fictional narrative to support our thesis. Like other illustrations, figures of speech such as analogies and metaphors can evoke an emotional response from the reader.

Scholars typically use specialized terminology to categorize different kinds of support:

- Evidence is a **primary source**, something that you can collect and analyze yourself.
- Verification is a **secondary source**, which means someone else has already analyzed or interpreted the evidence.
- Illustration is an **original source**, one that you create or borrow for a particular argument.

Of course, some kinds of support can cross over into more than one category. For example, sometimes personal experience can be used as evidence but also carry emotional impact. A hypothetical example can either evoke emotion or activate reasoning. Sometimes empirical data or statistics can build credibility. What's most important is that we think carefully about what we want a particular support to accomplish: Do we want it to build credibility, activate reasoning, or evoke emotion? We select the appropriate kind of evidence for our specific purpose.

Evidence tends to be the strongest kind of support because we trust most what we can observe. Evidence connects most clearly and certainly with reality and truth. Evidence also works well for different audiences, whereas verification may be culturally specific. For example, the US Constitution would provide convincing verification for an audience of US citizens but probably not for Canadians. Likewise, sociologists might not trust or find relevant the theories and research used by literary scholars. As the most speculative form of support, illustrations can evoke the most inconsistent but potentially powerful effects on audiences. We discuss ways to support arguments in much greater detail throughout the rest of the book.

For an argument to be successful, our audience must accept the support we present. Whenever an audience doubts or considers our support controversial, the bridge collapses. Sometimes collapses occur when the audience doubts the accuracy of evidence or misunderstands an illustration, but most commonly, supports fail when we haven't linked our claims and supports with a strong rationale.

Linking Support to Claims

We can walk, swim, run, and sit up straight because our musculature and skeletons work together. But these functions would be impossible without the tendons that connect our muscles and bones. Similarly, a rationale connects claims and supports together so they can function as an argument:

[Claim] BECAUSE [support].

A **rationale**, also known as a premise, explains the "because" part of an argument. Often, these rationales go unstated, but they are always present, whether or not we make them explicit. For example, we might argue that people shouldn't smoke *because* smoking is unhealthy. The unstated or assumed rationale is that *people should not do unhealthy things*. You might think that rationale is obvious or "common sense," and so it doesn't need to be stated explicitly, but you've probably heard what can happen when you assume. In this case, we shouldn't assume that rationale is obvious or uncontroversial when so many people who know the risks of smoking do so anyway. Countless doctors and government officials have warned people about the dangers of smoking, yet many people continue to smoke. Why? Because many people disagree with the notion that people should not do unhealthy things. For them, the rationale is open to question—another claim that needs support.

TRY THIS ➤ Practice Articulating Rationales

For this exercise, provide missing rationales for the following arguments:

- You're feeling sick (*support*), so you should go see a doctor (*claim*).
- Trendy jeans are worth the money (*claim*) because they're so stylish (*support*).
- American citizens should learn Spanish (*claim*) because there are so many Spanish speakers in the United States (*support*).
- Our candidate is tough on crime (*support*), so she deserves your vote (*claim*).
- Universities should pay student athletes (*claim*) because they earn substantial revenue for the school (*support*).
- Fraternities promote unhealthy behavior (*support*), so they should be shut down (*claim*).

Compare your answers with a classmate. Then, explain how you might support your rationales if your audience questioned them.

Rationales are just as important to arguments as claims and support. In fact, a distinguishing characteristic of scholarly argument is the extent that scholars go to scrutinize rationales and make them visible. That's why scientists use elaborate statistical calculations in their research: to validate the strength of linkages between evidence and the conclusions of investigation. In Chapters 5 and 8, we explain more fully how to develop and test rationales.

Table 4.2   ARGUMENT ELEMENTS AND THEIR FUNCTION

ELEMENT	FUNCTION
Purpose	The *inspiration* of the writer, the *functions* of the message, and the *implications* for the audience
Thesis or central claim	A debatable or controversial idea
Support	The *evidence, verifications*, and/or *illustrations* used to defend the claim
Rationale	An explanation of how a support holds up a claim

Can you imagine how these elements come together to form an argument?

An Everyday Argument

To illustrate the basic components of an argument, let's consider an example of an everyday workplace argument. Like many everyday arguments, this example begins with a claim supported by reasons. But remember, reasons are actually claims themselves—debatable statements—not evidence, verification, or illustration. As soon as the reader or listener disagrees with a reason, we must provide better support.

Everyday arguments often stack claims on top of other claims with little support. This kind of argument can work when we argue with friends or acquaintances who share extensive background knowledge, but whenever we encounter points of disagreement, we must support our claims with evidence, verification, and/or illustration. We must eventually base the argument on something that we agree about, something that's not open to question. This is especially true with arguments written for a demanding, sophisticated audience. In a later section, we'll show how a scholarly argument does just that.

Let's imagine a scenario where an employee is feeling financially strapped, so he approaches his boss to build a case for a pay raise. The dialogue goes like this:

EMPLOYEE: "I deserve a raise." (*thesis*)

BOSS: "Um, so do I. But why should I give *you* more money?"

EMPLOYEE: "Because I work hard, I'm indispensable, and I'm underpaid." (*reasons*)

The employee's argument should seem familiar, because the layout resembles the kind of argument that most of us learned in high school. His main claim, or thesis, asserts that he deserves more pay. To support his thesis, the employee gives three reasons that he thinks his boss will accept. **Effective arguments always build on some basis of acceptance or agreement.** If the boss agrees that her employee is hard working, indispensable, and underpaid, she's likely to give him a raise (if she has the authority to do so, her budget allows, and so forth). However, as we can see from the dialogue, the argument only works if the boss accepts the reasons provided. Note that the employee has not yet offered evidence or verification to support his claims:

BOSS: "I agree that you're a hard worker, but tell me more about how indispensable you are."

EMPLOYEE: "Well, I have more experience doing this work than anyone else in this office, and I'm a good problem solver." (*more reasons*)

BOSS: "Can you give me some examples of problems that you've solved that nobody else could?"

EMPLOYEE: "Sure. Remember that time. . .?" (*evidence*)

BOSS: "Okay, so now I see how you're a hard worker and sometimes indispensable. But so is everyone else. Why do you think you're underpaid?"

EMPLOYEE: "Because other employers keep offering me more money."

BOSS: "Can you show me some of those job offers?" (*verification*)

Getting to the Bottom of Things

Do you notice how difficult it may be to get to the "bottom" of an argument? Whatever reasons the employee provides, the boss can always dig deeper, asking for more support. With an especially complicated or controversial argument—or when addressing a demanding audience—this process might go on for a long time before reaching the bottom or finding some basis of agreement.

Let's look at the original argument once more in a graphic format that highlights how its structure can unfold (see Figure 4.1).

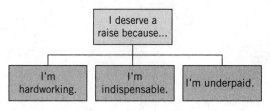

Figure 4.1
An Employee's Argument for a Raise

Notice that the employees three reasons are really claims.

Again, if the boss agrees with the basis provided, she might be persuaded. If not, the employee must dig deeper to build a stronger, more elaborate foundation for his argument, like the one shown in Figure 4.2.

Thus, we can imagine a brick building, where the thesis must rest on a strong foundation of support. Any block that's doubted or not accepted by the audience can cause the argument to teeter or crumble like a tower of blocks (think of the game Jenga). As we provide better reasons and more evidence to meet the needs of our audience, the basis of our argument grows larger.

In scholarly arguments, we drill down until we find much more solid ground to support our arguments. You can see how an everyday argument might work when both the person arguing and the audience share extensive background knowledge. But in the workplace example, the employee might need to provide evidence of his work productivity or examples of his contributions. Or he may need to verify that he has received job offers from other companies. His foundation would have been stronger if he had built these supports into his argument from the beginning.

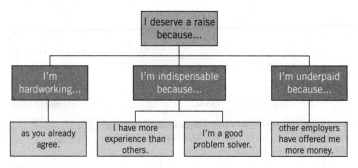

Figure 4.2

An Employee's More Developed Argument.

Can you imagine what evidence or verification the employee could use to support her claims?

TRY THIS ➤ Assemble the Elements of an Argument

For this exercise, practice building the elements of an argument. To identify a topic, brainstorm with other students about a problem or question at your school. Propose a potential solution (stated as a thesis) to resolve the problem, and think of what kind of support would convince faculty or administrators to implement your plan. Then create a block structure like Figure 4.2 to represent how you could present your proposal.

Learning to anticipate and meet the needs of a demanding audience (the way scholars try to do) can help you make more compelling and convincing everyday arguments, too.

Making Assumptions

Assumptions are any elements of the argument that either the writer or the audience are thinking but not saying. Assumptions can include things such as

- Evidence, verification, or other background knowledge that we assume our audience already knows ("You've seen my work, so you already know I'm a good problem solver.")
- Rationales ("You value hard work.")
- The inspiration or implications of the argument ("You know I've been struggling financially, and you can imagine how much harder I'll work if I get a raise.")

Assumptions lurk below the surface, like the immense base of an iceberg that is much larger than its visible top. Indeed, what's assumed in an argument is usually greater than what's said or written. That is, **assumptions make up the bulk of the total argument**, even though they're typically hiding, unstated, below the surface.

Of course, we always have to make some assumptions when creating an argument because we can never say everything we mean. In everyday arguments, we often leave most of our assumptions "submerged" when we argue with people we know well. We can rely on shared background knowledge, familiar culture, and so forth. When the employee in our everyday argument example provides reasons disguised as support, he is making assumptions. In this case, however, he wrongly assumes that the boss will not question his reasons or need additional support. And that's the problem: **Arguments often break down not because of what we've said but because of what we (wrongly) assume our audiences already know or believe.**

Let's examine another example: many politicians argue that wealthier citizens should pay more taxes in the interest of fairness. In this argument, politicians might assume a variety of things, for example:

- That economic equity creates "fairness"
- That fairness means that those who can afford to pay more taxes should owe more taxes
- That wealth causes political disparity and therefore higher taxes support equality by limiting the accumulation of wealth

It's easy to imagine how others may find these assumptions controversial or want additional support or explanation. Again, unless we know our audience well enough to anticipate what readers already know and believe, we must make our assumptions more explicit and possibly defend them.

When we engage in scholarly arguments, we're arguing with strangers—readers who don't know or trust us already and who will scrutinize our arguments carefully. (In fact, rigorous scholarly "peer reviews" are normally "double blind"—that is, the author's and reader's identities are not known to each other during the editorial process.) Scholarly arguments therefore seek to be as complete as possible so that readers can critique our work. Scholars know that writing is different from speech; we can't clarify, reword, add more detail, or respond to objections once we've published or "turned in" the argument. So we work diligently to ensure that our support is as solid and complete as space allows, that our rationales are clear, and that our "bridge" is fortified.

One way to avoid making assumptions is to make our unstated assumptions (reasons, inspirations, prior knowledge, and so forth) explicit. Metaphorically speaking, we raise as much of the argument above the water as we can.

"Above-Water" Arguments

Because arguments have the power to change our minds, behaviors, beliefs, and actions, scholars scrutinize their arguments carefully. As an apprentice, you might find the task of finding and fixing faults in your arguments daunting, and you might think they'll become too long or overexplained. But scholars leave little to chance. Every sentence in the argument is there for a reason, whether it be to prevent an objection, to answer a question, or to fully explain a controversial point. As much as is practical, we make our support and rationales visible to our audience. **Arguments that anticipate disconnects—that is, objections and unshared assumptions—have the best chance of changing our audience's mind.**

Taking the time and space to design a complete argument that will satisfy a skeptical audience usually pays off. Doing so not only helps

---

TRY THIS ➤ Build Support

For this exercise, take what you learned about making assumptions and apply it to a hypothetical situation.

1. Imagine that you're a teenager who wants to stay out later than usual for a party, but you need to persuade your parent to let you do so.
   a. What claims and support might your audience accept?
   b. What unstated assumptions must your audience share for your argument to work?
2. Now imagine that you're the parent, trying to convince your teenager that staying out late is a bad idea. What support and shared assumptions would make your argument work?
3. Based on how you answered 1 and 2, where are these arguments most likely to break down? What are the potential sources of disagreement or unshared assumptions?

---

us persuade readers, but we're also more likely to understand our subject in more depth and detail.

Rookie Mistakes and How to Fix Them

For apprentice scholars, one of the most difficult parts of college writing is imagining how much is safe to assume and how much must be made explicit. In other words, how much of our iceberg do readers need to see? As a general rule, **increased controversy requires increased explanation**. A truly "original" thesis will contradict what the audience already thinks, so we have to work harder to earn their agreement.

Here are three of the most common rookie mistakes made by apprentice scholars:

1. **Arguing the obvious**, or arguing about something the audience already knows or agrees with. Here, the writer wastes lots of effort supporting a conclusion (thesis) that really doesn't need to be argued.
2. **Arguing without support**, or underestimating how controversial a statement is—stating something *as though* readers already know or agree with it when, in fact, they don't. Rookie writers often use unsubstantiated claims to support an argument.
3. **Supporting without arguing.** Sometimes apprentice scholars present evidence, verification, or illustrations without telling the audience what point they're trying to make. Expecting that your audience will reach an unstated conclusion is a trick that works fine in everyday arguments, advertising, or politics. (For example, advertisers expect that handsome men can "sell" products to women.) However, experienced scholars state their claims clearly and explicitly.

So how do we avoid making these mistakes?

- **To avoid arguing the obvious:**
  a. **Read more.** When scholars think they have an original idea, they review other scholars' work to make sure that their research question or tentative argument isn't old news. (We discuss Research or Literature Reviews more in Appendix B.) You can do the same by consulting scholarly sources; if you find lots of sources that have made your argument already, you might need to find a new angle.
  b. **Ask an expert.** A good shortcut is to ask a scholarly mentor, such as your instructor, if the idea seems fresh and interesting. She'll tell you if she's already read too many papers about a "tired" subject like lowering the drinking age.

- **To avoid arguing without support:**
  a. **Highlight your argument.** Read your draft and mark the thesis and supporting claims in color (on your computer or with a highlighter). Then review the parts that aren't highlighted. Do the claims need more support? Is there anything that your audience might question?
  b. **Consult a reader.** Ask a trusted classmate, writing center tutor, or your instructor to review your draft with an eye for assertions that need more evidence or explanation.

- **To avoid supporting without arguing:**
  a. **Use topic sentences.** Like mini-thesis statements, topic sentences can alert your reader to the reason or claim that you're about to develop. Good writing doesn't always need topic sentences, but they can help weary readers (and you) keep track of your points. We discuss more organizational strategies in Chapter 8.
  b. **Search for stranded support.** Make sure that you have clearly linked your claims and support together. Is it clear what point you're trying to support with that evidence?

So What?

Arguments use evidence, verification, and illustration (what is known or invented) to support claims (what is unknown or controversial). In effective arguments, the writer's inspiration and the implications for the audience converge to answer the question: *so what?*

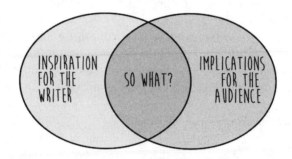

Now that you know that arguments are a complex network of inspirations, claims, support, rationales, assumptions, and implications, you might wonder how you can analyze arguments carefully enough to detect all of these features. Indeed, before we give any more advice on developing compelling arguments, we'll offer useful strategies for analyzing and responding to arguments. Responsible scholars wait to advance their own arguments until they have fully listened to what others have said. In order to develop persuasive arguments, we must first discover the most reasonable answers and the best courses of action for our audience. After all, our own thinking might be flawed, and it's certainly limited, so we need to take into account the intellectual work of others. Chapter 5 describes analytical techniques that you can use to understand others' arguments deeply so you can participate as an informed apprentice scholar.

What's Next
. . . .

Take what you've learned in this chapter and respond to the following prompts.

1. **Practice question and argument.** Integrate the various parts of an argument by creating an outline or graphic that develops one of the following questions:

   a. What major should I choose?

   b. Which profession should I pursue after college?

   Once you've selected a question, state your tentative answers to the question in the form of a thesis, such as "I should major in [Biology, Business, or Basket Weaving] so that I can get a job that is profitable and prestigious." Now, make a list of the kinds of support you would need to convince a friend or relative who thinks you should decide something different. Can you think of some evidence, verification, and illustrations that would answer the question more definitively?

2. **Explore current arguments.** For this exercise, explore the arguments surrounding a current social or political issue that interests you, like the local food movement. Read a few popular sources, such as newspapers or magazine articles, and at least one scholarly article, and then discuss the following in class:

   • Who are the various stakeholders in this issue (for example, individuals, organizations, and governments who have an interest in the matter)? What are their concerns? What arguments do you hear them making?

   • What questions or controversies do these arguments raise?

   • What characteristics of your community context promote or limit these discussions? For example, arguments about the local food movement might be different if you live in a farming community or a large city. What economic or cultural factors might influence the stakeholders? What is the dominant political affiliation, and how does that affect people's views on the issue?

Analyzing an argument in this way helps us understand an issue and its context more deeply. We can better recognize the complexities of an issue; understand the people involved and their different perspectives; and appreciate how the issue relates to other topics, values, beliefs, cultures, and customs within a social context.

CHAPTER five

How Do We
Analyze Arguments

chapter checklist

- How can we analyze rhetorical elements?
- How do we identify an argument's central controversies?
- How should we respond to arguments?

As you read more scholarly writing, you will begin to see texts not merely as unquestionable, lifeless, purely objective collections of facts and ideas, but as part of conversations that writers and their audiences use to create and recreate knowledge—and you will begin to participate in that discussion yourself. Closely studying an argument's rhetorical elements can deepen your understanding of its message.

Analyzing Rhetorical Elements

To read and analyze a text rhetorically, we break down the argument to see how it works, without judging or agreeing or disagreeing. The guiding questions of analysis are as follows:

- How is the argument designed?
- What choices did the author make in designing the argument?
- Why did she make those choices?

For example, why did she choose to open the essay with that particular illustration, or why did she choose that kind of evidence? Analyzing texts this way helps us read other writers' work as models for our own. In the next section, we will discuss additional rhetorical elements to examine while reading.

So What? The Inspiration, Purpose, and Implications

As we discussed in the previous chapters, authors write because they are responding to some *inspiration*: a problem, question, or gap in understanding. Something *motivates* them to write. Maybe they read something and disagreed with the author's argument. Or they discovered a problem that needed a solution. Or they became curious about a question. Something happened. We can better decipher a writer's inspiration if we ask ourselves: What happened? What is this writer responding to? Where did this idea originate? Why did this topic matter to him? Whether or not the writer explains or implies an inspiration, effective arguments usually leave clues about the author's motivation to write.

If the inspiration is the cause of the argument, the *purpose* is its desired effect: what the writer hopes his argument will accomplish. In general, arguments influence how our audiences think or act, so an argument's purpose will be to modify the knowledge, beliefs, or behavior of the reader.

Implications involve the larger outcomes of an argument: indirect and unforeseen consequences that go beyond its immediate purposes. Let's consider an everyday example that ties these elements together. Suppose someone becomes irritated about teenagers speeding through her neighborhood (*inspiration*), so she writes a letter to the editor of her local newspaper to raise awareness of the problem (*purpose*). After reading the published complaint, the chief of police sends a patrol car to the neighborhood to set up a speed trap (*implication*).

Now here's a scholarly example. A professor who tutors in a writing center notices many students who seem to obsess too much over "later order" concerns in their writing, such as grammar, punctuation, and citation formatting (*inspiration*), so he experiments with different tutoring techniques that shift students' focus to higher order issues, such as designing compelling arguments. He shares the results of his investigation in a journal read by faculty at other writing centers, hoping to enhance their tutoring practices (*purpose*). A few readers hold workshops for faculty across disciplines who want to improve how they teach writing, and the tutoring techniques are translated into strategies for teaching peer review in business courses, science labs, and so on (*implications*).

....

TRY THIS ➤ Practice with Inspiration, Purpose, and Implications

For this exercise, take what you've learned and try to imagine two or more possible inspirations, purposes, and implications for each of the following examples. Compare your results with a classmate.

- An editorial that criticizes a local politician
- A cigarette package that warns about the health risks of smoking
- A college academic department website
- A consumer survey that polls residents about their spending habits
- An in-class exercise in which you practice thinking about inspirations, purposes, and implications

....

Author and Audience

Knowing something about an author's credentials and background can give us insight into her assumptions, motives, biases, and credibility. We might investigate her background (by searching online) to learn about her expertise and what else she's written. We might also search for information about her political, personal, and community affiliations, if we think these factors might influence her argument. Similarly, we imagine the argument's intended audience—background and demographics (age, gender, income, education, political preferences), values, assumptions, and biases—because all of these elements can influence a writer's choices and an audience's reactions.

CONSIDER THIS ➤ Yourself as the Audience

For this reflection, think about what factors might influence how you interpret an argument. What are your values, assumptions, biases, and background? How might personal factors—such as your age, gender, ethnicity, education, income, or political preferences—influence how you interpret and respond to arguments? For example, how might your perspective on arguments differ from someone significantly older or younger than you?

Genre

Think of a genre as a **typical, recognizable *form* or *means* that achieves some *function* or *purpose*.** For example, to transport people from one location to another, humans have designed different types or "genres" of vehicles, such as bicycles, motorcycles, cars, trucks, trains, and planes. Each of these genres has a recognizable form. When we see an automobile, we immediately recognize it as an automobile, we know what it's designed to do, and we can distinguish it from a spaceship or unicycle or other kind of vehicle.

You already know about literary genres, such as plays, poems, or novels. Like vehicles, we immediately recognize their forms and functions because they're designed according to unwritten "rules" or conventions that audiences recognize and expect. Argument genres are no different. For example, we know that an editorial (*genre*) typically expresses a viewpoint about a current event (*inspiration*) in order to change public opinion (*purpose*). Or, we recognize a warning label (*genre*), written in response to a known health risk (*inspiration*), that cautions consumers about the dangers of using or misusing a product (*purpose*).

Arguments surround us, often in places we don't usually consider. For instance, think about stoplights as a kind of argument: their purpose is to *persuade* you to stop, go, or slow down. In contrast, exit signs merely *inform* you where you can exit a highway (or building). Their purpose is not to persuade anyone to exit—that's what billboard advertisements are for (EXIT HERE FOR THE BEST BARBECUE YOU EVER TASTED!).

Understanding the relationship between purpose and genre can dramatically improve our reading comprehension and give us an efficient starting point for analyzing an argument's effectiveness. When we recognize an argument's genre and purpose, we can evaluate it according to established, although often unwritten, rules and expectations. For example, when you watch a horror movie, you expect to be scared and startled—maybe even disgusted by blood and gore. There might also be some drama and humor, but like all genres, a horror movie has to follow the rules, mostly, or audiences will be disappointed. There's nothing worse than a comedy that isn't funny or a mystery with no surprises. Later chapters discuss expectations for appropriate styles, organizational patterns, and design features for genres of scholarly writing.

Context

In some situations, understanding an argument's content and genre will be enough to comprehend the message. But we've all communicated and miscommunicated enough to know how important the context can be. For instance, have you ever shown up to a party and realized that you were terribly overdressed? The style you wore last time was clearly too formal for this occasion. The context changed, so your choice was no longer appropriate.

Messages mean different things in different contexts. When reading something written long ago or far away, we may not be able to fully understand a text's meaning or purpose unless we know something about the time period, culture, community values, controversies, current events, and so on. Thinking about these elements gives us a richer picture. Arguments become more meaningful when we consider where and when they were created.

TRY THIS ➤ Examine a Scholarly Journal

For this exercise, find a physical copy of a scholarly journal and examine its features. Your school library should have copies of scholarly journals related to your major discipline. Find one, flip through it, and answer the following questions:

1. What do the article titles and topics indicate about the journal's intended audience?
2. What can you tell about the context or current scholarly conversations that are important?
3. Who publishes the journal, and how might that affect the journal's credibility?
4. How would you describe the genre and style of most articles?
5. Besides articles, what other kinds of content does the journal contain?

Identifying the Controversy

Beyond the basic elements of the rhetorical situation, rhetoric provides more sophisticated tools for reading and writing arguments. The most powerful tool of rhetoric, which we call the Controversy Categories, provides a systematic way to understand and create different types of arguments based on what kinds of disagreements an argument addresses. Because Controversy Categories are new to most college students, we introduce them here and provide opportunities for more practice in subsequent chapters. Table 5.1 describes the Controversy Categories in detail, but first we'll walk through an example to give a general sense of how this system works.

Our example is a murder case. During the trial, the first controversy that must be resolved is what actually happened—the facts of the case. If the prosecution does not have sufficient evidence to establish that, for example, the defendant was the person who stabbed his girlfriend (or his boyfriend, spouse, companion, or neighbor) to death, then he will go free. Once the prosecutors prove that fact, then they must establish that the accused person's actions fit the legal definition of murder. The cause (motive) and circumstances might affect the definition: Was it premeditated? A crime of passion? An accident? And the definition—first- or second-degree murder, involuntary manslaughter, and so forth—will determine the penalty or action to be taken according to the law.

In a trial, it doesn't make sense to skip steps and decide whether an accused person should receive the death penalty before we determine whether he was the person holding the knife. Indeed, that's why many countries, including the United States, base their justice systems on the presumption of innocence (innocent until proven guilty)—to guarantee citizens due process before enforcing penalties. The process doesn't always work, but if you were accused, would you rather face a lynch mob?

Note how the trial example shows the *sequential* or *hierarchical* progression of controversy categories. Until we agree about the facts, definitions, and interpretations (what's happening and what it means), there's no sense in finding solutions (enacting policies and

103

Table 5.1 CONTROVERSY CATEGORIES

CONTROVERSY CATEGORY	QUESTIONS FOR INVESTIGATION	EVERYDAY EXAMPLE	SCHOLARLY EXAMPLE
Existence or fact	Is it true? Did it happen?	Does country X have nuclear weapons capability? How do we know?	Do scholarly apprentices struggle with the demands of college-level reading?
Definition or interpretation	Does this case fit the definition? How do we interpret this information?	What kinds of weapons does country X possess?	What kind of reading problems do college students have?
Cause, consequence, or circumstance	What caused this? Was it intentional? Are there extenuating circumstances?	What prompted country X to develop nuclear weapons?	Why do college students struggle with scholarly readings?
Evaluation	Is it right or wrong? Is it serious enough to warrant our attention?	Do country X's nuclear capabilities pose an imminent threat to global security?	Do students' reading difficulties present a serious obstacle to learning?
Jurisdiction, procedure, policy, or action to be taken	What, if anything, should we do about it?	How should we respond to country X as a nuclear threat?	What actions might professors and students take to improve reading skills?

What controversy are you currently debating with friends, and which category would that issue fall under?

procedures). To further illustrate this logical progression, think about skipping a rock over water. Sometimes, the rock skips several times, and sometimes it just goes plunk.

Like a skipping rock, arguments that address fewer controversies can go deeper below the surface. Sometimes, writers skip over controversy categories that have already been resolved. For example, if the prosecution provides a video recording that clearly shows an act of murder and the identity of the accused and the victim, then defense counsel may concede that her client "did it" but argue about the circumstances or build a case for temporary insanity.

Sorting and prioritizing controversy categories allows us to skip over what's already well-established and focus our attention on the heart of the matter, or to locate places where multiple, competing disagreements have accumulated. Most complicated debates, such as gun control or abortion, involve multiple categories of disagreement. Complex arguments like these can be difficult to resolve because participants cannot agree to resolve a common "sticking point." For example, advocates for gun rights might focus too much on definitions (such as rights) and values (freedom to bear arms), whereas gun control advocates might fixate on competing values (safety) and policies (control measures).

Controversy categories can help us methodically navigate complex issues to get at the heart of the matter—the main controversy or point of disagreement. After all, arguments are designed to *resolve* controversies, so we can argue more effectively and efficiently if we can settle what we already agree about and direct our attention (argument) toward what matters most. As we discuss in Chapter 7, the main controversy is where we can find a compelling thesis.

TRY THIS ➤ Practice with Controversy Categories

For this exercise, identify as many controversies as you can for the following topics. Create a table with three columns: topic, stakeholders, and controversies. Here are the topics:

1. Grade inflation
2. Violent video games
3. Military conscription (draft)
4. [Choose a controversial topic that interests you.]

A Guided Analysis of a Scholarly Argument

Now let's put everything together to examine a scholarly argument by carefully analyzing the main elements of the rhetorical situation:

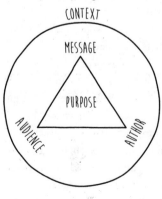

author, audience, message, purpose, and context. As we go along, think of how the elements connect with each other, as illustrated in this diagram that we introduced in Chapter 1.

Before we begin, read the article "A Wandering Mind Is an Unhappy Mind" by Harvard psychologists Matthew A. Killingsworth and Daniel T. Gilbert (reprinted in this book on pp. 243–247). Then, follow along in the essay as we model the analysis.

Identify the Audience and Context

Before we begin reading, we take note of the argument's publication information (where and when it was originally published) to help us identify the audience and understand the larger context. To identify Killingsworth and Gilbert's audience, we might ask ourselves:

- What do we know, or what can we find out, about the original publication context?
- Who are Killingsworth and Gilbert trying to reach? Who will read this article, and why?

This article originally appeared in the journal *Science*, which, according to their website, is "the world's leading journal of original scientific research, global news, and commentary." Journals like *Science* publish scholarly, peer-reviewed articles that typically attract particular kinds of readers (scholars and scientists). Knowing this information gives us some sense of the audience's level of education and expertise. We can assume that Killingsworth and Gilbert are writing for highly educated readers with a scientific background.

Identify the Author and Inspiration

A quick Google search for Killingsworth and Gilbert indicates that they are experts in their fields. They work at prestigious universities and regularly publish research in psychology. Their status influences their approach to the topic, their perspectives, and their purpose—and builds their credibility with *Science* readers.

In order to identify the authors' inspiration, we ask ourselves three important questions as we're reading the article:

- What initially motivated Killingsworth and Gilbert to investigate the connection between mind wandering and happiness?

- What gap in research or unanswered question prompted their attention?
- Why did *this* particular problem or question matter to these psychologists?

The researchers cite two pieces of information that stirred their curiosity and led them to hypothesize, or tentatively claim, that mind wandering might interfere with happiness. We can locate these statements in the first paragraph of the article. Can you find them?

If you still can't figure out the researchers' inspiration, look for an important clue in the introduction by asking yourself:

- What is their research question?

Identifying what prompted Killingsworth and Gilbert's investigation helps us understand how and why they developed their hypothesis, and how this led them to investigate people's thoughts and feelings. The inspirations and hypothesis that we detected are shown in Figure 5.1.

Inspiration:

Are philosophers and religious traditions correct, that "happiness is to be found by living in the moment"?

Research question:

Is our natural inclination to live outside the mind a help or a hindrance?

Hypothesis: "A wandering mind is an unhappy mind"

Figure 5.1

Do you notice how the psychologists' hypothesis responds to their initial questions or inspiration?

Identify Parts of the Message

An argument's message contains various components, including the thesis, support, genre, and style. For this sample analysis, we'll focus on thesis and supports. (Consult Appendix B for additional discussion about the generic layout of a research article.)

Identify the thesis. Arguments often state their thesis, or main debatable idea, in the introduction. Research articles like this one usually begin with a hypothesis, or tentative thesis. A hypothesis or thesis is simply the writer's answer to their research question. To locate the thesis or hypothesis, we ask ourselves:

- Where is a potentially controversial, overarching idea that Killingsworth and Gilbert will need to support?
- What controversy categories does the article address? How do the authors support their conclusions?

Knowing the thesis or hypothesis in advance helps us to evaluate the quality of the argument as we read along, because we already know what the writers are trying to discover or "prove." As we continue reading Killingsworth and Gilbert's methodology and results, we can be asking ourselves whether their research validates their hypothesis or not. In a research article like this one, the "conclusion" really is the thesis: the results or findings of the investigation. So, if the title didn't make the thesis clear, then the conclusion certainly should.

Identify the support. Although we typically find an argument's inspiration and thesis early in an argument (and perhaps again at the end), the body of the argument usually contains the support. In the case of empirical research like this study, the support is whatever information or data the writers collect to answer the research question. To find the support, we look for examples of evidence, verification, and/or illustrations that hold up the thesis. In "A Wandering Mind Is an Unhappy Mind," we note that the support is primarily evidence, in the form of empirical data (statistics), which provides "the results of observation and experimentation" (*Oxford English Dictionary*). When we diagram the elements of the argument, we see a strong base of support (see Figure 5.2).

Figure 5.2
The Elements of the Argument in "A Wandering Mind Is an Unhappy Mind"

What are some possible implications of these findings?

CONSIDER THIS ➤ Missing Support

For this reflection, find one claim in "A Wandering Mind Is an Unhappy Mind" that is not supported with evidence, verification, or illustration, and think about why the authors did not offer support. In order to understand this choice, ask yourself:

- Who is the original audience and what background knowledge would most readers have?
- How controversial or "open to question" is the claim for that target audience?

(continued)

Then, compare your answers with a peer and discuss the following:

- When writing, how do we decide whether claims, evidence, and rationales are open to question and therefore need support?

Develop a list of criteria for assessing whether we need to support claims.

Identify the rationale. Finally, we can identify rationales in the *Science* article when we look for places where the authors connect their statistical findings with their claim that "a wandering mind is an unhappy mind." To find these, we ask ourselves:

- Where do Killingsworth and Gilbert explicitly discuss the connection between their thesis and their research results—in order to tie up any loose ends?
- How do they help readers interpret the statistics they present?
- Where do they correct potential misunderstandings about how their data support their conclusion?

We often spot rationales at the end of paragraphs because that's an effective place to remind readers explicitly how the support verifies, illustrates, or provides evidence for a claim. As is common in many research articles, Killingsworth and Gilbert help readers interpret their data so that we can see how they have drawn their conclusions.

Identify the Author's Purpose

Knowing Killingsworth and Gilbert's audience, inspiration, and message helps us imagine their purpose—or the goal of their argument. Remember that a writer's purpose and thesis are *not* the same thing. The thesis is the main point that the writer attempts to support, whereas the purpose is the desired outcome of the argument—usually, how the writer wants to change the audience's understanding, beliefs, or behavior. To identify Killingsworth and Gilbert's purpose, we ask ourselves:

- What did Killingsworth and Gilbert hope to accomplish by publishing their findings?
- How could these findings change readers' behaviors or beliefs?

We imagine that Killingsworth and Gilbert wrote this article *to inform* or enrich readers' understanding about the consequences of mind wandering and *to convince* readers of its seriousness using empirical data. These actions (to inform or to convince) were likely their purposes. They may also have sought *to impress* their scholarly community or *to challenge* the thinking of other researchers who disagree with them. We suspect these latter purposes could be possible, knowing Killingsworth and Gilbert's intended audience and their chosen publication.

Identify the Implications

A scholarly argument's implications may be stated or implied. If they are stated, we usually locate them in the conclusion. But Killingsworth and Gilbert do not explicitly address the consequences of their argument or suggest specific changes readers should make (like learning to become more focused). To identify unstated implications, ask yourself:

- What are the potential consequences or effects of the argument?
- What is the larger significance of the argument? Why does it matter? *So what?*

Deciphering an argument's implications helps us discover what the writer wants us to *do* with the argument. We can also identify questions for further research, issues we might take up in our own writing, and other potential "leads" (inspirations).

Table 5.2 IDENTIFYING AND INTERPRETING A SCHOLARLY ARGUMENT'S COMPONENTS

ELEMENT	QUESTIONS TO ASK YOURSELF	PLACES TO LOOK
Audience	• Who is the author writing for? Who will read this argument? • Where was this argument originally published?	Publication context and writing style (word choice, organization, sentence structure, tone)
Inspiration	• What gap, problem, or unanswered question prompted the writer's attention? • Why did this problem or question matter to this writer?	Introduction
Thesis or central claim	• What is a potentially controversial, overarching idea that requires support and directly responds to the inspirations? • What controversy categories does the argument address?	Title, introduction, and conclusion
Support	• What evidence, verification, and/or illustrations hold up the thesis?	Body paragraphs
Rationale	• Where does the writer explicitly discuss the connection between a claim and support, in order to tie up any loose ends? • Where does the writer correct potential misunderstandings that readers might have about the link between the claim and support?	Near the end of all paragraphs and in the conclusion
Implications	• What are the consequences, effects, or larger significance of the argument (stated or implied)? • Is there a call to action?	Conclusion

How might this table help you read complicated arguments?

Analyzing Visual Arguments

Up until now we've discussed techniques for analyzing written arguments, but we haven't delved into the details of image-based arguments. Since many arguments that we encounter on a daily basis include visual elements, let's discuss ways of interpreting images and using them in arguments.

Often a picture, graphic, or video can be more persuasive than words alone. Advertisements, social media, television, and websites are only a few of the sources of visual messages we encounter. We use the same principles to examine visual arguments that we would to analyze and evaluate print-only arguments:

- Who is the author? Who is the intended audience?
- What is the controversy or debatable claim?
- What support does the argument contain?
- What is the purpose of the argument?
- How does context affect its meaning?

The strength of visual arguments—their vividness—can also be a weakness. Vividness makes these arguments memorable or "sticky," as advertisers say, and vividness can also evoke emotional responses easily. However, because images are often used as illustrations rather than evidence or verification, their success depends on them evoking the intended response, which doesn't always happen. Claims and rationales are often more implicit, so we must ask ourselves:

- What is missing from this argument? What has the author left to my imagination?
- What connotations, symbolic meanings, or cultural assumptions am I supposed to supply?

Let's examine the following visual argument, a cigarette warning label created by the US government. Figure 5.3 is one of a series of labels developed in 2011 to replace the surgeon general's warning.

When analyzing visual arguments, as with any others, it's useful to begin with the basic elements of the rhetorical situation. In this case, the label's purpose is to discourage women from smoking during pregnancy. From the stated reason, "Smoking during pregnancy can harm your baby," we can infer that the thesis of the label is "Don't smoke when pregnant." There may also be secondary claims, such as (a) "Don't smoke around pregnant women" and maybe even (b) "Don't smoke in the presence of babies." The illustration of an apparently unhealthy baby implies a connection between smoking and harm to infants, either born or unborn.

The primary audience is likely women who are pregnant or who are considering pregnancy, because the label explicitly warns about potential harm to "your baby." The label may also warn others about the dangers of secondhand smoke, particularly fathers, who might smoke in the presence of infants or pregnant women. To appeal to a younger audience, the creators may have chosen to use a comic book style, instead of the graphic photographs that other antismoking ads and labels use. Note, too, that unlike the old cigarette warnings, the surgeon general's verification is not emphasized. Instead, a small copyright of the US Department of Health and Human Services (HHS) appears in the background. Because the copyright is so small, the author of the government's warning appears to be the cigarette company or brand itself, whose name appears in large font at the

Figure 5.3

Cigarette Warning Label

How does this label activate reasoning, build credibility, and evoke emotion?

bottom of the label. Suggesting that the message comes from the manufacturer rather than the government might be more persuasive for some audiences.

In this advertisement—as in many visual arguments—illustrations and emotion dominate the argument. In fact, the only support offered by the label is an illustration, a drawing of a distressed newborn baby in an incubator. The baby faces the viewer, crying out, with a breathing tube and electrodes. This disturbing illustration may evoke a strong enough emotional response to provoke action from smokers who probably already know about associated health risks—even though the argument presents no evidence or elaborate verification.

One implication is that people quit smoking around babies. Beyond that, by including a phone number, 1-800-QUIT-NOW, the label connects its message to a larger antismoking campaign and clearly states what the audience should do.

What other implications or questions does the label raise? For example, how might people respond to an argument that's literally in their hands? Would this label be powerful enough to dissuade consumers from buying a pack of cigarettes? Would it be powerful enough to persuade smokers to call the QUIT NOW hotline or stop smoking around children? Why might this labeling campaign be considered controversial?

TRY THIS ➤   Analyze a Visual Argument

For this exercise, find a compelling print or video advertisement that argues with words and images, and then analyze the visual argument, using the following questions:

- What claims does the ad state or imply?
- What kinds of support are provided?
- How do the visual elements (images and document design features such as color and font) work together with the words?
- What makes the argument effective (or not)?

Responding to Arguments

Although reading may be your primary means of learning in college, writing is what typically provides evidence of that learning. Your teachers will often assign papers to test how well you comprehend what you read. They also expect that you can deepen your understanding *as you write* about a text, so they will ask you to "respond" or "critique" or "analyze." You should begin by asking your professor what he means by these terms, but a typical response assignment asks you to figure out what the text is arguing, either subtly or explicitly, and develop some kind of reply.

To respond effectively, you should think of your reading as a source for inspiration. A good place to begin such a response is by evaluating the argument made by your source. Evaluation is not the same thing as summary, which—as we explain on pp. 49–50—is a recap of what an author says. Sometimes apprentice scholars summarize an argument (that is, restate its most important parts) instead of evaluating it because they're reluctant to critique a published author, or they don't know how to evaluate an argument, or they simply prefer the easier task. Instead of regurgitating the gist of a message, evaluation involves judging whether the writer's strategies were effective for her intended audience and purpose (or for other audiences and purposes). Again, when evaluating an argument, we're still not arguing with the writer, but rather using her argument as a model from which we might learn what choices are more or less effective. Once we're done analyzing and evaluating, we will understand our source well enough to argue with it, to respond to it with our own opinion by agreeing or disagreeing—or, preferably, by adding something new.

It's important to realize that simply agreeing with your sources doesn't yield especially interesting results. Disagreeing is a bit more interesting, but we want to avoid a simplistic "I'm-right-you're-wrong" kind of debate. So, whenever we're responding to an argument, we agree or disagree in order to *extend* the argument and contribute something new. Think about it—in any conversation, the most interesting person is the one who introduces a new idea, a fresh perspective on the topic.

However, you might believe you have little to say in response because you don't know much about the topic. Or you might have been trained only to comprehend an argument, not to engage in a conversation with it. Summary, analysis, and evaluation enable you to dig deeper into *understanding* your sources (what other scholars have already said) in ways that can yield something fresh to say. Another way to come up with a significant response is to do some brainstorming. The "Believing and Doubting Game" can deepen your understanding of what you read and, at the same time, give you plenty to write about.

Play the "Believing and Doubting Game"

This strategy offers an efficient place to begin because you start with what you already know and think, focusing your attention on the writer's arguments. The questions are inspired by a brainstorming and peer review technique called the "Believing and Doubting Game," which was developed by writing expert Peter Elbow. The "Believing and Doubting Game" helps you think more carefully about how you relate to an argument as an individual reader (see Table 5.3).

The technique works like this. First, you "believe" the text fully by asking yourself questions that help you understand and extend the writer's ideas. Then, you "doubt" the text by asking yourself questions that help you challenge and even refute the writer's ideas. Running through these questions whenever you read can prepare you to design an argument of response, or even just to have more to say during class discussions of a reading.

Table 5.3 THE BELIEVING AND DOUBTING GAME

"BELIEVING" QUESTIONS	"DOUBTING" QUESTIONS
• What are the text's strengths? What does it do well? • Which claims do I agree with? • Which underlying values or beliefs do I share with the author? • How does the argument relate to my life? • What other ideas, examples, or scenarios fit the writer's argument?	• What are the text's weaknesses? • Which claims do I disagree with? • What are the writer's biases? • What does the writer overlook? What questions are left unanswered? • What claims need more support? • What rationales are faulty or missing?

Can you think of more questions that you could use to "believe" and "doubt" an argument?

TRY THIS ➤ Play the "Believing and Doubting Game"

For this exercise, practice playing the "Believing and Doubting Game":

1. Read the essay "With Liberty and Justice for Some" by apprentice scholar Emanuel Grant (reprinted on pp. 249–257). Then, spend 30 minutes playing the believing game, in response to his essay. Practice responding to the argument by answering questions that help you extend Grant's ideas.
2. Spend 30 minutes playing the doubting game. Answer resistant questions that help you challenge Grant's ideas.
3. Write a blog post that responds to Grant's argument and designs an argument of your own. You won't be able to address all of Grant's points, so select a few that interest you and compose a response that extends the conversation about this topic.

Mind and Mine the Gaps

Arguments can never address a controversy exhaustively. Writers inevitably leave unanswered questions, alternative interpretations, missing links, and things unsaid. These are opportunities for readers to join the conversation. We recommend that you "mind these gaps" just as subway riders do in New York City. *Minding the gap* means watching out for logical holes, missing examples, discrepancies, questions—spaces for you to insert your opinion. Along the same lines, once you find a gap, you can *mine* it: dig deeper, excavate the argument, and search for new idea "gold." When you plunge your shovel into the argument's holes, you can discover hidden gems and valuable, never-before-seen insights.

So What?

Keep in mind that we can't enter scholarly conversations (make our own arguments) until we're familiar with *what* others have said and *how* and *why* they've said it. The concepts and techniques we've introduced in this chapter can help you become a more efficient and effective scholarly apprentice who analyzes arguments carefully by categorizing controversies, looking for gaps in arguments, and developing interesting responses.

The next chapter explains how we collect and incorporate various kinds of support (verifications, evidence, and illustrations) to create messages that are more credible, logical, and emotionally appealing.

What's Next

Take what you've learned in this chapter and respond to the following prompts:

1. **Identify Controversy Categories.** Expand our "Guided Analysis of a Scholarly Argument" (pp. 106–114) by identifying the

controversy categories that Killingsworth and Gilbert address in their article, "A Wandering Mind Is an Unhappy Mind" (pp. 243–247). Use Table 5.1 to guide your analysis.

   a. Create a two-column chart, listing all five controversy categories in the left column. In the right column, list as many specific controversies as you can find in the article. Write the controversies as questions, following our examples in Table 5.1.

   b. Which controversy categories does the article not fully address? Which of these gaps could inspire further investigation? What kinds of research could you use to answer those questions?

2. **Multimedia presentation.** Go online to the TED Talks website (http://www.ted.com/talks) and find a video of Matt Killingsworth's presentation, "Want to Be Happy? Stay in the Moment." The presentation covers many of the same arguments he and his coauthor made in their article, "A Wandering Mind Is an Unhappy Mind." Watch the video and answer the following questions:

   a. What did the presentation accomplish that the article could not? How did it do so?

   b. Did seeing and hearing the author make his arguments more or less credible? Why?

   c. What kinds of multimedia did he incorporate, and how did that enhance his arguments?

3. **Analyze an argument rhetorically.** Analyze an argument's rhetorical elements in order to understand the author's choices. Follow these steps:

   a. Select a persuasive text (such as a magazine article, blog post, or even an advertisement) that interests you. Choose wisely by selecting something that has interesting rhetorical elements that you can detect and describe. It's generally best to stay away from strictly informative genres (like newspaper reports) and instead look at editorials, opinion pieces, and other persuasive genres.

b. While reading the article, analyze the argument's rhetorical elements:
- ○ Audience and author
- ○ Context: timing, publication
- ○ So what: inspirations, purposes, implications
- ○ Message: genre, style, thesis, supports, rationale

Refer to the list of questions on pp. 8–9 for guidance on completing a thorough analysis. Also, take note of the controversies that the author addresses. You might even list 5 to 10 of the main issues he discusses, and then categorize them according to the kind of controversy they are (existence/fact, definition, cause, evaluation, and jurisdiction/policy).

c. Write a three-page *rhetorical analysis* of the article. Your goal is to fully describe the argument's rhetorical elements and to explain *how* the text makes its argument. You can write for an audience of peers who have already read the essay (so you don't need to summarize the article). For assistance organizing your essay, read ahead in Chapter 8. You can also review the sample rhetorical analysis on pp. 267–273 and read the annotated article on pp. 259–265 to see the kinds of comments you might want to make.

CHAPTER six

How Do We Support Arguments

chapter checklist

- How do we build credibility, activate reasoning or logic, and evoke emotion?
- How can apprentice scholars incorporate original research?
- When do different kinds of support work best?

In this chapter, we'll explain some techniques that scholars use to collect and present various kinds of support. As we've discussed, scholars expect higher standards of evidence and reasoning than you might find in campaign advertisements or infomercials, but that doesn't mean that scholarly arguments can't include other kinds of persuasive techniques. Everyday arguments build credibility and evoke emotions that cannot be scientifically measured or predicted according to black-and-white rules of logic. Here again are the kinds of support that we introduced in Chapter 4.

Table 6.1   KINDS OF SUPPORT

VERIFICATION Something you can *look up*	EVIDENCE Something you can *observe*	ILLUSTRATION Something you can *imagine*
• Previous research • Law or precedence • Established theory	• Empirical data • Personal experience • Textual evidence	• Hypothetical example • Analogy or metaphor • Fictional narrative

Can you recall how different kinds of support activate reasoning, build credibility, or evoke emotion?

Building Credibility

Before most readers will trust new information that we present, they must consider us or our arguments to be *credible*. We've already discussed how audiences find some texts more credible than others. For example, scholars take the *Oxford English Dictionary* more seriously than Dictionary.com. They see scholarly journals as more credible than Wikipedia.

Credibility, or what the ancient Greeks called *ethos*, usually comes from three sources:

1. **Verification**, borrowed from trustworthy sources. Verification relies on "secondary" sources, which means someone else has already analyzed or interpreted the evidence. By integrating verification into our arguments, we demonstrate that we've read and understand what experts have already said (as in a Research or Literature Review). We assume that our audience will trust us only after we prove that we know what we're talking about.

2. **Reputation**, or what the audience already knows and thinks about the author before starting to read (for example, if he's a respected scholar or celebrity washout). Readers trust authors whom they recognize as experts. Similarly, readers trust arguments that appear in respected publications even before they begin reading.

3. **Presentation**, which involves using a style that's suitable for your audience and purpose. You wouldn't wear cutoff jeans and flip flops to a formal business interview. In scholarly writing, we can project credibility by using an appropriate style (effective tone, correct grammar and spelling, etc.) and by adhering to scholarly genres (using logical organization and support). Precise editing also demonstrates that we care about our writing and our audience. Additionally, we demonstrate trustworthy character by considering different perspectives (including counterarguments), by acknowledging weaknesses in our own arguments, and by treating sources respectfully (summarizing, quoting, and citing accurately).

Activating Reasoning or Logic with Evidence

Credibility helps us connect with readers by gaining their trust, but evidence and reasoning provide the strongest foundation for arguments.

To understand why, we must consider the concept of reliability, which indicates how closely the results of investigation come together to form a pattern. For example, if several professors graded the same paper differently, then we would consider their evaluation results to be unreliable. Reliability is a measure of consistency.

Audiences respond to evidence more reliably than they respond to credible or emotional appeals. Just as we all use different credibilimeters in different situations, we don't all laugh at the same jokes or cry at the same movies. But with the aid of instant replay and digital video, we can all agree when we see a football player stepping out of bounds. (Of course, without instant replay, referees generate lots of controversy.)

We're most "certain" of what we can observe and count because observing and counting don't seem like acts of interpretation. For instance, we're probably more confident in the conclusions we might reach if we conduct a biological experiment in a lab with carefully controlled methods than we might be confident in predicting next month's weather or developing a definitive interpretation of a Renaissance poem.

Quantitative Evidence

To seek reliable conclusions, scholars develop careful methods of investigation that will yield similar results each time. Scholars who engage in quantitative investigation use statistical analysis to test the quality of their results, which helps make evidence much more persuasive. Statistics also seem more precise. Compare, for example, the following statements:

- Most of Greenland's ice sheet has melted.
- Nearly 97% of Greenland's ice sheet shows evidence of surface thawing.

The apparent precision of the second statement seems more believable, right? The first statement sounds anecdotal—like something you might have heard from a friend who had a sister who knew some guy in Greenland who noticed a lot of melting. The second statement seems like something written by a scientist who might have planted a bunch of precise little instruments across Greenland, or, in this case, had access to sophisticated thermal satellite imagery. Also, "surface thawing" is more precisely stated than "melting." Statistics bring otherwise ambiguous information into sharp focus, like glasses that correct blurry vision.

Qualitative Evidence

Please don't think of evidence only as quantitative data. What "counts" as evidence varies across disciplines. Qualitative evidence includes information that must be interpreted, rather than counted.

In literary studies, for example, evidence might be actual words (quotations) from a novel, or known biographical information about an author. Similarly, scholars of theater, music, or visual arts might use a performance or a painting as their primary "data." Sociologists and psychologists might observe and interpret human behavior.

Whatever their discipline, scholars are careful to design reliable and precise methods for collecting, analyzing, and reporting evidence. As you continue your scholarly apprenticeship, pay careful attention and ask your professors lots of questions about what "counts" as evidence in their disciplines and how they determine whether that evidence is trustworthy.

Incorporating Original Research

Apprentice scholars often rely heavily on "library research" to support their arguments with verification. However, scholarly arguments become more interesting when we can collect some evidence for ourselves. To do so, we use a reliable research methodology, present and analyze our results, and draw conclusions.

Research Methods

Many scholars use empirical research—that which is based "on the results of observation and experiment"—to support their arguments (*Oxford English Dictionary*). Scholars collect empirical data in the lab and in the field through various means, such as experiments, observations, and case studies. Even if you can't carry out elaborate investigations, you can conduct interviews and observations or distribute surveys to practice gathering reliable data.

You'll find it helpful to consult with a more experienced scholar, such as your professor, when developing your research methodology. The research question will determine the appropriate methodology. For example, if you wanted to learn how a scientist approaches the writing process in general, you might interview a biologist, a physicist, and a chemist using somewhat open-ended questions. To answer a more specific, narrowly focused research question (such as "How much time do scientists typically invest in drafting a research article?"), you might survey several dozen different kinds of scientists.

To enhance credibility, we follow legitimate methods of data collection. Disciplines have specific guidelines and rules for conducting empirical research, which you might learn when assisting specific professors in their research. However, for many apprentice scholars, using legitimate methods mostly means following common sense:

- **Interviews.** Be courteous and respectful of your subject's time and expertise. Plan extensively beforehand, with carefully constructed questions, a clear sense of your purpose, and background knowledge about your interviewee. Record the interview, with permission, so that you can quote and paraphrase accurately.
- **Surveys.** Write clear and calculated questions that get at your research question but don't lead your audience too much. Invite a few peers to read over a survey before you distribute it to the masses so that you can catch any confusing phrases, misleading questions,

or errors. Collect enough survey responses to have a representative sample size.

- **Observations.** When possible, remain inconspicuous and limit the amount of influence your presence creates. When drawing conclusions about an observation, consider the possible effects your presence might have had on the behavior you observed.

Keep in mind the strengths and limitations of different methodologies. Surveys may yield high reliability (consistent results) but low accuracy. If a question is leading or confusing, the results might not really mean what we think. On the other hand, an interview or case study might yield high accuracy but low reliability or generalizability.

When conducting research that involves human subjects, most universities require a formal review and approval process to ensure that research is conducted with integrity, protects privacy, and keeps participants safe. Before beginning such research, consult with your scholarly mentor to learn more about the process and procedures.

Analysis

Once you've collected some data, you can begin to analyze it by asking yourself:

- What does this evidence suggest? What might it mean?
- How could this information help me answer my research question?
- Do these responses align with what other scholars have found, or are the results different?
- What questions remain unanswered? What else needs to be studied?

Be careful not to interpret your research results overzealously. Scholars hesitate to claim that their evidence "proves" their conclusions. Instead, they typically make limited claims about what their results "suggest." Again, remember the basics of argumentation: **Your claim can only be as strong as your evidence.** For example, interviews can help you collect rich, detailed data, but their results cannot be easily generalized. And even if you survey 100 college students and they all respond "yes" to the same question, you can't generalize this response to say that "all college students agree." You can say, "100 out of 100 college students responded 'yes,' which *suggests* that this is a popular response among college students; however, more research is needed."

Again, more experienced scholars can help you with analytical techniques.

Evoke an Audience's Emotions

Evidence and verification provide the foundation for scholarly writing, but like any form of human communication, scholarly arguments may also contain elements that arouse readers' emotions.

In everyday arguments, emotion often dominates. Consider, for example, television commercials that solicit donations for animal shelters by showing sickly, pathetic looking kittens and puppies. In fact, the term "pathetic" has roots in the ancient rhetorical name for a persuasive emotional appeal, *pathos*, which is also the root of the words "sympathy" and "empathy."

Emotion can be a powerful but dangerous force. Advertisers and politicians sometimes use emotional appeals to cloud their audience's judgment, to get them to act irrationally or to "go along" even when offered no evidence or logical reasons to do so. For example, cigarette advertisements might make teenagers think it's cool to do something that has potentially dangerous consequences. Political propaganda often uses emotions to motivate citizens to actions that are oppressive, violent, or not in their best interest.

The potential abuse of emotional appeals makes scholars cautious about using them. Writers who attempt to manipulate their audience's emotions risk losing credibility.

Besides, emotional appeals tend to be the most subjective, unreliable kind of "proof" available because emotional responses tend to vary so widely among different individuals and cultures. Using facts and knowledge as evidence builds a more solid, objective basis for argument because most everyone trusts them and finds them persuasive. If 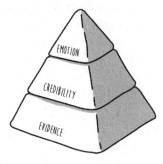 we built a pyramid of persuasive appeals, we'd place evidence at the bottom, then credibility, with emotion at the top.

Think of this like a food pyramid: use emotion carefully, in small amounts. Just like sugar, butter, or seasonings in a recipe, a little goes a long way. In limited doses, emotion can amplify an argument, especially if you want your audience to *do* something, like admit you to college or adopt a business proposal.

What are some safer ways to use emotional appeals in scholarly writing?

- Use vivid language and concrete imagery to illustrate your argument. Precise, fresh, lively words can stir interest and evoke a powerful response, even if the content isn't pulling at anyone's heart strings.
- As long as you build the core of your argument with evidence and verification, you could consider adding a touching example in your introduction or conclusion that arouses your audience's emotions.
- Perhaps the most efficient means to evoke emotion is to use symbolic cultural references that you know will resonate with your audience. For example, you might arouse a US audience's patriotic values with an iconic reference, either an image (Mount Rushmore or the American flag) or a verbal metaphor ("as American as baseball and apple pie"). Ancient Greeks characterized this persuasive

technique as *mythos*, which still resonates with us, for example, through heroes who are real (Abraham Lincoln or Martin Luther King, Jr.) or imagined (Wonder Woman or Captain America).

TRY THIS ➤ Credibility and Emotion

For this exercise, choose two current TV or magazine advertisements that pique your interest. As you examine the advertisements, reflect on the following:

- How do these advertisements build credibility or play audiences' emotions?
- Who would find these advertisements most persuasive? Why?
- How might these advertisements fail?
- What differences do you find between how these advertisements appeal to their audiences?

Share your analysis with some classmates. What do you notice about the roles that credibility, reasoning, and emotion play in advertising?

Crossover Effects

Supports often carry "crossover" effects. For example:

- We often use verifications, such as previous research or expert testimony, to build credibility. However, we might also use such sources as evidence (to activate reasoning) by borrowing another researcher's data set or using an eyewitness account of an event.
- Even when an audience cannot understand or judge the legitimacy of data or statistics, presenting gobs of such evidence can make an author or argument seem more credible.
- Illustrations can not only arouse emotions but also activate reasoning. Consider, for example, arguing that "the wars in the Middle

East are just like Vietnam." That statement uses an illustration to make a logical point. The reverse is also true: consider how we used pie charts in Chapter 2. Usually, these graphics represent data, but we used them as illustrations to help you imagine different versions of the writing process.

The most interesting and sophisticated crossover support might be personal experience.

Personal Experience as Support

Arguments often use personal experience to enhance credibility or emotion. In our first chapter, for example, we explained that we (the authors) are both experienced writing teachers and tutors, assuming that information would increase your trust that we know enough to write this book. In professional and everyday arguments, people often mention their experiences as credentials for speaking on a subject (though this is less common in scholarly writing). Personal experience can also amplify an argument's emotional appeal by creating a vivid illustration or by demonstrating empathy for your audience.

In scholarly arguments, perhaps the most common use of personal experience is as evidence. For example, someone writing an argument proposing improved support systems for students with learning disabilities might describe her experiences with dyslexia. We're careful not to overgeneralize from personal experience—after all, our sample size is only one—but personal experience can bring a depth of detail and perspective that other sources cannot.

As a scholarly apprentice, you can use personal experience as a powerful primary source of evidence, credibility, and emotion. Just be sure to use it carefully and ask your audience (if available) when you have questions about whether it's appropriate for the kind of argument you're trying to create.

Narrating

One way to incorporate personal experience, to use a more intimate voice, and to captivate readers is to compose a narrative, which uses elements of storytelling. For example, you might have written a personal narrative statement for admission to college. Narratives like this contain implicit arguments (for example, "You should admit me to college because of A, B, and C"). You might use narrative in a creative writing class, in a cover letter, or in a graduate school application essay.

Researchers also sometimes think of their writing as a kind of narrative. A good research report "tells a story": we found this problem, designed this experiment, and discovered these results. Scholars also use "micro" narratives to arouse emotion or interest, especially in their introduction or conclusion. When using storytelling this way, narrative becomes a kind of evidence or illustration. For example, if arguing about homelessness, a writer might begin with a story about a real person and his experiences living on the streets. Such graphic examples can serve as compelling evidence and can highlight the real world implications of an otherwise dry scholarly argument.

Using narrative elements may seem like a no-brainer, but it actually presents its own set of challenges:

- **You can't forget the audience.** When you're telling a story, particularly a personal one, it's easy to get wrapped up in what you already know and care about. But you have to connect with readers and make your experience relatable and meaningful to them so that the implications are evident. The story needs to be captivating, with a source of tension, a *so what?* Just because an experience is life changing for you doesn't mean that readers will see its significance. That means you have to think about your audience the entire time, asking yourself:
  - Why should readers care?

- ○ What's the larger significance here?
- ○ What's the takeaway message (implications) that readers haven't already heard a hundred times?

To keep your attention focused on your audience's needs, you might consider answering some of these questions explicitly by articulating clear claims and rationales, at least in your draft. If, in the final revision, you're confident that the audience will get your point, you can always remove those statements.

- **You still need evidence.** You may think that a personal story doesn't require proof, but all arguments need support. Whenever you're trying to convince readers of something—to think differently about an issue, to change their attitude, to embrace your message—you're writing an argument that requires support. Narratives typically incorporate evidence in more subtle ways, but it's still there. Usually, it's in the details. Elements of the story help to support the conclusion, the overarching thesis or argument. To incorporate this evidence, ask yourself:
  - ○ What story elements illustrate my message?
  - ○ What details can serve as evidence to prove my point?

Be sure to layer in these details so that you're not only saying something enlightening but supporting it, too.

Select Support According to the Controversy Categories

We can use the controversy categories as building blocks for larger arguments. Each category calls forth a particular kind of argument. For example, if we're writing an argument about women's changing roles since the turn of the 21st century, we recognize that we're writing an argument about *fact or existence* (because we would be answering the question "Have women's roles changed since 2000?") and *definition* (because we would be answering the question "In what ways have women's roles changed?"). Once we identify what kind of

135

argument we're developing, we can select the techniques that correspond to that category.

Arguments about Existence and Fact

Existence arguments can be difficult because audiences tend to hold stubbornly to what they already believe or think they know. Typically, existence arguments rely on observable evidence for support. Consider, for example, how emphatically people who have witnessed UFOs believe in extraterrestrial life, whereas people who have not seen flying saucers tend to remain suspicious. Even within the scientific community, an experiment must be repeated again and again before there's consensus about a major discovery.

Not everyone has a laboratory or can observe phenomena across the world. Therefore, we often rely on verification to support existence arguments; we trust others to observe evidence for us. How else would we know about galaxies or subatomic particles that we cannot see for ourselves? So, if an apprentice scholar were writing an existence argument, say about President John F. Kennedy's assassination, she might draw from different historical accounts to speculate on what really happened.

Sometimes existence can be presented through illustration, as is the case with science fiction and fantasy art that, for example, develops a political critique or proposes an alternative future (recall *The Hunger Games*). Michelangelo illustrated, through his drawings, the existence of flying machines long before we sent anyone to the moon. Illustrations can support arguments to bring into existence things we can only imagine.

Arguments about Definition

Many arguments begin with disagreements about how we define a term or concept. Arguments about abortion policy, for example, become bogged down before they begin if parties to the argument cannot agree about whether abortion is "murder." And arguments about whether abortion is murder also depend on when we define an embryo or fetus as "human"—that is, when human life begins. (Note how we use quotation marks to call attention to terms in dispute.)

Public controversies often hinge on the definition of a word or phrase. In a famous White House scandal, President Bill Clinton famously asserted that he "did not have sexual relations with that woman, Miss Lewinski," prompting vigorous debate about what specific kinds of physical interactions constitute "sexual relations."

Knowing that vaguely defined terms can cause arguments to stall, scholars tend to be very careful about the language they use, often explaining potentially controversial terms in the beginning of their arguments. Often, we present small definitional arguments as building blocks for larger arguments. For example, in order to argue against "corporal punishment," we would need to define what we mean by the term. Does spanking of children by their parents fit the definition? In most states, parents can legally use "reasonable force" to discipline their children. But what actions are "reasonable"? It's worth thinking through any terms that might be open to question before proposing a larger evaluation or proposal argument.

Usually, we argue whether a case fits an existing definition. But sometimes we discover a case that doesn't fit existing definitions, or we can't agree on a definition and need to create one. For example, we might redefine the term "marriage" by comparing different types of marriage and looking for patterns across groups.

Some definitional arguments can be so interesting, significant, and substantial that they can take an entire essay or even book to examine adequately. For example, rhetoric scholars Celeste Condit and John Lucaites wrote a book-length study of definitional arguments about the term "equality" in American history. Their book, *Crafting Equality: America's Anglo-African Word*, traces how public arguments transformed the very meaning of equality—from how the US

Continental Congress referred to equality ("all men are created equal" but not women or slaves) to the present.

To craft a definitional argument, we must first settle on a definition that our audience will accept. Sometimes we can simply define a term explicitly and hope that the audience will accept our definition, as in "for the purposes of this argument, we will define 'reasonable force' as physical contact that does not cause bodily harm or long-term emotional damage."

Another strategy is to verify a definition with a credible source. Sparingly, we might use an everyday dictionary to validate our meaning: "*Merriam Webster's Dictionary* defines murder as...." For a scholarly audience, a more credible place to start would be the *Oxford English Dictionary*, or *OED*, which gives a richer set of definitions and some historical background of how a word has been used over time. (Sometimes it's also interesting to see where words came from, what they originally meant, and how their meanings have evolved.)

For a more specialized scholarly audience, we consult specialized encyclopedias, such as Thomas Sloane's 837-page *Encyclopedia of Rhetoric*. Scholarly encyclopedias are written by experts who provide extensive discussions and bibliographies to help sort out the nuances of key terms and concepts in a specialized subject. Check your local library's reference section for a range of scholarly encyclopedias, from the *Encyclopedia of Paleontology* to the *Encyclopedia of Management*.

Once we've established an agreeable definition, we then explain how our subject "fits" that definition using evidence and illustration. For example, a law that bans assault rifles will clearly define its characteristics so we can determine whether the Colt AR-15 fits the legal definition. If we wanted to argue that energy drinks are dangerous or unhealthy, we would need to explain what we mean by "dangerous or unhealthy" and then cite evidence that energy drinks have those effects.

TRY THIS ➤ Write a Definition

For this exercise, brainstorm with peers to identify an issue that is controversial because of people's conflicting definitions. For example, public funding for art sometimes raises the controversy of "What counts as art?" After you select an issue, write a one-page argument that develops and defends a specific definition of a term or phrase that is central to the controversy. Afterward, compare your definitions with your peers and discuss the implications of your definitions.

Arguments about Cause and Consequence

Arguments that try to establish a causal link are one of the most difficult cases to make. That's because it's difficult to definitively link a cause and effect without confusing cause with correlation. Often, when writers try to argue about cause and consequence, they commit logical fallacies like the ones we discuss in Chapter 9. However, you may have read persuasive essays or watched documentaries that build compelling cases against social or environmental problems, such as *Food Inc.* or *An Inconvenient Truth*. If you look back at these films, you might notice that they are causal arguments.

Arguments about Evaluation

Like definitional arguments, evaluation arguments sometimes stand alone and sometimes become part of larger arguments. For example, an argument proposing a solution to international copyright infringement would probably begin by describing the problem and then evaluate why copyright violations are wrong and deserve our attention. This last part is especially important because ethical issues can help motivate an audience to act by highlighting an argument's implications.

TRY THIS ➤ Examine a Causal Argument

For this exercise, select and analyze an essay or a film that makes a causal argument. To find an example of a causal argument, think about topics that yield debates about cause and consequence. Then, read or view the argument to identify and analyze specific techniques the author uses to build her case. As you analyze the argument, consider the following questions:

- How does the author organize the argument? Why do you think she chose that structure and sequence of ideas?
- How does the author build a case that the consequences or effects are not merely coincidental?
- How effective is the argument, overall?

We begin evaluation arguments by establishing criteria by which we will judge the case at hand. Those criteria must be based in values shared by the audience. Let's consider the argument against corporal punishment that we discussed earlier. In this example, the definition hinges on the phrase "reasonable force," which we defined as "physical contact that does not cause bodily harm or long-term emotional damage." Here, we're making a kind of evaluation argument, counting on our audience to share our belief that causing bodily or emotional damage to children is morally unacceptable.

Because evaluation arguments depend so much on values and beliefs, they tend to be complex and compelling, especially when they involve competing values. For instance, most Americans value national security and individual human rights, but the use of aggressive interrogation techniques on suspected terrorists (defined by critics as "torture") places security and rights in apparent conflict. In cases like this, we must argue why we hold one value more dearly than another.

To fully evaluate an issue, we might have to compare (find similarities among) and contrast (find differences among) components of the controversy. In fact, many arguments compare and contrast theories, texts, artifacts, events, concepts, and so on. For example, a research or literature review compares sources in order to describe and analyze the scholarly "conversation" about an issue. When using this mode of analysis, it's important to synthesize—bring items together in a new, enlightening way so that readers learn something new about a subject—rather than just look at each item or subject separately. **The structure we choose can help promote synthesis**. For example, if we compare similar items alongside each other, perhaps even within the same paragraphs, we're more likely to show off our good thinking by explaining exactly how we've arrived at our evaluation. Doing so can help us avoid the worst kind of comparison/contrast analysis— the one that says little more than "These things have some things in common but are still different." When we compare and contrast items in close proximity to each other, we can examine the intricacies of each, as they relate to the other.

TRY THIS ➤ Evaluate a Film or Restaurant

For this exercise, choose a film or restaurant that you want to evaluate. Before viewing the film or dining at the restaurant, identify a list of criteria against which you will evaluate your subject. Then, write a 500-word review of the film or restaurant. Post your evaluation on a blog or a social network for others to read and comment on.

Arguments about Policy

When we write a proposal argument, we typically (a) describe a problem, (b) present potential solutions, and (c) justify a course of action. We might not spend equal time on every section but instead think about the primary source of disagreement. For instance, if readers already understand the severity of a problem, we can focus more on the solution and justification sections. However, if readers don't recognize a problem, we need to spend more time proving that there's actually cause for concern. To determine which controversies you can skim or skip, do your research, test your arguments on a real audience (such as a classmate or a writing tutor). Or ask your professor: How much can I assume my audience already knows or agrees with my argument?

So What?

Effective scholarly arguments use reasoning and evidence and connect with an audience through credibility and emotion. However, each rhetorical situation requires a different dose of these supports. Scholars typically prefer evidence over credibility and emotion, but that's not to say that values don't influence how we investigate and reach conclusions—or that we shouldn't pursue questions that involve human emotion. As Aristotle taught, we must appeal to the whole person; although evidence provides a stable foundation, it doesn't always motivate people as powerfully as credibility or emotion.

In the next chapter, we argue that the best way to develop a compelling argument—one that your audience will want to read—is to pursue a stimulating question. We offer concrete strategies for finding important and inspiring questions, and we detail the steps of refining and narrowing a thesis to make it more complex. This chapter also recommends some arguments to avoid and gives alternative options like the evolving thesis and ones with a stylistic flair.

What's Next

Take what you've learned in this chapter and respond to the following prompts.

1. **Analyze an everyday argument.** Find an everyday argument or persuasive text that interests you, such as an advertisement,

political cartoon, letter to the editor, or magazine article. Map out the uses of evidence, verification, and illustration, and then consider how well they work. Are you persuaded? Why or why not? You might also consider creating a pie chart or another graphic representation that illustrates the ratio of evidence to illustration to verification.

2. **Debate.** Practice debating a controversial issue. As a class, list several potential issues, and then vote on the most interesting one. Some topic suggestions might include genetically modified foods, salary caps, grading practices, drones, paid college athletes, adolescent plastic surgery, and single-sex schooling. Next, divide into groups for each position on the controversy, and develop a plan for your argument. Develop a potential list of evidence, verification, and illustrations that support your position. You might spend time outside of class gathering more support and then present your arguments to the class. After each group defends its position, take some time to develop and present rebuttal arguments.

3. **Evaluate a persuasive campaign.** Watch a couple short films from Dove's Beauty Campaign, such as *Dove Evolution*, *Beauty Pressure*, or *Body Evolution*. Discuss the following questions with a peer and then as a group:
   - What and where is the thesis (argument)?
   - How does the film develop credibility? Is the use of credibility effective for its intended audience and purpose? Is it relevant and sufficient?
   - How might this use of credibility fail?
   - How does the film arouse emotion? Is the use of emotion effective?
   - How might this use of emotion fail?
   - How does the film use evidence and reasoning? Is the use of evidence and reasoning effective? Is it relevant and sufficient for supporting the argument?

- How might this use of evidence and reasoning fail?
- What additional techniques do you notice? How effective are these?

After analyzing the films, write a 1,000-word response to the arguments presented in these films, or write a rhetorical analysis essay. We explain the purpose and features of this kind of essay on p. 122.

CHAPTER seven

How Can We Create a Compelling Thesis

chapter checklist

- How do we find a question worth pursuing?
- What are the right questions to ask?
- Can (and why should) you change your thesis?
- How can you jazz up your style?

Even though you might have been taught to decide on your thesis *before* you start writing your argument, experienced scholars typically begin with a really good question. Remember, every argument answers a question.

Every Great Thesis Grows from a Stimulating Question

Scholarly investigation builds new knowledge or understanding by posing questions, gathering information (conducting research), and processing that information to draw conclusions. When scholars publish their discoveries, they must "show their work" by building a case to support those

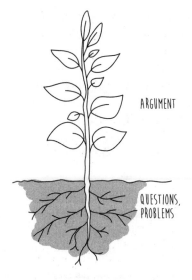

ARGUMENT

QUESTIONS, PROBLEMS

conclusions. In their introduction or research review, scholars often tell the audience explicitly what question they were trying to answer so readers can focus their attention on whether scholars have "earned" the conclusion by providing adequate support.

Ideally, questions grow organically from the work that scholars do. Scholars notice gaps in previous research, such as a historical archive or literary work that has never been examined, or an experiment that needs to be extended or updated using the latest scientific techniques. This kind of problem solving also applies to work outside of school, such as when a business manager develops a model for promoting her services to a new audience or an engineer designs a factory to be as safe, sustainable, and cost effective as possible. Although we may not always get to solve problems as significant or practical as curing Alzheimer's disease, scholars and professionals use similar methods to answer questions that matter to them and their readers.

Notice, though, that scholars, engineers, and business managers already have extensive training and experience in their field, which means they have the expertise to identify and solve these important problems. The originality of their arguments depends on that expertise. It's easier for a medical scientist to discover a cure for cancer if he's intimately familiar with state-of-the-art research trends and methods.

Lacking this expertise, how can an apprentice such as yourself know what question to ask or problem to solve so that you can create an original thesis? How can you possibly develop an argument that experienced scholars, like your professors, have not already fully considered?

- **Keep reading.** Remember, scholars write from sources. Ask your scholarly mentor to recommend readings on your topic. Once you find a good source, scour its bibliography for related readings that will take you deeper or in new directions.

- **Apply your perspective.** You undoubtedly have knowledge or life experiences that your professor does not. Use that expertise to bring fresh perspective to a subject. Realize, too, that ignorance (meaning lack of information, not lack of intelligence) can be a strength. Knowing little about something may help you to ask questions or see things that are invisible to experts.

- **Make your own luck.** Just like seasoned scholars, apprentices sometimes stumble accidentally on a research topic, a piece of evidence, or an insight that others have overlooked. Discovery often happens by mistake, so be brave and curious.

- **Challenge yourself.** Arguments demonstrate evidence of thinking. Discovering something for yourself can lead to a good thesis, even if it's not "news" to the experts.

- **Talk with others.** Conversation often sparks great ideas. Talking with trusted friends and mentors helps us refine fuzzy ideas and discover more original angles from which to approach a topic.

- **Try free writing.** (See the following TRY THIS exercise.)

TRY THIS ➤ Freewriting

For this exercise, experiment with a technique called *freewriting*, which simply means drafting with abandon. When freewriting, we don't plan ahead or stop to edit; we just write. Freewriting works well for getting started when you're not sure what you want to write about, or when your brain gets clogged with too many ideas. Freewriting can also cure writer's block (which often happens to perfectionists who

---

(continued)

edit too much while composing). Here's a technique inspired by Peter Elbow's classic book *Writing Without Teachers* that you could try alone or in class:

Step 1: Open a new document in your word processor. Save it with an awesome manuscript title.

Step 2: Turn off your computer monitor and write for 15 to 20 minutes. (Laptops: swivel the monitor flat or cover with paper.) Don't stop writing for anything.

Step 3: Turn on the monitor. Save your work. Check your word count to see how much you've written. Gloat.

Step 4: Repeat Step 2 for another 10 minutes; then repeat Step 3.

Step 5: Spellcheck the document so it's readable. Do not edit. Save again.

Step 6: Close the document and take a 10-minute break.

Step 7: Return to your computer and read the document. Do not edit. Locate the most interesting, controversial, or promising sentence. Cut and paste that sentence into a new document and begin again at Step 1. Repeat until you become lightheaded or you complete your first draft.

Ask the Right Questions

Scholars cannot always identify significant questions and problems without some help. A great tool for getting started is to explore the kinds of controversies that arguments address, as we explained in Chapter 5. These five categories are all that we need to discover a great question because most every argument you can think of belongs to one of these categories. To illustrate how to use these questions to discover an argument or a thesis, let's work through an example.

Imagine that you want to write an argument about the media's influence on body image, but you don't know how to come up with a compelling thesis. You initially thought that you could write a thesis like "The media negatively influences teenage girls' self-image," but your professor told you that such an argument would be a cliché, because most people already know that. You're frustrated, and you don't know how to develop an alternative focus. Here's where you might start:

Use the five controversy categories to brainstorm potential questions about your topic. Write down as many questions as you can. Your goal is to examine the topic exhaustively so that you can find a question worth pursuing. Just like with freewriting, when brainstorming a list of questions, try to "catch" as many ideas as you can. You don't need to decide right away about whether your questions or thoughts are stellar or weak. Like a fisherman trawling the ocean for as many fish as possible, your goal is to sweep up every last sardine.

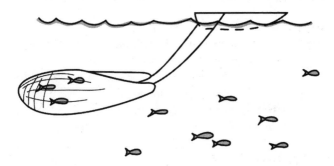

A preliminary list of controversy questions might look like the ones found in the next section.

Potential Questions about the Media's Influence on Body Image
Controversies of existence or fact (Is it true? Did it happen?)

- Does the media actually influence teenage girls? How do we know?
- Who else does the media influence?
- How much influence does the media have on teenage girls?
- Has the media always influenced teenage girls? Did this influence accelerate at a certain point?

Controversies of definition or interpretation (Does this case fit the definition? How do we interpret this information?)

- What kind of "influence" are we talking about? Does the media influence girls' thoughts, choices, feelings, aspirations, values, or something else?
- What are the signs of media influence?
- What kinds of media (magazines, film, television?) are most influential?
- What other cases would fit the definition of media influence?

Controversies of cause, consequence, or circumstance (Was it intentional? Are there extenuating circumstances?)

- Who is to blame?
- Does the media intentionally target teenage girls? Why are teenage girls profitable targets?
- Do current problems such as exercise addiction and eating disorders also result from the media's influence?
- Why are teenage girls particularly vulnerable? What other factors affect the media's influence?
- What are the consequences of this problem? What are the effects of a poor self-image? What other personal and societal problems are related?
- What theories (maybe from psychology) help explain why the media can have such a strong influence on teenage girls?

Controversies of evaluation (Is it right or wrong? Is it serious enough to warrant our attention?)

- Are the media's influences good or evil?
- Should the media take some moral responsibility for its influence?
- Is this problem more serious than other issues adolescents face?
- Is the problem serious enough to deserve immediate action?
- Do we have a moral obligation to address this issue?

Controversies of jurisdiction, procedure, policy, or action to be taken (What, if anything, should we do about it?)

- Should the government regulate media more closely?
- What can parents do to protect their teenage girls?
- How can teenage girls avoid or counteract the media's influence?
- What existing laws, policies, or solutions developed for similar controversies might apply?
- Should magazines develop a rating system like films do (G, PG, PG-13, R, NC-17) to limit adolescents' exposure to harmful messages from the media?

Once you develop a long list of questions, select the questions that are most stimulating and original. These are your starting points. From here, you can speculate on the answer to a question (develop a hypothesis or tentative thesis statement), or you can begin reading other scholars' views (verification) or collecting data (evidence). We describe methods for data collection in Chapter 6.

TRY THIS ➤ Practice Using the Controversy Categories

For this exercise, reflect on which controversy categories are most compelling, and then develop a list of questions yourself.

1. Review the media influence example and identify which questions are most interesting.
   - What makes these questions particularly thought provoking?
   - Which controversy categories seem to yield the most interesting possibilities? Why do you think so?
2. Following our example, select a topic that interests you, such as an issue related to your major or a problem that you have observed on your campus, and develop a list of questions using the controversy categories. Organize the questions in a table that outlines the controversy categories and then lists four to six

---

(continued)

questions per category. For example, you could brainstorm questions for any of these topics:

- Cost of higher education
- College admissions criteria
- Extracurricular funding in college (for example, student clubs or athletics)
- Relationships in college
- Campus diversity
- Characteristics of "good" writing

You might find it helpful to imagine stakeholders—potential audiences who care about this issue and would be affected by its implications. For example, students, parents, employers, legislatures, college administrators, and lenders might raise different questions about college funding.

So What's a Good Question?

Believe it or not, you *can* ask a bad question, at least when it comes to creating a thesis. Some questions just won't lead you down a path toward an interesting argument. Bad questions can be too simple, too obvious, or just plain boring. Good questions—ones that lead to good answers (strong thesis statements)—are challenging, compelling, and controversial. Keep these three Cs in mind when developing research questions.

Challenging questions. Scholars prefer thoughtful questions that require more sophisticated proof, scientific data, or investigation. These questions challenge scholars and their readers intellectually because they inspire careful, critical, and creative thinking. For example, compare the following:

- Too easy: "Do students abuse Adderall and Ritalin to improve concentration and test performance?"
- Better: "Are universities morally obligated to create educational programs and policies that prevent students from abusing prescription drugs?"

Compelling questions. Good questions have significant consequences or implications for real people or real situations, even if the effects are mostly theoretical. Scholars can appeal to larger audiences when they investigate issues of greater significance.

- Trivial: "Is the cafeteria's food service on weekends convenient for on-campus residents?"
- Better: "What are the economic costs and benefits of colleges providing accessible and convenient services (beyond academic support)?"

Controversial questions. Great questions don't need to be scandalous (although they can be), but they usually inspire some degree of disagreement among readers concerning the best solution to a problem or answer to a question. Selecting a question that has a spark of tension can lead to a more provocative argument.

- Pointless ("No duh"): "Is smoking unhealthy?"
- Better: "If smoking poses a public health risk, shouldn't it be illegal?"

CONSIDER THIS ➤ Using Examples

For this reflection, consider the difficulty of choosing effective examples, which is something we tried to do in this last section.

Examples help us "show" our ideas, rather than only talk about them abstractly. But we have to think carefully about how audiences will interpret our examples, or they'll misfire. Consider the previous examples of "better" questions. Do you think they work? Do you understand and agree that the "better" examples are actually stronger? Can you think of more vivid examples than the ones we provided? How might you use examples in your own writing?

When you're brainstorming possible research questions, see whether they fit the criteria of stimulating questions by asking yourself:

- Which questions are most controversial, interesting, or complicated to answer?
- Which questions already have obvious, simple, or commonly known answers? (Avoid these.)
- Is this question expansive and sophisticated enough for me to fulfill my assignment's page requirement, yet narrow enough for me to investigate it deeply within the page limit?
- How might I answer this question? What methods (for example, surveys, interviews, library research) could I use?
- Do I have the time and resources—such as access to relevant books and articles, labs, contact with experts—that I'll need to answer this question?

These practical questions help us determine what we can accomplish within the *constraints* of a writing task, which are:

- Available time (for thinking, reading, research, drafting, revising)
- Available knowledge (about methods, background information)
- Available space (literally, constraints of page and word counts, plus assignment guidelines, genre and style conventions)

When writers select a question or thesis that's simply too big, their arguments typically lack *focus*. Apprentice scholars often think they need a huge problem to fill the pages, but really they need a small problem to investigate deeply. Our advice: **Dig narrow and deep, rather than broad and shallow**. Burrow into the shores of the beach, not the confines of a sandbox.

It's difficult to demonstrate much thinking (develop a really good idea) if you're only scratching the surface of a problem. You'll likely just say things most people already know (obvious or uncontroversial thesis) or leave readers hanging (advancing a thesis that's more controversial than you realize, leaving holes in your argument). Instead, you need to select a focus that gets to the heart of an issue by unraveling layers of complexity.

"Great," you might say, "but how do I do that?" More insight into the controversy categories can help.

Picking Juicier Questions

As you might have noticed, controversies move from yes/no questions involving controversies of fact or existence (for example, "Do students cheat a lot? Check yes or no") to more complicated and usually more interesting questions involving definition, cause, evaluation, and policy (such as "Why do students cheat so much?" "Is cheating really unethical?" "What can or should be done about it?").

Questions from the latter categories are typically the ripest for picking because they're sweeter and more complex. Consider, for example, a yes/no question that examines a controversy of existence versus a question that involves policy:

- Simple question: "Should the drinking age be lowered to 18?"
- More complex question: "What kind of public policies might protect young adults from the dangers of drinking while safeguarding their civil rights?"

The second question gets at the heart of the matter, the *so what?* Plus, it gives the writer a much clearer plan of attack. You can imagine exactly what the writer might research in the library, what she might include in her outline, and what pieces of evidence she might collect. The first question doesn't give the writer a specific focus, so she probably wouldn't know where to start.

Turning Clichéd Arguments into Better Ones

Clichéd arguments restate common wisdom ("We can learn important lessons from tragedies in our lives") or rely on an overused idea ("Capital punishment is unethical"). Clichés don't work in scholarly writing because their life has already been sucked dry; there's nothing left to discover or add to the discussion. Also, clichéd arguments don't answer the *so what?* question. They may be interesting, but they don't solve an important problem or get to the heart of the matter. Your passion for a topic may not be enough to motivate your audience. Professors often discourage students from writing about clichéd subjects such as abortion, gun control, or the death penalty—not because such topics are uncontroversial but because it's so difficult to tell your audience anything they haven't already heard many times before.

Choosing a clichéd topic can also lead to *confirmation bias*. If you have already made up your mind about your topic, then you might only consider information that confirms your existing viewpoint rather than approaching the subject from a fresh or objective perspective. Most people will stop listening to someone who thinks his viewpoint is the only one that matters. Besides, *what if you're wrong?*

You might gravitate toward familiar topics because you know them well or can easily find plentiful sources. If you discover that other writers have already addressed your topic the same way, then your planned argument may bore your readers. You can still discuss something familiar if you can find a fresh or unique "take" on the subject that will transform a cliché into something more compelling. Using the controversy categories to focus and complicate your topics can help.

Let's walk through an example. Many students are concerned about their right to drink alcohol. Therefore, essays that argue for a lower drinking age are painfully common. Unfortunately, most of these arguments will be overly familiar to your audience. The problem you face, then, is trying to write about something that interests you but needs an angle to engage your audience. Starting with a less familiar question can help. We can use the controversy categories to develop more compelling, complex questions, such as the following examples:

- What's the real problem: underage drinking or alcohol abuse? (*Existence/fact*)
- How should Americans define an "adult"? What are the underlying assumptions about adulthood in American culture, and what are the implications of these assumptions? (*Definition/interpretation*)
- If young people have wanted to lower the drinking age for many years, why hasn't anything changed? What causes political apathy among 18- to 21-year-old voters? (*Cause/consequence*)
- Is the real problem that the legislative process takes so long? Should we be worried that many citizens are unhappy with the government but apathetic about change? (*Evaluation*)
- How can we encourage young adults to become more politically active? How can we make the process of enacting new laws more efficient and possible? (*Policy*)

Through investigating related issues using the controversy categories, we can find underlying issues that are more compelling and fresher for our audience.

So, to sum up: you can find the strongest thesis statements by doing the following:

1. Investigating a controversy thoroughly to identify the best questions that people haven't answered fully yet
2. Selecting challenging, compelling, and controversial questions
3. Focusing on the later controversy categories

Use Sources to Generate Ideas

The controversy categories can help us discover an inspiration and begin collecting support for a potential thesis. However, you don't have to develop thesis statements entirely on your own. Conducting library research and reading other scholars' work can also help you develop ideas for a thesis. The following techniques help us generate ideas:

1. **Play the "Believing and Doubting Game"** with sources to discover new applications and arguments. Get in the habit of asking yourself the questions that we describe on pp. 118–119 every time you read a new source. Reading actively in this way can inspire new ideas in response to existing ones.

2. **Find a source with which you strongly disagree.** Reading alternative viewpoints can help you clarify your own perspective.

3. **Create a table that compares and contrasts various sources.** You can use this table to do a number of things: (a) to outline diverse perspectives; (b) to identify the heart of the matter, according to these sources; (c) to find points that the sources overlook; (d) to highlight central disagreements; and so forth.

4. **Pair two sources in conversation with each other.** Imagine what two authors might say to each other if they were together. Imagine what new insights they might reach, given the chance to converse. Predict the answers that one author might give to the other author's questions, given their respective positions.

5. **Look at one source through the "lens" of another source.** This strategy allows you to do a couple of things: (a) apply a theory that one source describes to another source's examples or case studies or (b) consider the implications of one scholar's argument on another scholar's position. For example, in order to discuss how cloning might enable survival of the fittest, you could apply Darwin's theory of natural selection to an anticloning article.

All of these strategies can prompt an original thesis. However, keep in mind that some of these strategies require you to speculate and build a case for your interpretation. In those instances, you'll need to explain and support your thinking.

TRY THIS ➤ Use Sources

For this exercise, select two reliable and useful sources on a topic of your (or your instructor's) choice. Then, use one of the five techniques we outlined for using sources to generate ideas. Record your brainstorming by taking notes, freewriting (see pp. 147–148 for a description of this technique), or creating an outline or table.

Alternative Competing Hypotheses

Sometimes scholars develop multiple tentative answers, or hypotheses, to answer their research questions. For example, following the scientific method, early researchers may have used the following hypotheses concerning tobacco use:

1. Smoking improves health.
2. Smoking is unhealthy.
3. Smoking has no significant effect on health.

Next, researchers might collect evidence—by studying correlations between disease and smoking via health records, experiments on rats, or maybe just sitting around smoking a lot—and then measure which hypotheses have the most and least amount of support. The amount of support, of course, determines the strength of the conclusion (thesis). As evidence accumulates, the hypothesis intensifies from a possibility to a probability, evolving from something we *suspect* to something we think we *know*.

Investigating simultaneous, competing hypotheses helps scientists reduce bias. Even if a researcher favors a particular conclusion, the scientific method allows the evidence to speak for itself. Good researchers generate as many potential hypotheses as they can to increase their chances of discovering the best possible answer, which is sometimes something truly original.

Can I Change My Thesis?

Yes. Not only can you change your thesis, but you often should. The purpose of investigation is to *discover* knowledge—not just to reinforce what we already think. Experienced scholars allow their investigations to change their perspectives on a subject, which is why we begin with questions and hypotheses, rather than making up our minds before we begin our research.

Many inexperienced writers think that they should select a thesis early in their writing process and then stick with it at all costs. They see the thesis as an unchanging guide for the paper's direction. But this notion of a fixed thesis disregards the writing process that experienced writers follow. Scholars typically have a tentative thesis or hypothesis in mind when they begin researching and writing, but they refine and change their views as they encounter better evidence and other scholars' findings. Their thesis ultimately *evolves*.

For example, a writer might begin her first draft with a fairly simple thesis, like "SAT scores are unfair and unreliable predictors of college-level success." After some preliminary research, she discovers evidence that higher SAT scores do often correspond to higher college grades, so she revises her thesis: "Although SAT scores can predict many students' college-level success, universities should not value SAT scores over other aspects of a student's application, such as grades and extracurricular activities."

Then, in her next draft, she might refine those ideas even further by developing a solution, or proposal argument (a genre that we describe in Appendix B), for a specific audience of university policy makers:

> Colleges should use new technologies such as FaceTime and Skype to interview applicants online, rather than relying primarily on outdated assessment tools that reflect students' abilities in very

limited contexts, such as exam environments. To gain even more perspective on the "whole student," admissions offices might even employ current students to assist with the selection process.

Notice how the writer's final thesis is more specific and more original? It demonstrates the writer's *thinking* on the issue. Also, notice that this final thesis falls under the last category of controversies (controversies about jurisdiction, procedure, policy, or action to be taken). Not surprising—given what we said earlier about picking juicy topics. This final category is where you'll find your strongest thesis statements when readers already agree on the issues in the previous categories. Here's why. Facts, as the basis of argument, are often based in the past; there's less to argue about because we know more about the past than the present and the future, which are still unfolding. Knowledge and beliefs (controversies about definition and evaluation) are juicier because we're still struggling to get a sense of them right now. Controversies about what we should do in the future are juiciest because we really don't know what will happen (it's anyone's guess).

In the case of our example, many readers would already know that SAT scores are imperfect predictors of college-level success, but they might be unsure about alternative criteria. The writer's evolved thesis would address the heart of the issue: "What should we do about this problem?" In her final draft, the writer may show how her thesis evolved, or she may just revise the original thesis by changing the introduction. Readers may never even know her previous thoughts on the topic. What's important is that she remains open to different ways of seeing a controversy so that she can understand its complexity and select a thesis that takes into account multiple perspectives and objections.

Why Would I Change My Thesis?

You might oppose such a flexible stance because of the extra time involved. After all, if you write your paper with one thesis in mind and then change your argument, you could face extra hours of researching and revising. How will you ever finish a paper if you keep shifting the focus of your argument?

Remember, the point of scholarly argument isn't only to finish a paper but also to discover and communicate knowledge. Scholars don't write for the sake of writing; they write to communicate (and sometimes discover) what they think. **Settling on a thesis before writing closes off opportunities to learn.** Usually, you're not really *changing* your argument so much as *focusing* and *refining* so you can learn more.

How can you do so more efficiently? Spend more time reading and thinking and brainstorming *before* actually writing a formal draft. Anticipate problems in your thinking and objections to your position before they pop up in your paragraphs. Keep in mind, too, that for scholars, writing grows out of investigation.

Moreover, let's be honest: most of us have trouble identifying exactly what we're trying to say until we talk it out. Drafting can achieve that. We might have a blurry idea of a thesis but once we start writing, we realize we really mean to say something different. Embrace that process. Allow yourself to discover first and organize later.

Peer review can also help us identify a good thesis. When someone reads a scholarly draft, the best question to ask is this: What do you find most interesting? (Consult Appendix A on "How to Benefit from Peer Review and Collaboration" for advice and additional questions to guide peer review.) Often, the most interesting—and thus potentially best thesis—lurks somewhere toward the end of a draft. This makes sense, if a thesis is really the conclusion of your thinking, right?

Because conventional scholarly arguments lead with the thesis, once you find it, all you have to do is put it at the beginning and pretend you knew that all along. It's as if you're saying: here's what I discovered, now let me show you how I arrived there and why you should believe me. Alternatively, if you change your thesis midway through your writing process, you might want to tell readers how and why you've arrived at a new conclusion. You can do this with the "evolving thesis."

Writing an Evolving Thesis

You might be pleased to hear that there are other options available than leading with your thesis.

We're all familiar with the five-paragraph essay that keeps a consistent thesis throughout. Historically, though, the "essay" was exploratory and evolving. (The French word *essai* literally means an "attempt," "test," or "experiment.") Similarly, an argument with an evolving thesis builds and becomes more complicated, narrow, or detailed as the paper progresses. This kind of thesis offers different advantages, such as:

- **Showing readers your evolving thoughts.** If you want to illustrate exactly how you've reached a particular conclusion, you can begin your paper with your initial hypothesis and then introduce counterarguments, evidence, or verification that influenced your thinking. By showing what has expanded and changed your perspective, you can take your readers on the intellectual journey that you followed while investigating the issues.
- **Building a complicated argument.** Sometimes you simply can't articulate your entire conclusion before you've explained its various subpoints. In these cases, you need to explain or prove one part of the thesis before moving on to the other parts. The evolving thesis allows you to defend each claim separately and then—like a staircase—to build to the precipice, your overarching thesis. This strategy can make your logic clearer for your reader to process and understand.
- **Developing a controversial argument.** When you take a controversial stance, one that your readers might reject outright, it's smart to begin from a position that your readers are more likely to accept. That way, you can establish some common ground. Then, you can gradually evolve your thesis by proving claims one at a time, in the same way that you would develop a

complicated argument. With this strategy, you essentially say to readers: "We can agree on X. Now let me explain Y. . . . After you agree with me about Y, I'll support Z. . . . Once you understand why I think Z is true, you might reconsider your position." The evolving thesis is useful when you need to persuade your audience gradually and methodically, when you want to get them on your side before fully exposing your position. For example, Charles Darwin used this technique in his groundbreaking book *On the Origin of Species by Means of Natural Selection*. Can you imagine why?

- **Keeping the reader interested or surprised.** You can introduce an element of surprise and engage readers when you initially hold back a bit. We're not advocating that you mislead your audience or intentionally frustrate readers, but you can unravel your ideas dramatically, like a ball of yarn. For example, instead of giving your full position in the first paragraph, you might give readers a taste of it but leave out the complicated details. Then, you can incorporate the intricacies of your thesis as the paper evolves. This strategy is especially enticing when your audience expects you to take one position and you actually support a different one or when your topic might otherwise be dull.

As you might suspect, thesis statements raise ethical implications. On the one hand, showing your cards at the beginning of an argument can be more ethical because it's less sneaky. Because the readers already know where the argument is going, they can evaluate evidence within that context, according to that purpose, as they go along.

On the other hand, the deferred or evolving thesis can also treat the audience as a partner investigator. If you present evidence without telling readers how to interpret it, they're free to draw conclusions for themselves. Of course, audiences might not reach the same conclusions as you do, so you lose some "control" over the argument. But that's okay if you consider your audience to be equals and remember that the point of arguing isn't just to win but to seek understanding and make the best decisions together.

The bottom line is: **Wherever you place it, the best thesis is somewhere you arrive, not a place to begin.** A thesis states the results of thinking. Sometimes you need to investigate a topic, consider the controversies that surround it, weigh evidence, and activate reasoning before you know what to think. After all, jumping to conclusions often gets people into trouble.

Thinking carefully and considering all the available evidence and viewpoints? That's the work of scholars.

TRY THIS ➤ An Evolving Thesis

For this exercise, study the structure and the strategies of an evolving thesis by reading the apprentice scholar's essay "With Liberty and Justice for Some" (on pp. 249–257) and discuss the following questions in class or with a peer:

1. What is the thesis? How does it change? To answer this question, mark each time the writer's thinking seems to shift.
2. What makes this evolving thesis effective?
3. What, if anything, doesn't work for you as the reader? What could the writer do differently?

Infuse a Little Style

Thesis statements can engage readers through their ideas and through their form. **We aim for thesis statements that are both provocative and clear**: vivid in their expression and evident in their meaning. Actually, thesis statements can be more than one sentence long, and they don't have to be as dry and tasteless as a cafeteria sheet cake. When we write—and rewrite—thesis statements, we search for words that convey our meaning clearly and precisely, using language that will stimulate readers. We talk more about writing with style in Chapter 10, but for now, we want to encourage you to avoid boring, tasteless, and overly general statements that don't invigorate your reader.

"Although" Statements

One concrete way to engage readers is to use an "although" clause in your thesis statement, which positions your idea against an opposing idea. A thesis with an although clause looks like these samples:

- "Although many scholars support _____, new data suggest that, in fact, _____ is more accurate."
- "Although you might at first believe _____, once you see evidence to the contrary, you'll be convinced that _____."
- "Although it is true that _____, the real issue is _____, which many scholars have overlooked."

Try Something Unexpected

Another way to make your argument stand out is to select a purpose, style, or genre that your reader may not expect. If you're having trouble writing a thesis statement because you can't find something interesting (original) to say, try to find an interesting way to say it. Specifically, try a style or genre that's different (such as satire, or using a metaphor to structure your argument), or maybe pick a different purpose—for example, to amuse your readers or even to provoke them. You could direct the argument toward an overlooked audience who doesn't yet know they have a stake in the issue. Any of these strategies would put a different spin on the topic and bring something new to the conversation.

Checklist for Thesis Statements

After you've composed a thesis statement, test its quality by making sure it meets these criteria:

- Answers a challenging, compelling, and/or controversial question
- Gets at the heart of the controversy
- Breathes new life into an issue and avoids overused, common wisdom
- Is appropriate for the argument's audience, purpose, and context
- Engages readers with specific and interesting content and style

So What?

How many times have you heard a friend make an argument that you've already heard a dozen times before? Contrast that feeling of boredom or exasperation with the way it feels to hear something new and think, "I've never thought about it *that way* before." Developing a significant question and compelling thesis is about finding that slightly different angle, fresh perspective, or personal twist that will give readers a beautiful "aha" moment.

With a compelling inspiration, you're ready to begin developing an argument. We recommend doing some preplanning before you start drafting, and in the next chapter, we offer several organizational strategies to use throughout the writing process. We encourage you to experiment with these and adapt them according to your (and your audience's) needs. We describe organizational "moves" that scholars typically use, such as referencing other scholars' important discoveries, controversial claims, or shared knowledge at the beginning of an argument or proposing solutions at the end. Additionally, we offer techniques for developing and expanding arguments to fill in gaps and improve coherence.

What's Next

Take what you've learned in this chapter and respond to the following prompts.

1. **Analyzing arguments.** Select a controversy debated in your community. Find two arguments (editorials, blog posts, opinion pieces, etc.) that express opposing viewpoints, and try the following:
   - For each argument, outline the author's main claims and identify which controversies each claim addresses. For example, what is the author's first main point, and is it an argument about fact, definition, cause, evaluation, or policy?
   - Compare the authors' claims. Do they address the same categories of controversy? Or are they arguing about different things (for example, one is an argument of fact, whereas the other is an argument of policy)? In other words, are they arguing effectively with each other, or are they arguing past each other?

2. **Using sources as inspiration.** Practice using sources as inspirations for your own argument. Pick a controversial topic that you might be interested in writing about. Find two to three sources that approach the topic from different vantage points or perspectives. While reading the sources, ask yourself:
   - How do these essays relate to each other?
   - What ideas, questions, viewpoints, and so on, do they have in common?
   - What issues are they both interested in?
   - What might the authors agree on?
   - Where might the authors disagree?
   - What new questions or issues do you want to explore?

   Then, develop three to five research questions, new angles, or controversies that you could explore in an essay.

CHAPTER eight

How Do We Organize and Develop Arguments

chapter checklist

- What strategies can we use to organize and reorganize our ideas?
- What are some typical organizational patterns?
- How can we develop and expand our arguments?

Communicating ideas accurately is incredibly difficult. That's why, when writing or speaking to others, we work hard to structure our ideas as clearly and deliberately as possible. Thoughtful organization and development aim to reduce our readers' *cognitive load*, making it easier for them to access our good ideas. Our goal is not to oversimplify or "dumb down" arguments but to make them easier to follow by carefully organizing and elaborating, as needed by our audience.

Rather than just following rules and templates, imagine elements of organization and development as tools for reducing readers' workload. Using these techniques can help us cultivate a more creative and purposeful writing process. For example, rather than thinking of an introduction as paragraphs that just fill space at the beginning of our argument, we think of what we can *accomplish* with an introduction: introduce our topic and inspiration, provide background information, establish our credibility, and forecast our argument's main claims.

Although we can arrange claims, supports, ideas, and paragraphs in many different ways, we design arguments deliberately by **putting everything in its place for a reason**. Generally, we use two guiding principles to reduce reader workload (and thus increase coherence and readability):

1. Move from known to unknown information, general to specific ideas, and accepted to controversial arguments.
2. Create smooth connections and fill in any gaps that might interrupt the "flow."

Following these guidelines will not only help you organize your writing but also help your readers process your ideas more easily.

Organizing Rhetorically

Because there are many ways to arrange an argument, we must think carefully about our audience, purpose, and message in order to select the best structure. We don't have prescribed formulas that work in all cases, and we don't make things up as we go along. Instead, we can use moves that have been practiced before, like the "plays" that sports teams use for practice and competition.

You might even consider your time as an apprentice scholar as a scrimmage, an opportunity to practice plays that pros in your academic discipline use. With time—and especially in the big game when it really counts—you can begin to adapt the playbook to specific situations, even calling "audible" modifications when circumstances change.

Eventually, you may outgrow certain basic plays. For example, sometimes apprentice scholars get stuck on the familiar five-paragraph essay format. That's a useful foundation for writing, but most college writing requires more than five paragraphs, and most arguments involve more than three main claims. Complex concepts and complicated arguments demand more sophisticated structures that allow us to expand our ideas, explore subclaims, and address readers' objections.

Before we start drafting—while we're still brainstorming, freewriting, and outlining—we begin thinking about the best way to arrange our ideas to suit a particular audience and purpose. We analyze our rhetorical situation and ask ourselves:

- What's my purpose? What am I really trying to accomplish (for example, to change readers' opinions, to offer a solution, to help readers understand a concept or event)?
- What role am I playing? What persona do I want to create?
- What's my audience's stance toward this issue? Will readers likely welcome or resist my ideas?
- How do writers typically organize this kind of argument? What kind of organization will my readers expect? Should I try to meet these expectations or "bend the rules"?
- Should I conduct original research, such as collecting data or performing experiments? How will I organize and present my results?

Rather than just picking a pattern that worked well last time, we think strategically about our purpose and audience: what we want our message to accomplish and who we're trying to reach. We then select a structure to meet our readers' needs and help us achieve our purpose.

Techniques for Organizing Your Thoughts

Different writing situations call for different strategies of organization. Sometimes we know most of what we want to say before we start writing. In those cases, we can compose an outline and mostly stick to it. Other times, we may lack a clear sense of our argument, so we need to begin writing, see where that takes us, and design a logical structure later. Still other times, we need to use creative organizational techniques that help us arrange and assemble our thoughts. Let's look at a few of those techniques next.

Visualize Your Organization

Every writing toolbox needs some techniques for conceptualizing your argument visually. One way is to imagine your paper as a building that has various rooms, each with a different function. We envision how the rooms (ideas, paragraphs) connect together in a way that will make sense to our readers. For example, if we imagined our argument as a museum that displayed ancient Egyptian artifacts, we could arrange the rooms chronologically (separate rooms for each time period), or we could organize the rooms topically. Either way, in the first room of our museum, we would want to greet visitors, arouse their interest, introduce our main ideas, and preview the tour. After all, we want to motivate our audience from the start and keep them from getting lost.

In addition, we would need to post clear signage (transitions and rationales) throughout the building to help visitors move easily through the exhibit. This would help the audience see how the rooms connect and how the contents of each relate to each other.

Finally, we'd want to conclude our audience's experience in some meaningful way. If, like many museums, our exhibit potentially overwhelmed our visitors with complexity and detail, we might want to synthesize what they saw—tying everything together so they didn't miss the point. We might also want to elaborate on the implications of our argument, perhaps by showing ancient influences in present-day Egypt, or even how ancient Egyptian art and culture has influenced the rest of the modern world.

Thinking metaphorically and visually about our argument helps us to imagine how its various parts fit together and to consider the argument from our audience's perspective so that they don't become lost, sidetracked, or overwhelmed.

CONSIDER THIS ➤ Using Metaphor

For this reflection, take a break from the chapter's content to examine and experiment with some choices that writers make.

We chose to use a museum metaphor to explain organizational concepts for two reasons. First, similes and metaphors allow us to illustrate a concept using something that's already familiar, or relatable, to the audience. Second, metaphors are vivid. "Showing" rather than "telling" will help our audience "see," understand, and remember an idea more accurately.

Using metaphors can be risky, though, because our audience might not recognize what we're referencing, or they may think we've oversimplified the issue. In our case, you might not be familiar with the typical layout of a museum. Even worse, you might apply the metaphor strictly and decide that all arguments are organized chronologically or topically. Despite these risks, we decided that the

---

(continued)

benefits of vivid illustration outweigh the potential risk of misguiding our readers.

Do you think the museum metaphor works? Is it placed wisely, or is there a better place in the chapter for the metaphor? Can you think of another metaphor that would illustrate this concept? What does this example teach you about the complexities of using metaphors in your writing?

Experiment with Maps, Graphics, and Software

Maps, cluster diagrams, or technology can be helpful tools for arranging our ideas while brainstorming. We might simply sketch out ideas on paper or use a word processor to design a graphic. Visuals can help us explore a topic in depth, discover key issues, find missing rationales, and tighten connections among our claims.

We can also use presentation software to visualize our argument. For example, traditional software can help us generate a plan for organizing our argument if we think about each of our main points as a slide. We add subclaims and support in bullets under each slide's main claim. Then, we can rearrange the slides according to the most logical outline. We can transform our presentation blueprint into a paper by adding rationales and more in-depth support. Newer online presentation software alternatives can also be used for planning purposes because they allow us to organize ideas with more complicated structures and interconnections. For example, we can illustrate how one claim connects to three subclaims that are all components of a larger idea.

TRY THIS ➤ Create a Visual Representation

For this exercise, create a concept map or other graphic as a way of developing and organizing an argument that interests you.

Patterns for Organizing Arguments

While drafting an argument, you can also experiment with some common "moves"—steps and strategies—that scholars use to develop arguments. For starters, you can follow the conventional argument structure used by many disciplines. In the sciences and social sciences, for example, scholarly research articles typically contain eight major sections:

1. Abstract
2. Introduction
3. Literature (or research) review
4. Research methods
5. Results or findings
6. Analysis and discussion
7. Conclusion
8. Bibliography

We describe the purpose of each of these sections more below and in Appendix B, but this outline provides a good starting guide, based on the typical way that many scholars arrange ideas and information.

Start with What Others Have Said

After introducing the topic of investigation, most scholarly arguments provide some background by highlighting related work by other scholars. We do this for three reasons:

1. To familiarize readers with the subject's context and to place our argument within a scholarly conversation
2. To verify our assumptions, methods, or the research question, as in a research or literature review
3. To demonstrate that we've done our homework by reviewing previous research. Neglecting to cite or at least refer to previous,

relevant scholarship damages our credibility within the scholarly community.

The length and style of the research review depends on the paper's length and on the audience's familiarity with our topic. A formal review of previous research (or "literature review") can span several pages, or it might only appear in an opening paragraph that contextualizes the argument. Regardless of what the review looks like, **scholars rarely assert their own position before they've first acknowledged what others have said**. They situate their perspective within the larger scholarly "discussion" about a topic. For example, a writer might begin an argument by citing predominant theories that inform an issue and quoting important viewpoints. We describe these techniques for verifying arguments in Chapter 6.

These strategies allow us to present what is already known about a subject before complicating it. That is, we can establish what others have already "said"—what our audience knows to be true—before we challenge these perspectives, add our own discussion to the mix, and explore new questions. Moving from known to unknown also reduces cognitive load, as mentioned above.

Follow Scholarly Models

As we've discussed, scholarly investigation proceeds from a question or problem toward an answer or conclusion—also known as a thesis. Scholars often don't know what their thesis will be when they begin investigating, but they lead with the thesis when reporting their results, as if to say, "Here's what I've discovered. Now let me show you how I got there."

Although not all forms of writing follow this conventional structure, many of them still use the generic moves and structure of the classical argument, which was developed by ancient Greeks and Romans. If you grew up in Europe or the Americas, this form of thesis-first argument probably seems familiar. Other cultures sometimes meander toward their conclusions or don't proceed through their points in a straight line, allowing their arguments to unfold more like a narrative journey. In fact, some non-Western cultures think we're rude for being so blunt, but American academic and professional audiences generally expect to hear the "bottom line up front"—a familiar move that also reduces cognitive load. Learning to get to the point early will serve you well not just in scholarly writing but also in business and scientific communication, where audiences don't want to work too hard or wait too long for you to answer the question, *so what?*

The conventional structure we offer next provides many potential moves we can make to organize an argument, but we never follow these lockstep. Rarely do we make *all* of these moves, or even sequence the sections in this exact order; rather, we thoughtfully select the ones that suit our particular rhetorical situation. Think of this structure not as a detailed outline to follow strictly but as a series of options to use according to your audience's needs. Imagine the format as a menu to select from—deliberately and thoughtfully—when you're determining what your audience might need. Notice how the Scholarly Model is compatible with the scholarly research framework described above.

The Scholarly Model

1. **Introduction**
   - Identify the controversy, problem, or research question and its significance and relevance (inspiration, implications).
   - Establish your qualifications to write about the topic.
   - Create common ground with readers.
   - Demonstrate fairness.
   - Arouse readers' attention and interest, often with a vivid illustration or a personal narrative.
   - State or imply the thesis.
   - Forecast the structure of the argument.

2. **Background**
   - Summarize important sources and previous research on the subject.
   - Describe the topic's history and its theoretical foundation.
   - Give an overview of the situation or problem.
   - Explain the process you used to answer a research question or to study a problem (for example, methods used to collect and analyze data, or theories applied to a particular subject).

3. **Support**
   - Present verification, evidence, and illustrations that support the thesis, organized in a clear and thoughtful pattern.
   - Report and tabulate data and results gathered through investigation, sometimes using figures and charts.
   - Explicitly link subclaims and support back to the thesis.
   - Analyze, interpret, and apply research findings.

4. **Consideration of alternative arguments**
   - Examine alternative points of view.
   - Note advantages and disadvantages of alternative positions.
   - Acknowledge limitations of your research or viewpoint.
   - Explain why your argument is better.

5. **Conclusion**
   - Briefly summarize and synthesize the overall argument.
   - Identify the implications of research findings.
   - Make clear what readers should think or do.
   - Add a strong emotional or ethical appeal.
   - Raise questions for further research.

Remember: this structure is a useful starting point that we approach creatively, adapting the template to particular rhetorical situations. It's not a cookie-cutter model for all arguments.

Also, there is no prescribed formula for how long each section should be. We might devote several pages to one part and only a few paragraphs to another. We select a ratio and scope that meets the needs of our purpose and audience. As an apprentice, try to notice these moves while reading and practice them yourself in different genres as you learn what your audiences expect.

TRY THIS ➤ Design an Argument Based
on the Scholarly Model

For this exercise, begin organizing an early draft of an argument using the menu of options offered by the Scholarly Model. Answer the following questions to help you decide what to include in your argument:

- How many of the Model's main sections will my audience need? For instance, will they expect to hear about alternative arguments? Are readers already familiar with the topic, or will they need extensive background information?
- What other "moves" will you need to make in order to develop your argument?
- Do you need separate sections for all of these "moves," or can some be combined?
- Which moves will be most effective in the conclusion?

Highlight or list all the points on the outline that you may want to include in your argument.

Use the Controversy Categories

Exploring an argument's various controversies, like we do when we're brainstorming, can also help us decide where to begin a paper and how to arrange our ideas. The hierarchy of these controversy categories (outlined in Table 5.1) offers a natural progression to follow. We can organize an argument around these categories by first addressing controversies about fact or existence, then discussing definitions and consequences, then evaluating, and finally offering solutions.

Organizing with controversy categories creates a logical progression of ideas and allows us to focus on the issues that are most controversial and interesting. In fact, we typically don't cover all of these categories: we skip over the issues that our audience already agrees with, knows, or understands. For instance, if we're writing about global warming, and we know readers agree:

- That climate change actually *exists*
- That it is *defined* as "an alteration in the regional or global climate" (*Oxford English Dictionary*)
- That it is *caused* by excessive carbon emissions

Then we skim over the first three kinds of controversy (existence, definitions, causes) and get right to the heart of the matter to discuss:

- Whether climate change is *serious enough to deserve our attention* (evaluation)
- Which *solutions* would be most realistic and effective (policy)

TRY THIS ➤ Use the Controversy Categories to Brainstorm and Organize

For this exercise, develop a list of questions about a topic that you are writing about, using each of the controversy categories (Fact/existence, Definition, Cause/consequence, Evaluation, Policy). Then, select key questions or points from each category, and create an outline that follows the order of the controversy categories. For a refresher on how to use the controversy categories to develop ideas, consult Table 5.1.

Techniques for Organizing Paragraphs

The following techniques are useful when organizing your argument overall (macrostructure) and when arranging individual paragraphs (microstructure). You might use these techniques when you're drafting your argument for the first time or when you're revising. Keep in mind that organization isn't only something we work on before we start writing. Often, when a professor asks you to revise your essay, one of the primary changes she expects is improved organization. Here are some ways to improve an argument's organization while you're drafting and revising.

Highlight Agreement before Disagreement

As mentioned previously, sometimes we skim over issues that our audience already knows. However, jumping into the center of the controversy may be a strategic mistake when making arguments that are especially divisive or when we imagine that an audience will resist our thesis. In such cases, we first try to build some common ground with our readers.

For example, we might begin by acknowledging opposing arguments to show our readers that we respect their perspective. This move is typical in Rogerian argument (inspired by American psychologist Carl Rogers, who coined the phrase "unconditional positive regard"), which focuses on negotiating and empathically listening to another side. Rather than blindly starting with our own position, Rogerian argument starts with the audience—prioritizing their views and building bridges to reach consensus—rather than pushing our own agenda in order to win or prove we're right. This organizational move shows how our organizational choices can enable or undermine our purpose and invite or alienate our readers.

Stick to the Point

As we discussed in Chapter 5, scholars dig deep rather than shallow when creating arguments. Focusing on the main argument helps readers, too. Try to keep things simple for you and your reader by eliminating irrelevant information. To figure out what's needed and what's tangential, use your thesis as your guide. Ask yourself "Is this point directly related to my thesis?" or "Does this information directly support my argument?" You might find it helpful to think of your thesis as an umbrella: Does every claim and detail support the spokes and fabric of the umbrella? Or is something better suited under a different umbrella—and therefore another argument?

Repeat Key Terms

When editing, we can highlight connections and create a sense of unity by repeating key words throughout an argument. Weaving in terms that are central to our argument can create a more consistent and memorable message. Successful orators often use this technique, such as in Martin Luther King, Jr.'s "I Have a Dream" speech.

We're careful not to overdo it, though. In limited doses, repetition can reinforce and unify our argument. For example, throughout this book, we've used the term "strategic" frequently to remind readers that writing should be deliberate. Has this word stuck out to you? Does it unify and reinforce our message, or has it been too repetitive?

Create a Reverse Outline

A "reverse outline" can show us how well paragraphs come together to form a coherent, well-organized whole. This outline looks very similar to a prewriting outline, but it's called a "reverse outline" (described on p. 50 in Chapter 3) because it's composed *after* a draft is written. To write a reverse outline, list the main points of each paragraph, which will give you a schematic of your draft's layout. You might also list the function of each paragraph within your draft, using the Scholarly Model as a guide. (For example, mark where you review previous research or examine alternative points of view.) Reverse outlines function like rearview mirrors; they help us navigate our way forward by showing where we've already been from a different perspective.

Once we create the outline that reflects what we've already written, we can see whether our paragraphs are focused, our main claims are evident, and our ideas progress logically. Then, we can make adjustments to keep us on the right track. Our goal here is to improve our argument's *coherence*; we don't want our audience to struggle through making sense of an incoherent message.

TRY THIS ➤ Disassemble a Draft

For this exercise, disassemble a draft to improve its organization. Print a draft of something that you're currently writing and cut it into separate paragraphs. Mix up the paragraphs and play with different sequences to decide which arrangement works best. Then, trade your piles with a classmate to ask for feedback on paragraph sequence and discuss possible transitions.

How to Develop and Expand Arguments

Organizing and reorganizing a draft will likely expose gaps and disconnects among ideas. Arguments "flow" better not only if we arrange each part carefully but also if we make sure to weave our ideas together and fill in any missing parts for our audience. Let's look at some ways of tying ideas together and eliminating gaps.

Build Transitions

When revising, we look for places that lack explicit transitions between paragraphs or sections of an argument. Think of transitions as signposts that direct the reader. Like a travel guide who points out important landmarks along the tour or a road sign that indicates when drivers need to exit, a writer guides his audience through his argument with strategically placed signposts. These markers tell readers, either explicitly or implicitly:

- What's coming next
- How ideas are connected
- When a change in subject or tone will occur
- How to interpret the argument

Signposts make our writing clear and readable so that readers don't need to work too hard to follow our meaning. Signals can be as simple as transitional words or phrases such as "however," "moreover," "similarly," and "on the other hand," or they can be as sophisticated as lengthy sections that clarify the relationship between one idea and another. What we don't want to do is just insert a transition whenever we sense a gap. Transitional words are powerful tools, but they won't magically create a connection where one does not exist. They're not love potions.

To create tighter connections among ideas, we consider the hierarchy of our claims—how they relate to one another—and we use signposts to highlight that relationship. It's important that we send the signal that communicates exactly what we mean. For example, we don't want to write "in addition" (which would connect two equally weighted ideas), when we mean "accordingly" (which would indicate a cause and effect). To be precise, we ask ourselves:

- How are these ideas related? What is their relationship?
- Are these claims equal, or is one a subpoint of another?

In addition to linking sentences, signposts can help readers move smoothly from one paragraph to the next. Paragraphs typically begin by referring back to something familiar, such as a previous paragraph, a concept explored earlier, or the thesis. Readers become confused when they encounter paragraphs that don't clearly relate to something they've seen before. We can help readers feel comfortable in a new paragraph by beginning the paragraph with something *old*—something touched on earlier—and then using this reference as a bridge to *new* material. For example, review our previous paragraph, where we began by saying: "To create tighter connections between ideas, we consider the hierarchy of our points." Note how the first part of this sentence is old information (because we made this point earlier). The second part of the sentence introduces the new material, which is easier for readers to interpret within the context of the familiar statement. Imagine how the sentence would read without a reference to something already known.

Add Metacommentary

You can also develop your argument by incorporating *metacommentary*, explicit statements about your intended meaning that clarify your message and address any confusion readers might have. Scholars use metacommentary to talk explicitly about their data collection methods, their rationales, and their thought processes. For example, we might say:

- What I mean by that is . . .
- The point I'm trying to make is . . .
- I'm not saying _____. What I am saying is . . .
- Let me clarify: _____ is my central argument.
- The gist of the matter is . . .
- In other words . . .

These statements allow us to interrupt the flow of our writing and step in as "the author" to clarify any misunderstanding or speak directly to the reader, which is what narrators do when they interrupt a movie scene to explain something to viewers. We use metacommentary sparingly, though. Like any snazzy trick, we don't overuse it, for fear of diluting its power.

TRY THIS ➤   Look for Metacommentary

For this exercise, review your favorite chapter in this book to find examples of metacommentary. Look carefully for places where we incorporated statements to clarify our meaning or address any confusion readers might have. As you investigate, think about the following:

- What effects does this metacommentary have?
- Why do you think we chose to incorporate these statements where we did?
- What gaps in our logic would remain, without this metacommentary?

Provide Rationales to Fill in the Gaps

When arguing, scholars typically provide a *rationale* or explanation of how their evidence, verifications, or illustrations support their thesis. When writers leave out this important ingredient—the metaphorical glue or linkage that holds the argument together—readers must make logical leaps on their own. For example, imagine that a writer argues that "We should invest in clean energy (claim) because 97% of Greenland's ice sheet shows surface thawing (evidence)." The argument is difficult to follow because the audience has to supply the missing rationale, such as "Clean energy will reduce carbon emissions, which cause climate change that results in melting ice sheets. So, if the ice begins to melt, we should invest resources in clean energy development and maybe avoid an environmental apocalypse."

In contrast, a scholar might connect his claim and evidence by saying, "We should invest in clean energy [claim] because excessive carbon dioxide is causing climate change [rationale], as demonstrated by the fact that 97% of Greenland's ice sheet shows surface thawing [evidence]." **Rationales connect claims with their supports.**

One of the best ways to develop rationales is to probe an argument for missing controversy categories. In the climate change example above, we provided a fact (thawing) to support a proposal (for clean energy). The missing explanation is a subclaim about cause and consequence: "excessive carbon dioxide [causes] climate change." Readers need this rationale to understand how the evidence supports the main argument. If we think they may not make that leap, we provide the rationale for them. And why take the risk that they may not make that leap?

Again, scholarly argumentation is case building. We want to "show our work" as much as possible so that the audience can follow along with less cognitive load and less chance of misunderstanding.

TRY THIS ➤ List and Define Key Terms

Often, arguments lack shared definitions of key terms. For example, in order to argue about "justice," you may need to explain what you mean by the term, which also may require some discussion of "freedom," "equality," and other related terms.

For this exercise, brainstorm a list of 5 to 10 terms that you think are central to an argument that you're currently writing. Decide whether you will need to define any of these unfamiliar or controversial terms for your audience. Consult pp. 136–138 for a description of how to write definition arguments.

Aim for Reader-Centered Writing

One way to show our work is to transform our arguments from *author*-centered writing (stuck in the writer's head) to *audience*-centered writing (focused on readers' needs and expectations). Audience-centered writing anticipates readers' needs: places where they could stumble, disagree, misinterpret, or need more explanation.

Experienced writers view their writing from this audience perspective and build or clarify rationales to link their claims and evidence. They also watch out for (a) supports without claims and (b) claims without support. When these elements are missing, arguments can fall apart because readers can't see the logical pathway that guides our thinking.

Adding rationales makes our assumptions more explicit, and they elucidate implications for claims. To see what we mean, look at the following example of a paragraph from a job application essay (or "personal statement"). This first draft doesn't offer much rationale at all, and many claims are missing:

> I am qualified for this job because I am hard working, work well in teams, and have top-notch experience in the field. During my senior year in college, I worked as an intern at Awesome & Super-Awesome Law Firm. During that time, I conducted research for one of the senior partners, filed confidential papers, and represented the firm at college fairs. I also have experience working extensively with my peers in group projects, and I studied abroad for six weeks during the summer.

The writer cites impressive experiences as evidence, but she expects the reader to understand *why* these experiences are valuable and *how* they make her a competitive candidate. She doesn't make an argument that would translate her experience into something meaningful.

The writer could improve her argument by adding rationales that explain why her claims matter. For example:

1. (Claim) My self-reliance and my ability to handle adversity blossomed
2. (Support) . . . when I studied abroad . . .

3. (Rationale) . . . [and you should care because] my self-reliance will be an asset to your company in a position like this, which operates independently of the main office.

Now, see how adding rationales and missing claims (marked in boldface) can enhance the paragraph:

> I am qualified for this job because I am hard working, work well in teams, and have top-notch experience in the field. During my senior year in college, I worked as an intern at Awesome & Super-Awesome Law Firm. During that time, I conducted research for one of the senior partners, filed confidential papers, and represented the firm at college fairs. **The fact that the partners trusted me to preserve client confidentiality demonstrates that I am reliable, honest, and responsible.** Moreover, the experience I gained as a company representative refined my presentation skills, **which shows that I am articulate and comfortable speaking in public.** I initially developed these professional social skills by working with my peers in group projects. **These assignments developed my ability to work independently and as part of a team, showing that I am both a self-starter and a collaborator. My self-reliance and my ability to handle adversity blossomed** when I studied abroad for six weeks last summer, **which required me to manage my own time, adapt to a new culture, and live independently.**

See the difference? Now readers know exactly why she is qualified for the job. The writer added revealing explanations that support her argument ("You should hire me because . . ."). These details fill in the gaps of her logic so that readers interpret her experience more like the writer intends. The evidence no longer stands alone, without any bridge to her implied thesis.

This elaboration adds something else, too: length. It is not mean-ingless filler but substantive additions to the paragraph that also increase the word count. That's a win-win outcome, since many apprentice scholars worry about meeting an assignment's length requirement.

> **TRY THIS ➤** Incorporate Reader-Centered Writing
>
> For this exercise, select a paragraph in a paper that you are writing or have written recently (for this or another class). Imagine the para-graph from your readers' perspective, and ask yourself:
>
> - Is it clear what I mean exactly?
> - Where might the reader be confused? What could be mis-leading?
> - How does this information support my thesis?
> - Where do I need to provide additional rationales?

Explain Relevance and Sufficiency

Scholars and other well-educated thinkers use two kinds of power-ful rationales to evaluate and develop arguments: relevance and sufficiency.

Relevance indicates the quality, or qualitative strength, of a con-nection between a claim and its supports. For example, grades are sup-posed to measure learning, but are they a *relevant* measure? Do grades accurately reflect learning? In the sciences and social sciences, scholars carefully explain the relevance of evidence by making clear distinc-tions among correlation, causation, and coincidence. Just because, for example, parents see a correlation (or connection) between increased use of vaccines and increased rates of autism doesn't mean that we can claim for certain that vaccines *cause* autism. In this case, the evidence is circumstantial. And as we all know, any good defense lawyer will object to the relevance of circumstantial evidence against his client because the evidence might indicate something different.

Sufficiency reflects the quantitative strength of a rationale. We cannot claim more than we have evidence to support. Again, think about a courtroom trial. A jury will only find someone guilty if the prosecution offers sufficient evidence. In fact, in a criminal trial, where the defendant is "presumed innocent" until proven otherwise, guilt must be established "beyond a reasonable doubt." Civil trials have different rules and standards. For example, sufficient support in a civil case is the "preponderance of evidence." Can you imagine why a criminal trial requires an overwhelming majority of proof, whereas a civil case needs only a simple majority of evidence to render judgment?

Invest in a Good Title

Apprentice scholars oftentimes underuse compelling titles. Titles are important because they are our first chance to capture the audience's attention and to inform readers about the argument's content. A strong title tells what the paper is about (topic) and arouses the reader's interest (with a hint toward conclusions or implications). That's why titles like "Paper 1" or "Rhetorical Analysis" don't work well—they're neither specific nor interesting. Scholars frequently use two-part titles with a main title that engages readers and a subtitle that states the main idea. Another option is to write a title that poses a compelling question or that states the thesis explicitly. Here are a few examples of titles that we like:

- "Seeing Red? The Mind-Bending Power of Colour" (by Tom Chivers)
- "Accents and Ebonics: When the Hood Goes to College" (by Taylor Callwood)
- "Will We Use Commas in the Future?" (by Matthew J.X. Malady)

- "Get Stadiums out of Our Churches" (by Alan Levinovitz)
- "Let's Give Chivalry another Chance" (by Emily Esfahani Smith)

In these examples, we can predict what the argument might be about, and we're inspired to read further.

Elaborate

Writers can never cover an issue entirely, so we can always find more room for development. As readers, we can mine these gaps to discover unanswered questions, missing evidence, and places to insert our ideas. As writers, we can identify gaps in order to expand and refine our arguments. For apprentice scholars who struggle to meet an assignment's page length requirement, gaps are a productive place to expand a draft. Keep in mind that if you don't have enough material to fill the pages, chances are good that you need to develop your argument by conducting more research or digging deeper into your analysis. But if you're absolutely sure that you have selected an appropriate scope for your writing task, you can use the following strategies to enhance your argument. (Note that the last three suggestions can help you answer the *so what?* question, too.)

1. Incorporate more examples.
2. Respond to more objections.
3. Relate the argument to real-life contexts.
4. Discuss the larger implications of your argument.
5. Make connections to other related issues.

Although these strategies help us expand our points, we do not "pad" arguments with unnecessary fluff. Like most audiences, professors typically would prefer that you get to the point and, if necessary, write less. Busy readers value conciseness almost universally.

So What?

Effective writers use structure to ease their readers' cognitive load and reduce misunderstanding. They consider their audience's needs and put everything in its place for a reason. And they present their arguments as completely as possible by providing rationales to connect claims with relevant, sufficient supports.

We can use various strategies to structure arguments effectively for particular audiences. For instance, creating an idea map might reveal connections among our thoughts, adapting a recognizable structure might ease your readers' cognitive load, and reverse outlining our points might help us rearrange the argument. Because there are many techniques for organizing ideas, we recommend experimenting with different strategies to find ones you're most comfortable with. The larger your tool bag of options, the more likely you will be to find a technique that works when you get stuck or that gives you a starting point when you encounter a new writing task.

In the next chapter, we explain how to locate an argument's weak spots. Faulty reasoning and misuse of credibility and emotion can undermine a writer's purpose and deter readers, but they can also present opportunities for improvement. When we notice gaps and faults in our argument, we can investigate holes to fill, new ideas to explore, and other hidden possibilities.

What's Next

Take what you've learned in this chapter and respond to the following prompts.

1. **Examining a publication.** One of the best ways to learn about effective organization is to study examples. To see how scholars in your discipline typically arrange their arguments, find a scholarly article that is published in one of your discipline's prominent journals.

Your library most likely has access to these scholarly journals online; if so, you can begin by searching in a database such as Academic Search Complete or EBSCOhost. You might also ask your advisor or a professor in your major to recommend an article that represents the typical features of scholarship in your field. For example, if you wanted to know what scholarly articles look like in writing studies, we would recommend examining articles in the journal *College Composition and Communication*.

Once you've selected an article, look carefully at the organizational moves the argument makes and discuss the following in class or with a peer:

a. How does the author begin? What "moves" does she make? For example, does she reference other scholars, raise important questions, or define key terms?

b. How and where does the author address the argument's *so what?*

c. Is the paper divided into different sections with headings?

d. Are there major shifts in the paper between different topics? How does the author transition between different ideas?

e. How does the author handle potential objections or different perspectives on the topic? Does she give voice to any opposition? Where?

f. Are there graphics and charts? How do they relate to the text?

g. Are there footnotes or endnotes? What purposes do these serve?

h. What moves does the author make in the conclusion?

Now, write an e-mail to an incoming student who is planning to major in your discipline. Give him some tips for writing in your discipline, particularly for organizing and formatting scholarly papers. Provide links to useful resources and examples.

2. **Proposal arguments.** Watch the documentary *An Inconvenient Truth* to investigate its techniques and evaluate it as a proposal argument. Consider the following questions:

   a. How is the film organized? Why do you think the film's creators chose this arrangement? What effects does the order have on the audience?

   b. Who is the intended audience for this documentary? What clues in the film hint at this audience?

   c. How does the documentary convince viewers that a serious problem exists? Are you convinced by the support?

   d. What unstated assumptions does the film rely on? What values and beliefs must the audience share?

   e. How well does the film respond to opposing views?

CHAPTER nine

How Can We Find Faults and Gaps in Arguments

chapter checklist

- What are fallacies, and how do we avoid them?
- How much can we rely on credibility and emotion?
- How do we anticipate and respond to objections?

Whenever we buy a product we don't need because of some advertising gimmick or use a lame excuse to avoid a traffic ticket that we know we deserve, we participate in arguments that persuade when they should not. Most of us do so often, and all of us do so sometimes.

Why are weak arguments so appealing? According to social psychologists, we use mental shortcuts to save energy. For example, we generalize what we observe. When we notice a pattern—say, several drivers from a neighboring state driving like maniacs—we conclude (or argue) "people who live in [insert neighbor state here] are terrible drivers."

Of course, we shouldn't make such a sweeping claim after observing such a small sample of drivers from a neighboring state, many of whom probably drive more responsibly. But you can certainly imagine making this kind of reasoning mistake without giving it much thought. Hasty generalizations like this are mental shortcuts that we rely on to make sense of the world with whatever limited information we have at hand. Often, the conclusions we reach also involve preexisting biases or emotional reactions that further cloud our thinking.

Shortcuts work okay when the consequences are slight. You probably won't go bald because you bought a bottle of lousy shampoo based only on a celebrity endorsement. However, shortcuts certainly matter when an argument can send a person to prison; create a new law; or, in the case of news reporting or scholarly arguments, change how we view the world.

Scholars since Plato have warned against the potential abuses of rhetoric as a tool for poor decision-making, manipulation, and tyranny. That's why, from ancient times to the present, a key function of education has been to improve the quality of arguments that we make or follow. Lawyers, legislators, and scholars have developed rigorous standards to minimize the potential abuses of argument. They scrutinize each other's claims and support, honing their reasoning and accounting for multiple perspectives so their arguments will be more acceptable to demanding audiences.

Fallacies and Critical Thinking

Rooted in the critical reading skills described in Chapter 2, this chapter presents methods to locate gaps and faults in our own and others' arguments. Fallacies reflect poor thinking. Learning how to identify fallacies, qualify claims, and anticipate and respond to alternative views will strengthen your arguments and your thinking. Knowing how to avoid fallacies can make you a better learner, communicator, consumer, and citizen.

Written arguments provide your audience with a window to view your thinking. Being able to build fallacy-free arguments will demonstrate effective critical thinking and make you more credible in school and in professional settings. Arguments based on sound reasoning can withstand harsher scrutiny, and in most cases they can help us find better answers to our questions and solutions to our problems.

When reading or listening, recognizing fallacies can also make us smarter consumers of arguments made by advertisers, politicians, bosses, and so-called friends. Learning about fallacies can inoculate citizens against being manipulated by others because we'll be more likely to think twice (or more) about whether we should believe an argument—especially when we're already inclined to do so.

Fallacious Arguments

Fallacies are arguments built on unsound rationales. In other words, a fallacious argument weakly, or even mistakenly, connects a claim and support.

Let's consider an everyday example. How often do you buy more expensive name-brand products instead of cheaper generic alternatives? The underlying argument might look something like this:

Smucker's Grape Jelly is better than its generic equivalent (CLAIM)

→ *because* (UNSTATED RATIONALE)

it carries a brand name (SUPPORT)

In this case, we assume that, in general, name-brand merchandise has superior quality compared to generic products. Indeed, Smucker's advertising tag line says so: *With a name like Smucker's, it has to be good.*®

But wait. How did we ever make the connection that name brand equals quality? What's our unstated rationale? Have we tried Smucker's Concord Grape Jelly in a side-by-side taste comparison with, for example, Walmart's generic Great Value equivalent? Have we compared ingredients on the labels? (Hint: the ingredients and nutritional information are identical.) If not, then what do we base our conclusions on: that our grandmother always bought Smucker's, that we've had a few bad experiences with other generics, that we don't want to be seen buying or serving "off brands," or that we've seen one too many Smucker's commercials? In each of these cases, our rationale is weak, and we may be wasting our money.

Educated consumers resist fallacious arguments because they impair our best thinking. **Fallacies may seem persuasive, but they do not build the best possible case for reaching a conclusion.** Regardless of their potential persuasiveness, arguments can and should be evaluated more carefully when based on a weak rationale.

Scrutinizing assumed rationales is what most people mean by the phrase "critical thinking." You can learn about dozens of different kinds of fallacies in critical thinking or philosophy classes or via books and websites on the subject. In this chapter, we focus on describing some general categories and how they work rather than trying to cover every type of fallacy. In general, fallacies typically follow one of three patterns:

1. Faulty use of reasoning or logic (activated by evidence)
2. Faulty use of credibility (built with verification, reputation, or presentation)
3. Faulty use of emotion (often evoked by illustrations)

Faulty Reasoning

Mistakes in reasoning are the most common fallacies, but they are often easy enough to find and correct.

Jumping to Conclusions

You already know one of the most common fallacies—the overgeneralization, sometimes called a "hasty generalization." The faulty rationale here involves *insufficiency*: reaching a conclusion before sufficient evidence accumulates, as in the case of horrible drivers discussed above.

Again, it's human nature to seek patterns and sort our experiences into categories. But when generalizations become stereotypes that influence how we treat others, they raise serious ethical issues. The best way to counteract the risks associated with "jumping to conclusions" is to slow down and scrutinize an argument's rationale—especially when it's unstated.

CONSIDER THIS ➤ Sufficiency Fallacies

For this reflection, consider these three generalizations, and then reflect on the bulleted questions that follow.

1. Students are lazy.
2. Professors lack common sense.
3. High school graduates make less money than college graduates.

- How do you think someone could reach each of these conclusions? What evidence would they use?
- What rationale would make each of these statements persuasive?
- Which audiences would find these most persuasive, and why?

Qualifying Your Claims

You can avoid sufficiency fallacies in your arguments and in your own thinking by *qualifying* your claims. **A qualification is a stated restriction that limits a claim's strength.** For instance, you might say something like "I don't know about *all* [neighbor state] drivers, but I've seen lots of knuckleheaded ones in my neck of the woods." Qualifying claims helps us avoid exaggerating our conclusions.

Let's consider ways to qualify the claim "Students are lazy." We could do one or more of the following:

1. Weaken the verb: "Students *seem* lazy."
2. Narrow the subject: "*Some* students seem lazy."
3. Limit and clarify the modifier: "Some students seem *to devote inadequate efforts to studying.*"
4. Add verification: "*Recent research indicates that* some students devote inadequate efforts to studying."

Note that in these examples, the precision and length of each statement increases as the scope of the claim decreases. It's almost as if scholars use more words to say less—but really, we're just careful not to overstate our claims.

One qualification that bothers many scholars is using the phrase "I think" to introduce a claim. (Even worse may be using "I feel" when discussing what you think or believe, rather than your feelings.) Beginning claims with "I think" is probably why many English teachers ban "I" from student writing. It's not that they necessarily discount students' thoughts or experiences, either. As we discussed in Chapter 6, personal experience can provide very persuasive evidence. Teachers dislike "I think" because the phrase often precedes an *assertion*, or unsupported opinion. Students sometimes think they can avoid the work of building an argument (supporting their ideas and providing strong rationales) if they simply qualify their claims as "personal opinion." Also, characterizing an assertion as "just my opinion" can shut down conversation for people who believe that "everyone's entitled to her own opinion." For public arguments, especially scholarly arguments, audiences agree that everyone is entitled to her opinion—but they expect that writers will provide support and rationales for the audience to scrutinize.

Really, every claim contains an implied "I think" before it. Trust that your readers will know that: take ownership of your arguments rather than "hedging" your claims.

TRY THIS ➤ Qualify Claims

For this exercise, use the techniques you've learned here to qualify the other two claims from the previous CONSIDER THIS.

Fallacies of Relevance

Another main category of reasoning errors involves *relevance*. Even when there's sufficient support, the linkage between that evidence and the claim or thesis may be weak.

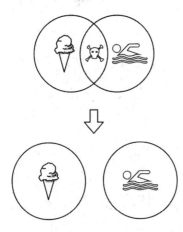

Correlation versus Causation

A common kind of relevance fallacy confuses correlation with causation (initially described on p. 139). A famous example involves ice cream sales and drownings. As you can imagine, both phenomena increase during the summer, so we might imagine that there is a *correlation* between increased ice cream sales and drownings.

But that doesn't mean that increased sales of ice cream in the hot summer months actually *cause* more drownings. Folks just like to swim more when it's hot. And more people frolicking in pools and ponds means more drownings.

Scientists and other researchers who use data to answer research questions employ statistical analysis to test the strength of the relationship between variables (like ice cream sales and drownings, or smoking and lung cancer). When a correlation becomes more than coincidental, the evidence becomes "significant." Scholars and others who have been well educated about quantitative methods habitually scrutinize scientific findings by asking questions such as:

- How large was the sample size?
- What's the margin of error?
- What other variables may be involved?

Changing the Subject

A second type of relevance fallacy intentionally introduces information that's only weakly related to the conclusion. Politicians often use this fallacy, changing the subject to avoid answering a question:

REPORTER: Can you describe your proposed tax plan?

POLITICAL CANDIDATE: We need a tax program that supports the middle class and creates new jobs.

REPORTER: Yes, but can you talk specifically about how your plan will accomplish those goals?

POLITICAL CANDIDATE: We must work together, across political parties, to solve these issues. I believe my track record demonstrates my ability to get things done in Washington.

In this case, the candidate simply changes the subject, or controversy category, so as to avoid providing any specifics, drifting from the original question of *how* the tax plan will work to *what* it should accomplish to *why* he's the person who can make things happen.

Philosophers who study informal logic or reasoning sometimes call the "changing-the-subject" technique a kind of "red herring" fallacy (after the distractingly stinky fish). Experienced scholars avoid extraneous information that might sidetrack or mislead their audiences.

Other Reasoning Fallacies

In addition to fallacies of sufficiency and relevance, there are several common mental shortcuts that educated communicators are careful to avoid.

Straw Man Arguments

A "straw man argument" presents an oversimplified, exaggerated, or simply inaccurate version of an opposing argument to make alternative perspectives seem weak, foolish, and easily refutable—like a scarecrow that we could easily knock over. One of the most common straw man techniques is to misquote or use someone's words out of context. Another popular trick is to misrepresent or oversimplify opposing views. Think about the following examples of claims, drawn from straw man arguments we see and hear around us daily:

- "Pro-life advocates don't care about women's rights."
- "If you're not with us, you must be against us."
- "My opponent's tax plan will target the poor and destitute, while giving the wealthy a free ride."

We look out for the straw man whenever we encounter arguments, especially opinion pieces, political ads, campaign speeches, and product advertisements. These sneaky moves tell us a lot about a writer and his message, mainly that his case probably isn't very strong if he has to weaken the other side in order to look good. We also scour our own arguments for faults like these.

CONSIDER THIS ➤ Mistreating Opposing Views

For this reflection, think of a time when you or a friend treated each other's perspectives unfairly during a disagreement. Reflect on the consequences of mistreating different perspectives. How did this affect the way that you responded to the argument? What kind of character did you or your friend exhibit? Was the argument improved at all by downplaying the other side?

Slippery Slope Arguments

Sometimes we get caught up in dire predictions about the future. If, for example, you ask someone for a date and she or he rejects your offer, then you might conclude that there's probably no future in that relationship. And if that relationship won't work, then maybe none ever will and you'll eventually die alone, miserable that you could never find love.

Obviously, we try to take rejections less seriously. And we should also question political, social, or economic arguments based on some rationale that the worst will inevitably happen, or that the present so definitively determines the future. The future is, after all, unknown. Ask any weather forecaster.

CONSIDER THIS ➤ Using Humor

For this reflection, weigh the costs and benefits of using humor in your writing.

You may have noticed our occasional attempts at humor, such as suggesting that someone might interpret rejection as a sign that he will "eventually die alone." We try to use humor to enliven the text and give our reader a break from otherwise serious discussions.

(continued)

Although most people enjoy a chuckle, humor also incurs risk. The audience may read literally and become confused, or they might interpret the tone as inappropriate and not take us seriously.

Do you think our (sometimes lame) attempts at humor work? How do they affect how you read or process our ideas? How does humor affect the style of a piece of writing? (We continue discussions of style in Chapter 10.)

False Dilemmas

Also known as an either/or fallacy or binary thinking, a false dichotomy is a kind of oversimplification. For example, in a special State of the Union address in September 2001, President George W. Bush famously stated that "You're either with us or you are with the terrorists." Obviously, there were probably groups who favored neither terrorists nor the US, and maybe even some who sympathized with both. (And to be fair and not create a straw man argument by taking this often quoted statement out of context, Bush's next sentence made his position somewhat less extreme: "From this day forward, any nation that continues to harbor or support terrorism will be regarded by the United States as a hostile regime.")

Scholars try to imagine many possibilities, rather than basing arguments on the rationale that there are only two choices when there obviously are more.

Circular Reasoning

Sometimes people back up a claim with the exact same claim, disguised as support. For instance, someone might say, "That food is unhealthy because it causes cancer" or "That action will be beneficial because it will help you." In both examples, the reason given is the same as the stated claim. This fallacy is also called "begging the question" (although you may notice that many people mistakenly use that expression when they actually mean "raising a question").

Truth as Support

Truth is a special category of support. Here we're not talking about facts or reality but about a "Truth" that's not really open to question, such as religious beliefs or patriotism. Verifying an argument with a Truth can be very tricky; those who believe the Truth will probably believe the argument, but of course, not everyone believes the same Truths. Truths, after all, are usually matters of faith more than logic or evidence.

Invoking a Truth often shuts down arguments, because once a discussion gets down to matters that are not "open to argument," there's little left to debate. Furthermore, in the United States, where we generally consider matters of faith to be private, scholars typically refrain from supporting arguments with Truths.

Whenever scholars can, they build their arguments on the least controversial, most accepted support available. When invoking values, public sources of verification make more effective scholarly arguments because they build on commonly held agreement. For example, Martin Luther King, Jr. condemned racial injustice by invoking shared American values that had previously been articulated by the nation's founders and Abraham Lincoln. For an audience who shares those values, King's arguments were, and remain, quite persuasive.

Relying Too Much on Credibility

Writers and readers commonly make mistakes with credibility, just as they do with evidence.

We must be careful about using shortcuts to assess a source's credibility. For example, a website domain (.com, .edu, .org, .gov) is not sufficient for determining its trustworthiness. You may have been taught to be more suspicious of .com websites because they only want to sell their brands or products, but company websites can be informative, if biased, sources for researching a business and its products or services. Also, don't jump to the conclusion that other websites (like .orgs) have no agendas. One look at organizations such as the NRA, PETA, MADD, and MoveOn proves different.

We misuse credibility whenever we trust or agree with an argument because of the author's reputation, rather than the verification and evidence presented. We might make this mistake, for example, when thinking that everything we read in a textbook (like this one) must be correct. It wouldn't have been published otherwise, right?

Advertisements often use this kind of *false authority* fallacy because they know that consumers will buy products based on celebrity endorsements, rather than on what they know about the quality of the product itself or whether it really works. Of course, endorsements like these can backfire with disastrous effects when a celebrity's reputation changes (think of Lance Armstrong or other sports heroes gone bad).

There's good reason not to be swayed or try to persuade others by relying too much on credibility. Think about it. **Credibility is a kind of oversimplification.** Reputations are often inaccurate or not well deserved, and they can change or even be faked fairly easily.

Credibility can also be used in deliberately or inadvertently negative ways. An ad hominem, or "against the person," fallacy intentionally emphasizes negative credibility, rejecting an argument just because of the arguer's reputation. This happens in politics when diehard Republicans or Democrats refuse to consider the other side's arguments because of party affiliation, rather than evaluating the strength of support provided. Another credibility fallacy is the "bandwagon effect," when we decide to do something just because it's popular with others. Here, our unstated rationale is that "what's good for others must be good for me." The fashion industry frequently exploits the effectiveness of the bandwagon effect in its advertising with the implied rationale, "Buy this product in order to belong."

One of the most commonly used credibility fallacies is an appeal to tradition, when we support present or future actions not on good reasoning but on what's been done before. These arguments often seem appealing, but their rationales are weak—often some nostalgia for the past or fear of change. In either case, doing things the same old way without question inhibits progress and does not represent strong critical thinking.

As we discussed in our chapter on supports, credibility is the gateway to persuasion: Before most audiences will trust new information that we present, they must consider us or our arguments to be credible. Indeed, Aristotle identified credibility, and especially the perceived character of the speaker or writer, as the most authoritative form of persuasion. Even experienced scholars are not immune to the lure of credibility. Scholarly journal articles are sometimes wrong, despite rigorous review by disciplinary experts. And despite being written mostly by novices, Wikipedia articles are mostly accurate and often well supported.

As with other kinds of fallacies, we should always ask two questions. How sufficient and relevant are these supports? Are these rationales strong enough to connect these claims and supports?

Getting Emotional

Emotions provide the least reliable but typically most compelling kind of support. Consider how much money charities raise by showing cuddly puppies or starving children to evoke sympathy. Emotion can make the difference between an audience agreeing with an argument and doing something about it. However, emotion can also cloud good judgment. Consider the last time you became overly emotional in an argument. Did you make the best decision possible?

As we discussed in the chapter on supports, arguments often arouse emotions with vivid examples, narratives, or personal experiences that may not represent the larger picture. Such illustrations may seem persuasive, but on closer inspection, they are insufficient supports when they represent small sample sizes, ignore substantial counter evidence, or hide faulty reasoning.

TRY THIS ➤ Identify the Fallacies

For this exercise, use what you've learned about fallacies to explain why the following statements might not persuade your professor. What rationales does each of these statements assume, and why might those rationales be fallacious?

Sample claim: None of the other writing classes are this hard and their teachers give all A's.

Assumed rationale: Classes can and should all be equally difficult and grade the same way.

Problem: Just because one person does something a certain way doesn't mean others should automatically follow suit (bandwagon appeal).

1. My mom said this paper was really good.
2. I'm an "A student"; I don't deserve a B for this course.
3. This paper is just as good as the ones that earned me As in high school.
4. Maybe my paper isn't that good, but I tried *really* hard.
5. What did you expect? I'm a math major.
6. If you fail me, it'll ruin my life.

Answers

1. Rationale: What mom thinks is relevant. Problem: Appeal to false authority—your mother isn't teaching this class.
2. Rationale: Past performance guarantees future results. Problem: Relevance/overgeneralization—just because you get good grades in most classes doesn't mean you'll earn them in every class.
3. Rationale: High school is the same as college. Problem: Relevance—college is not high school.
4. Rationale: Efforts should count more than quality. Problem: Relevance—quality counts.

(continued)

5. Rationale: Math majors are not good writers. Problem: Hasty generaliza-tion/stereotype or relevance—being good at math doesn't limit your writ-ing ability.

6. Rationale: Consequences are relevant to evaluating performance in a course. Problem: Manipulative emotional appeal based in weak reason-ing (slippery slope). This one's especially complex because it can be interpreted as any of three different fallacies: (a) an emotional fallacy, playing on the pity of the teacher not to harm the student with a bad grade; (b) a sufficiency fallacy, because one course grade typically does not cause success or failure in life; (c) a relevancy fallacy, be-cause grades reflect performance in a course, not success or failure afterward.

Hidden Benefits of Studying Fallacies

Humans don't simply operate according to cold, hard logic like robots or Mr. Spock. In fact, fallacies are often quite effective (that is, persua-sive), even when audiences pay close attention. It takes practice and constant attention to recognize fallacies in everyday life, and, as humans, we often believe what we choose to believe. This isn't to say that you should willfully use fallacies to manipulate an audience, but you should also not reject arguments outright when they contain weak reasoning, either. Just be mindful of these faults as part of the larger picture.

Remember, too, that **fallacies aren't necessarily false.** Making a hasty generalization or invoking a Truth may very well be an error in reasoning, and using such techniques may cause a critical audience to question your conclusions. However, just because such fallacies use weak reasoning doesn't mean that they're false. For example, consider the fallacy "If you fail me, it will ruin my life." We can cer-tainly imagine a situation where this might be true. Perhaps a stu-dent is at risk only for failing this particular course, he needs this course to graduate, and he's been offered the job of a lifetime but cannot be hired without the degree in hand. Still, his grade depends on his performance in the course, not the consequences of that performance.

Finally, consider the usefulness of fallacies as gems for further research. For example,

- You might think of a hasty generalization as a hypothesis worth testing.
- You might notice red herrings as potential issues to investigate further.
- You might introduce evidence to support an argument that typically evokes only emotion.
- You might search for credible sources to replace the false authorities that a weak argument relies on.

Anticipate and Respond to Opposing Views

In addition to avoiding fallacies, we can make arguments stronger by addressing alternative perspectives. When we fail to anticipate our audience's objections, readers are left thinking, "Yes, but what about _____?" or "How could you overlook the fact that _____?" These omissions can annoy readers or imply that we haven't thought through our argument fully. At the very least, readers won't be fully convinced. At the worst, they'll be offended, angry, or unwilling to read any further.

Sometimes we feel this way when we view political advertisements that only show one side of the story, such as when a candidate attacks her opponent for one poor decision while disregarding all the good work he's done. This kind of ad hominem attack can diminish our trust in the candidate's good will. Writers can make similar mistakes, whether they mean to or not. There are several ways to avoid misrepresenting the other side.

Anticipate Objections

Imagining potential objections is one of the best ways to fortify our arguments against resistance. After all, it's much better to anticipate readers' objections while we're drafting an argument than it is to hope that our readers won't think of that one counterargument that could unravel our whole case. Unlike in conversation, writing can't be supported or clarified any further once it's published. Once it's in print, we can't add or take anything back, so we use strategies such as the following to *anticipate* objections.

Walk in the Reader's Shoes

In Chapter 8, we introduce Rogerian argument, which teaches us the importance of honoring our audience's perspective and their life experience. Whether or not we're writing a Rogerian argument to a resistant audience, we imagine what readers will think as they're interpreting our argument, what they value, what they know, and how they might respond to claims. We examine each of the argument's components from the reader's perspective and identify places where readers might object, asking ourselves:

- What elements of support are weakest and most vulnerable?
- What might readers have to say in response? If I were reading this aloud to another person, where might he stop me and say, "Wait a minute! What about _____?"

Identify the Potential Controversies

To avoid missing a key component of an argument, we make sure we've covered all our bases. We explore an issue comprehensively and identify different ways of approaching it by examining all five controversy categories, which we outlined on p. 104. We figure out the heart of the issue—the place where our readers will likely disagree with us—before we start writing, or we review the various controversies as we're revising to identify alternative viewpoints.

Play the Devil's (or the Angel's) Advocate

Peter Elbow's "Believing and Doubting Game" that we mention in Chapter 5 helps us explore controversies from perspectives that differ from our own. It's worth spending time getting in the mindset of someone who thinks very differently from us because it can help us see an issue's complexity more clearly—rather than through our limited tunnel vision. We also ask trusted readers to play devil's advocates for us by directly challenging our ideas, pretending to support an opposing position, and pushing us to consider all the implications of our claims.

TRY THIS ➤ Locate Missing Objections

For this exercise, review a piece of writing that you have recently composed or are currently working on. Use the first two strategies we recommend (walking in the reader's shoes and identifying the controversies) to discover alternative viewpoints and possible objections. Then, work with a partner to play devil's advocate for each other. Help each other identify possible gaps and faults in your arguments.

Respond to Objections

Once we pinpoint the objections readers could raise, we acknowledge and respond to them. Doing so demonstrates to readers that we've done our homework and understand the complexity of the controversy. Also, if readers have reasonable objections, we need to show how we've thought through those issues and reconciled our views. Basically, we have two ways of responding:

1. **We can concede.** When our readers' objections are valid, we typically acknowledge their legitimacy. We don't think of conceding as "giving in" or undermining our argument; rather, we concede to

show readers that we're honest, open-minded, and reasonable. However, we're careful about the way we frame the concession so that we don't *sound* weak or unsteady in our position. We use statements such as the following to acknowledge the alternative view and then explain why our argument still works, despite an objection:

a. Scholars who claim _____ make a good point because _____; however, what they overlook is _____. This is actually more important because _____.

b. I concede that _____, but I still maintain my position because _____.

c. Although _____ is a relevant concern, the heart of the issue is _____, which means _____ needs to happen.

d. It is true that _____. However . . .

Notice how many of the above statements contain words such as "however" and "although"? These terms are *conjunctive adverbs*. Also, most of the sentences contain two parts: a deemphasized portion (the first "although" part, called a *dependent clause*) and an emphasized portion (the second part where our message comes through—the *independent clause*).

These examples show that sentence structure and word choice can bolster our message. We can emphasize our position by using conjunctive adverbs and a sentence structure that basically says, "I'll give you this minor thing, but look at what's more important." Subtle but effective, don't you think? We talk more about stylistic choices like these in Chapter 10.

2. **We can refute**. If we disagree with our readers' objections, we can explain how we've arrived at an alternative position. We describe an opposing view and then present the evidence, verification, and illustrations that convinced us to think differently. We imagine this refutation as a mini-argument that needs support. Still, we

maintain a respectful tone and treat others' objections fairly, without oversimplifying or inaccurately representing their views. Usually, this means that we summarize the opposing view in a way that shows we understand where scholars are coming from, like this:

a. Some scholars argue _____ because they inter-pret evidence to mean _____ .

b. Many well-intentioned people have said _____ , which is understandable because _____ .

c. Another way of viewing this issue is _____ .

After we give voice to the opposition, we explain and defend our point of view. This refutation may take a few sentences, a paragraph, or an entire section. It all depends on how relevant the objection is to our central argument. To decide how much attention to give it, we consider the building blocks of our case and what claims our readers must accept in order to move forward in the argument.

So What?

People don't change their minds easily. An audience that disagrees with an argument naturally tends to pick apart the argument, whereas when audiences hear arguments they already agree with, they tend to think less critically about the quality of the rationale and support.

What's difficult about creating arguments is knowing how picky or objective an audience will be. Generally speaking, we assume that scholarly audiences will be "neutral"—that is, rigorous but open-minded. Recognizing fallacies can help us scrutinize arguments and avoid taking shortcuts with our thinking. Finding faulty rationales while reading can make us less gullible. Filling gaps while writing can make our arguments more convincing for demanding audiences in school and beyond. Although we can't always see the faults and blind spots in our own arguments, we can ask others to review our work and help us refute counterarguments or elaborate and build stronger rationales.

Throughout the book, we've described writing as deliberate and flexible. Similarly, in our final chapter, we describe how to adapt your writing style to different rhetorical situations. Rather than prescribing strict rules, we explain the effects of stylistic and grammatical choices. We answer specific questions such as "What is passive voice?" and "Can I bend the rules on purpose?" as well as share fun techniques you can try to vary your sentences, liven up your language, and add some pizzazz to your prose. Finally, we offer proofreading and editing advice that you can use on your own or with a trusted reader.

What's Next

Take what you've learned in this chapter and respond to the following prompts.

1. **Fallacies scavenger hunt.** Fallacies can be found everywhere. (Okay, maybe that's an overgeneralization.) Spend a day noticing as many fallacies as you can find—in the news, in advertisements, and in your daily conversations. Collect and analyze the most interesting examples. Bring your artifacts to class and discuss which ones you think are most persuasive and why.

2. **Critical thinking.** Imagine yourself in a job interview. Your potential employer asks you about your critical thinking skills. To help you prepare for this question, write a page about how finding and fixing faults in arguments can help you solve workplace problems.

3. **Satirical argument.** Write a short, satirical argument that relies heavily on fallacies. Here's an example that one of our

students, Trygve Rorvig, wrote. Before writing your own satirical argument, try to identify each of the fallacies in this
example:

The drinking age of America is too high because everyone who en-
dorses it is horrendous. The legislators of Virginia should change it
back to 18, like it was at first. Other countries have a lower drinking
age so we should, too. Charlie Sheen drinks alcohol, and that man is
a legend so it should be legal for 18-year-olds. If we legalize a lower
drinking age, the students in college will have higher morale, which
will cause less depression, which will cause higher life satisfaction for
all. So if you're not for a lower drinking age, you are for the depression
of 18-year-olds. Some people say 21 is a good age, but I might offer a
rebuttal by sharing the many kinds of alcohol there are, such as wine,
beer, liquor, or moonshine (which should be legal, too). Legalization
of a lower drinking age will be beneficial to America because it will be
good for the people of the United States. Almost all 18-year-olds want
a lower drinking age, so they cannot be wrong.

CHAPTER ten

What about Style

chapter checklist

- What are the features of style?
- How can we develop a range of styles?
- How do we edit and proofread?

You may have learned "never" to use the first person ("I") in academic writing. But what should you do when a professor asks you to write about your personal experiences? When faced with a question like this, or another stylistic dilemma, keep in mind that "rules" for good writing are not universal or unchanging, because what works in one context for a specific audience and purpose might not work for another. In other words, **writing is a series of strategic choices**.

Writing with Style

What is stylistically appropriate in one argument might be a faux pas—or even a colossal blunder—in another situation. Just as you wouldn't wear pajamas to the club or a bathing suit to a presentation, you probably shouldn't use slang in a lab report. But you might use popular colloquialisms in an article for the student newspaper because such language could help you connect with readers. As with fashionable attire, what constitutes a smartly chosen writing style depends on the rhetorical situation.

CLUB   GYM   PRESENTATION

Therefore, we define style as "thoughtful flexibility"—the ability to customize our writing for different situations and expectations. With practice, style is something that you can change and adapt according to the needs of different audiences, purposes, and contexts.

To be clear and precise, scholarly style doesn't have to be boring, nor does it require unnecessarily fancy expression. The universal rule for good style, in scholarly writing or elsewhere, is for it to *seem deliberate*, with every word and sentence carefully chosen for its particular audience, purpose, and situation. Effective scholars try to **write compelling prose that reduces your reader's workload.**

Although we can't offer foolproof advice for every writing situation, this chapter will help you think deliberately about your stylistic choices. Before we delve into the details of style, let's focus on some fundamental terms and concepts.

CONSIDER THIS ➤ Style for Different Occasions

For this reflection, consider how writers adapt their style for different audiences, purposes, and contexts.

1. How would you describe the overall style of this book? How does our style compare to other textbooks you've read?
2. You probably use different styles in different situations. Describe your favorite writing style, and explain why it's your favorite.
3. What elements of style have you noticed in the scholarly writing that you've read? Create a list of common characteristics.

Compare your answers with those of a classmate.

Clarity and Vividness

Imitating good writing can be an effective technique for improving style, but it often backfires when apprentice scholars try to emulate the dense, highly technical style that they read in published scholarship. Trying too hard to sound smart can sacrifice clarity. The result is often wordy, convoluted, confusing prose that overworks readers.

Remember, the primary goal of writing is to communicate. If our style interferes with our ability to communicate, we've adopted the wrong style. To avoid an overly academic, pretentious style and reduce your readers' fatigue, consider the following suggestions.

Start Easy

As we discussed in Chapter 8, how we sequence information affects our reader's cognitive load. Generally speaking, we can reduce their workload by easing them into content that is newer or more complex. This works at the essay level when we state our thesis in the introduction ("bottom line up front") before introducing supporting details. This works at the paragraph level when we use topic sentences to announce the main idea of a paragraph. And it works in sentences when we make the most general "big" idea the subject of the sentence. Consider, for example, the following sentences:

A. Trauma to the face that damages capillaries near the eye causes a black eye, or periorbital hematoma.

B. A black eye, or periorbital hematoma, is caused by trauma to the face that damages capillaries around the eye.

Which do you prefer? Which is easier to read? These sentences both contain the same information. Sentence B begins with the concept or term, and then provides details. For most readers, sentence A is more difficult to read. (Notice, too, that sentence B uses the passive verb construction, "is caused," which in this somewhat rare case enhances clarity.)

Remember, Less Can Be More

While explanations and descriptions are necessary to communicate our full arguments, most readers appreciate when we spare them from wading through more words than necessary.

Use Strong Verbs

Sometimes writers nominalize verbs by turning them into nouns. For instance, "express" becomes "expression," and "communicate" becomes "communication." Nominalized sentences can become clunky or unclear because they are overloaded with prepositions and excessive words. Helen Sword from *The New York Times* (July 23, 2012) calls nominalizations "zombie nouns" that "cannibalize active verbs," leaving the sentence desiccated and lifeless.

To see what we mean, consider which of the following sounds better:

- "The study of rhetoric *is the investigation of* how persuasion and communication work."
- "Rhetoric *investigates* how persuasion and communication work."

Nominalized verbs sometimes help us express abstract ideas or vary our sentence structure, but nominalizations can also make our writing less lively, concise, and readable than using the original verbs.

Notice, too, how the first example sentence uses the verb "is" with the nominalization "investigation." The verb "to be" is not inherently evil, but it rarely enhances clarity. As a general rule, editing "to be" out of our writing can help us avoid using nominalizations and passive

---

TRY THIS ➤ Eliminate Nominalizations

For this exercise, practice translating nominalizations into active verbs, and then look for nominalizations in a draft that you're currently writing.

To practice reviving stilted language, turn the following sentences into more lively constructions:

1. The demonstration of her character was shown through her consideration of others.
2. The examination of multiple views made the essay interesting.
3. The discussion of the issue was resolved through consideration of everyone's viewpoints.

Now, look for nominalizations in a draft that you're currently writing. Replace as many nominalizations as you can find with more lively, precise verbs. To make the process easier, try using the "find" function in your word processor to search for word endings such as *-tion*, *-ism*, and *-ity*.

---

voice, which we discuss later in this chapter. Replacing "to be" with more precise verbs that reflect our exact meaning makes our writing more engaging and fluid.

Use Vivid and Precise Language

Descriptive language can help you incorporate details into your writing that help readers feel, see, and experience your message. However, this style doesn't work in every situation. When the audience values brevity and clarity, as is often the case in business or scientific writing, literary flourishes fail. Chemists don't want flowery lab reports, and bosses don't necessarily appreciate business proposals that rhyme.

We are very careful not to overembellish our writing if the genre or audience calls for concision, but that doesn't mean that we can't use vivid and precise language. In fact, readers generally prefer specific and clear phrasing, details, and examples that express ideas precisely— so long as every detail is there for a reason. For example, consider a vague word like "beneficial," which communicates very little substance. If we said, "Our class was beneficial," readers wouldn't know exactly what made it beneficial. Was it informative? Intellectually challenging? Motivational? Transformative? (Who knows?)

We use descriptive language to select words that transmit our exact meaning without interference or distortion. Think of this as "showing" readers exactly what we mean, rather than just "telling" them. The difference is in the level of detail. When we "show" readers, we give them something concrete to grasp—evidence of our intended meaning. When we "tell" them, we claim more abstractly.

Telling and showing come together like a claim and support. For example, if you "tell" your audience to vary their vocabulary, then they might need for you to "show" them how.

Telling: "You might use synonymous phrases . . ."

Showing: ". . . for example, refer to a puppy as a 'wee canine.'"

Showing is more precise and lively because it's less abstract.

Mechanics

Often we hear students clump all local concerns together under vague headings such as "grammar" or "flow," but these imprecise terms don't convey *exactly* what students are referring to—punctuation, transitions, sentence structure, grammar, or something else. Accurate, precise terminology can enable writers to think and communicate more carefully about their writing. For example, writers can ask for specific assistance from peer reviewers or tutors when they use terms that communicate their exact needs. Writers who talk vaguely about their writing often are less sure about what they really need to improve. To be more precise, we use the term *mechanics* to refer to sentence-level concerns, which include spelling, punctuation, capitalization, grammar, and usage.

Errors and Mistakes

Even though hardly anyone speaks or writes with perfect mechanics all the time, most educated readers expect standard academic English in formal writing. Sometimes mechanical errors do significantly affect meaning. For example, you've probably seen the T-shirt or poster that says: "Let's eat grandma." This statement implies serious bodily harm, whereas the corrected version is an invitation: "Let's eat, grandma."

Although punctuation may not actually "save lives," as these comical T-shirts claim, mechanics can certainly modify meaning. Punctuation, in particular, can be a powerful tool that affects a message. Consider, for example, the following versions of a sentence:

- A woman, without her man, is nothing.
- A woman: without her, man is nothing.

Do you notice how these sentences mean something very different? This is the main reason why educated readers value proper mechanics;

they value precise meaning and want readers to say what they mean clearly and deliberately. **Errors add confusion.** Errors cause readers to work harder to make sense of what we're trying to say.

Even when they don't seriously impair meaning, **mistakes can diminish credibility** because of the potential for imprecision or miscommunication. Educated readers will likely interpret mistakes as signs of laziness (like the writer didn't edit carefully and therefore don't care about our work) or ignorance (as though the writer doesn't know the rules). Just as when preparing for a job interview, when submitting a final draft, we make every effort to make sure our appearance is polished and professional. There's no reason to lose the job over a bit of toilet paper stuck to your shoe or an errant apostrophe.

With that being said, deviations from standard academic English can result from nonstandard dialects and written accents, not from "mistakes." What may look like a grammatical mistake may actually be an accepted form in another English dialect. We like to think that people are becoming more open-minded about variations of English, but we also know that standard English carries power in many circles. Those of us who are multilingual writers or speakers of nonstandard dialects need to decide when to use standard academic English and when to use other dialects. It's generally helpful if writers can use these dialectical differences intentionally, so becoming well versed in the rules of standard academic English can make you a more versatile writer.

Grammar versus Usage

Grammar and usage are not the same, and experienced writers know the difference. Simply put, "grammar" involves the rules for how we use language traditionally or formally, whereas "usage" is how most people actually use language in everyday conversations.

Here's an example that explains the distinction. In Chapter 1, we mention that many scholars avoid sexist language by alternating between "she" and "he," or just using "she" (since "he" had his turn for hundreds of years). The same usage formula applies to the other forms of third-person singular ("him," "her," "his," and "hers").

Third-person plural makes matters more complicated. Grammatically speaking, personal pronouns should "agree" in number with the noun to which they refer. In the previous sentence, for example, "they" refers to and "agrees with" the word "pronouns." This gets tricky, though, when a pronoun refers back to a singular noun phrase. Take, for example, this sentence: "Every student should bring [insert possessive pronoun] laptop to class." From a strictly grammatical perspective, "every student" is singular, so the pronoun should be "his" or "her": "Every student should bring *her* laptop to class." However, because gender-neutral language has become accepted usage for writers and speakers who are less finicky about grammar, people now commonly say, "Every student should bring *their* laptop to class." Experienced writers know this distinction and deliberately shift between formal and informal registers, or language styles, according to the particular audience, purpose, and context. Also, sometimes, writers use "their" as a singular pronoun to refer to a person in gender-neutral terms for political or social reasons. Although the singular "their" is becoming increasingly

CONSIDER THIS ➤ The Politics of Language

For this reflection, consider how language choices can carry political and social implications. Language use is complicated, especially because the words we use shape our perceptions. For this reason, people debate instances when language use causes "microaggressions," everyday offenses that intentionally or unintentionally target minority groups. For instance, consider the following examples and discuss the political and social implications of these language choices:

- Names of athletic teams, such as the Washington Redskins and the Atlanta Braves

(continued)

- Terms such as "homeless," "foreigner," "opposite sex," "elderly," "disabled," and "American"
- The practice of standard and nonstandard English
- Other language issues you have encountered

accepted in everyday conversation and in writing, writers need to be aware of how their audiences may respond to their language choices.

When you think about it, many mistakes don't significantly impair meaning. Because we usually read words and punctuation in the context of sentences, paragraphs, and pages, we can often understand what a writer's trying to say even if a word is misspelled, missing, or incorrect (substituting "their" for "there," for instance). However, if you're writing something more formal, especially for a professor who knows and cares that "every student" is singular, then try to conform to standard academic English, or you might damage your credibility. In either case—informal or formal writing—try to avoid mistakes that confuse your readers and increase their workload.

You can find detailed discussions of mechanics in style handbooks and credible resources online, such as Oxford Dictionaries Online and Purdue University's Online Writing Lab (OWL). Even if you're not ready to memorize the rules for using *who* versus *whom* or avoiding dangling modifiers, we highly recommend finding helpful resources that you can consult on a regular basis.

Punctuation

Punctuation marks, such as commas and colons, make our writing more readable; we can prevent confusion and reading fatigue by correctly punctuating sentences. But punctuation marks do more than help us communicate clearly—they can even help us emphasize our argument and persuade readers subtly. When deciding how to punctuate a sentence, we ask ourselves:

- How are the ideas in these sentences related?
- What level of connection do they have with each other?

Punctuation marks create a spectrum of connections among ideas. For instance, periods offer complete separation, whereas commas produce a tighter relationship between similar ideas. If you think of a paragraph as a group of people, imagine how sentences mingle with and relate to each other.

1. A **period** fully separates ideas. Each sentence can stand on its own, independently.
   EXAMPLE: "Experienced writers know that sometimes they have to write first to discover what their argument will be. Often, they allow writing to inspire their thinking, rather than the other way around."

2. A **dash** separates—especially to emphasize or to elaborate—one portion of a sentence from another. Often, dashes direct the reader's attention toward the end of a sentence, but they can also highlight the middle portion of a sentence (as in the previous sentence). Writers can also use commas or parentheses to mark off a part of a sentence, but the dash has a different effect. Putting commas or parentheses around something suggests that it's less important, while dashes are used to *emphasize* the separated portion.
   EXAMPLE: "Scholars typically take advantage of every opportunity to have someone read and respond to their work in progress—either their real audience or a peer who can play substitute."

3. A **colon** is used in two main ways: (a) to introduce a list (as we're doing right now) and (b) to combine two independent sentences, where the first part of the sentence introduces the ideas of the second part. The colon is placed after the introduction or the "spoiler" regarding what comes next.

229

EXAMPLE: "A similar phenomenon occurs with writing: practicing effective habits can help them feel more natural, but practicing bad habits will further instill them."

4. **A semicolon** connects two sentences that express closely related ideas. The semicolon allows the writer to elaborate or clarify one idea with another closely related one.
EXAMPLE: "You can build knowledge about writing through practice; however, practice alone won't make you a better writer."

Bending the Rules

As you've probably noticed through reading this book and elsewhere, writers sometimes bend or break the mechanical rules—especially rules of usage—for dramatic effect. This can be appealing, stylistically, as long as the audience knows you're doing so intentionally (and as long as it's appropriate for your purpose and context).

Like this, for example.

Sometimes we use incomplete sentences, extra punctuation, one-word answers, or even miniature paragraphs because the prose reads better with the intentional deviation. We like the way it sounds. Or the alterations actually enhance the meaning or clarity of our message. We make these choices deliberately, after we've considered the full effect of our style selection, based on how we expect our audience to respond. However, because professors normally expect proper mechanics, apprentice scholars should intentionally "break the rules" sparingly and only when the effect will magnify the message.

Like any writer who reads her audience carefully, you have to figure out whether your creativity will be praised or scorned. Stylistic decisions provide practice for the choices you have to make when composing work e-mails, communicating with clients, or writing online in public spaces. The style you choose determines the way you present yourself, and carefully selected rule violations can demonstrate your rhetorical dexterity. To be on the safe side, you can show your professor that you know what you're doing by pointing out intentional mechanical variations in your paper (mark them with asterisks, or add footnotes or penciled comments to explain), or you can always get permission ahead of time.

Active Voice

You've probably heard teachers talk about finding your authentic "voice" when you write. Readers in the humanities often like to "hear" a human voice as they read. In other disciplines, such as the sciences, audiences commonly expect a more objective-sounding, "voiceless" style. Neither approach is wrong. In fact, the more styles writers can master, the more flexibility they have to adapt to different situations.

Verbs make a big difference in how readers "hear" our writing. Scholarly writing often employs active voice, where the doer of the action (the actor) comes before the object that is acted upon (the action receiver), like this:

EXAMPLE: "The scientist (*actor*) conducted (*action*) the experiment (*action receiver*)."

Passive voice reverses the sentence order, placing the object that is acted on before the action and the actor, like this:

EXAMPLE: "The experiment (*action receiver*) was conducted (*action*) by the scientist (*actor*)."

Neither order is grammatically incorrect, but **many readers prefer active voice because it's usually clearer and easier to read.** In active voice, the action progresses in the order that it occurs—from the actor, through the action, to the object—rather than placing the result before the cause. This linear order creates a steady rhythm that keeps readers moving forward. On the other hand, passive voice is usually wordier, which increases the reader's workload and slows him down.

In addition to being cumbersome, passive voice can be vague when the actor is missing because we may not know who performed the act. At its worst, passive voice intentionally hides the person responsible for the action. Consider, for example, the notorious statement "Mistakes were made," which doesn't indicate *who* made mistakes. The culprit can evade blame.

The bottom line is that scholarly writing values agency, clarity, and full disclosure. We aim to write sentences that help readers move smoothly and understand both what happened and who is responsible.

You can pinpoint passive voice in your own writing by spotting sentence structures like the example above (action receiver–action–actor). Another trick is to notice the way the verb changes in passive voice. Passive voice always uses a "to be" verb (am, is, are, was, were, be, being, been) along with another verb in its past participle form (usually ending in -ed or -en). You can also set most word processor's grammar and style checker to help you identify instances of passive voice.

To transform passive voice into active voice, ask yourself: Who is responsible for this action? Who is performing this action? Then place the doer, or the cause, before the action or result.

TRY THIS ➤ Transform Passive Voice into Active Voice

For this exercise, practice transforming the following sentences into active voice.

1. Well-educated people know that everyone's perspective, including their own, is limited by ignorance and bias.
2. In college, you will often be judged more on how you develop and defend your ideas than the ideas themselves.
3. Arguments are built on a basis of acceptance or agreement.

(continued)

4. Opinions can be shared by many, but are understood as subjective, or open to interpretation, debate, and revision.
5. As an apprentice, you will get to practice the same active approach to reading that scholars take—one that is fueled by curiosity, authentic motivation, and a desire to respond.
6. If your mind is not actively engaged, you will not remember what you read, let alone be able to comprehend or analyze new information and difficult text.
7. Experienced scholars mistrust sources that haven't been scrutinized by experts.
8. Scholars don't want to repeat research that has already been conducted or pursue questions that have already been answered.

Does changing voice change the meaning? If so, how? Which versions sound better? Why?

Now, inspect a piece of your own writing for signs of passive voice, and rewrite sentences that would be clearer in active voice.

Creative Choices We Make to Improve Style

The best news about improving style is that it's something you can practice on your own.

Imitation

One way to develop a range of styles is to practice imitating other writers whom you admire. Imitation is an ancient and useful technique for learning to write. Imagine, for example, that you were going to apply for a job but had never written an application letter or resume. Unlike in school writing, your audience (a prospective employer) would likely not provide detailed instructions for this assignment. Your best bet would be to ask someone who's recently been on the job market (and who scored a good job) to borrow her application documents to use as a guide.

Scholars often do the same thing when they want to write an article. Once they find a journal that their intended audience reads and that fits their topic, they study articles in the journal to create a set of instructions:

- What's the typical length of articles?
- How are they usually organized? For example, how much space do authors devote to reviewing previous research?
- What style is typical? Do writers tend to write more or less formally? Are there lots of graphs or charts?

TRY THIS ➤   Practice Imitating

For this exercise, select a short piece of writing by an author whose style you admire. Study the passage carefully, noticing the author's voice, word choices, and tone. Then, write a paragraph about any topic of your choosing, trying to adopt the author's style. In class, compare imitations and describe the style you were trying to mimic.

Sentence Variation

Another technique for improving style is sentence variation, which was popular during the Renaissance and used by great writers such as Ben Franklin. You can begin with a statement (like "I love ice cream") and then write multiple versions of the sentence, changing the style each time. Here are a few strategies for revision:

- **Rhetorical variation**: Change the audience, purpose, or context.
- **Amplification**: Elaborate; exaggerate; or use an analogy, metaphor, or simile (EXAMPLE: "I pine for ice cream just as reality stars crave drama").

- **Linguistic variation**: Substitute vocabulary or rearrange the order (EXAMPLE: Yoda from Star Wars might say, "Ice cream, I love" to emphasize the object of his affection).
- **Genre translation**: Rewrite the sentence in verse or as a Tweet (EXAMPLE: "Can't wait to eat this bowl of Rocky Road! #homemadeicecream").

Sentence variation helps writers assemble a richer stylistic tool kit, which can help them write more engaging prose. It also helps writers develop effective paraphrasing skills. And sentence variation can make writing more fun. Even with boring assignments, playing around with style can make the writing process more stimulating. If you can't write something interesting, write interestingly.

Figures of Speech

Rhetorical "figures" are useful tools for enriching style. You probably learned some of these while studying literature, for example:

- Metaphor: "the stench of fear"
- Analogy: "quiet as a mouse"
- Hyperbole or exaggeration: "a pea-sized brain"
- Sarcasm: "I never let schooling interfere with my education" (Mark Twain)

Brigham Young University's "Forest of Rhetoric" website (*Silva Rhetoricae*, http://rhetoric.byu.edu) provides scores of other examples and explanations to expand your repertoire.

Figures of speech can incur also some risks, such as:

- **Reference failure**. Much figurative language depends on the audience being familiar with specific cultural references. The common analogy "as annoying as nails on a chalkboard" may no longer make sense to younger readers who've only used whiteboards and digital projectors in school.

- **Inappropriate style.** Using figurative flourishes in a lab report might not go over well with an audience that wants an objective tone and "just the facts."
- **Misinterpretation.** Attempts at humor, especially through sarcasm, can fail when the audience takes them literally.
- **Clichés.** Because audiences expect figurative language to explain something in fresh terms, overused expressions can seem stale and bland.
- **Offensiveness.** Phrases like "neat freak" or "grammar Nazi" may seem harmless, but imagine how someone with obsessive-compulsive disorder would feel about being labeled as a "freak," or whether a Holocaust survivor would want grammar scrutiny equated with mass genocide.

Despite these potential pitfalls, figures of speech can be powerful argumentative devices, useful for more than stylistic embellishment. Scholars often use metaphors and analogies to introduce radically new concepts to each other or to explain specialized ideas to nonscientists (for example, explaining atomic structure as a solar system of subatomic particles).

Figures of speech can create fresh understanding and even be used beyond the sentence level as argumentative techniques. For instance, *anticategoria*, the "I'm-rubber-you're-glue" argument, turns a thesis back on the person making it. After the 9/11 attacks, for example, President George W. Bush condemned al-Qaeda as terrorists, to which Osama bin Laden responded by accusing the United States of acts of terrorism in the Middle East. This example raises the most important risk of using rhetorical figures:

- **False comparison.** Using figures of comparison to make an argument may provide a new way to make sense of your topic (for example, "America's involvement in the Middle East is like the Vietnam conflict"). However, such comparisons might also cause an audience to claim that you're using fallacious reasoning (that is, you're using irrelevant support for your argument).

In any case, think carefully about your audience's background and expectations when using figures of speech. If you think there's a chance that your figures will misfire, provide more explanation—or maybe just take it down a notch.

Revise Globally and Edit Locally

As we discussed in Chapter 2, experienced writers typically concentrate on big-picture concerns in early drafts and more minute concerns later. Like painters, they select the "tool" that best suits the job: a large paint roller for the wide strokes and a fine brush for the details and touch-ups.

Revision focuses on global (or "higher order") concerns—such as focus, development, organization, and whether ideas make sense. Successful scholarly writers invest ample time in revising before editing for local (or "later order") concerns, such as grammar, punctuation, and so forth. Here are three good reasons not to worry about polishing your prose until you have your ideas carved out.

1. **Perfectionism can cause writer's block**. Your mind has enough to do without trying to articulate your ideas perfectly the first time, especially when you're grappling with complex concepts and arguments. As an alternative, we like to freewrite during early drafts, which allows us to develop and organize our ideas before we

nitpick over punctuation and sentence-level choices. (We describe this technique of drafting without editing in Chapter 7.)

2. **Polishing can waste time and energy** while you're still sculpting. Every time you reorganize, add, or delete content, you'll have to refinish your writing.

3. **Editing while drafting is less effective** because it's difficult to concentrate on everything at once. Returning to our writing after putting it down for a day or more gives us a fresh perspective, which helps us find more mistakes and opportunities to improve style.

Remember that you don't have to proceed through the writing process in a linear, lockstep way. Still, we do recommend that you prioritize and try not to do everything at once. We prefer to read for content and organization first, giving less attention to mechanics. Then we can pay more attention to style and grammar, targeting the quality of writing. Once we're ready to edit and proofread, we review our writing multiple times, always with a specific, focused purpose.

Proofreading and Editing

Reading your writing aloud is a very effective technique that doesn't require much expertise but yields great results. Doing so slows down your reading and exercises more parts of your brain and body (eyes, ears, and mouth), so you can be more successful editing for clarity and correctness.

Hearing your own sentences can also help you better imagine how your reader will experience your writing. Reading aloud may be unnerving at first, but it can be a tremendously helpful way to detect confusing sentences, grammatical mistakes, or just an awkward tone.

Reviewing with Others

You can also **invite a trusted friend, classmate, or writing tutor to read your work aloud**. You can check whether your main points come across clearly by asking the reader to pause after each paragraph and paraphrase or summarize what he just read.

We also ask reviewers questions such as:

- How does the writing "sound"? Is the tone appropriate?
- Are there any sentences that are confusing, awkward, or otherwise unclear?
- Are there any word choices that are vague, confusing, or overly technical?
- Where can the writing be more concise? Where can I reduce unnecessary wordiness?
- Where should I combine or divide sentences?
- Where do you see mistakes, such as missing commas, subject-verb agreement problems, or misspellings?
- Where, if appropriate, might I add more personality, through humor or vividness or other stylistic devices?

Appendix A, "How to Benefit from Peer Review and Collaboration," offers more guidance for giving and receiving feedback.

Using Technology

Technology can help with editing, too. Spellchecking tools can be useful, though they usually won't catch things like homophones (their/there) or misused contractions and possessives (its/it's). For help with that, some word processors offer advanced proofing features, with options for activating grammar and style checking. In the settings, look for where you can select features you want your word processor to check, from spacing after punctuation to passive verbs and clichés. Some style checkers will also find sentences overloaded with prepositions (of, to, for, with . . .), accidental instances of "I," and other oversights. Just be sure to **think carefully before you take your word processor's advice**. Computers are careful readers, but they're not as smart or subtle as we are when it comes to writing.

Speaking of which, be very careful with your word processor's the-saurus. Synonyms carry similar but not equivalent meaning. **Don't use words unless you know how to use them.** Trying to sound smart by using words you really don't know often has the opposite effect.

We also use the "find" function to identify boring verbs (is, are, have . . .) and grammatical mistakes we are likely to make, such as in-correct uses of "their" or "affect." The "find" function will search for any of these examples, giving us the opportunity to make changes.

Taking these extra steps makes it less likely that we'll annoy or ex-asperate readers. We all know readers who experience a visceral reac-tion when they encounter a split infinitive or a rogue apostrophe.

Developing More Style

Good writing connects with its reader. We begin creating that con-nection when we select a question or problem that matters to us and our audience and then write an argument that generates fresh under-standing. However, in school or at work, we often cannot choose to write about a topic that naturally inspires our audience or us. Still, what appeals to readers almost universally—and can make any writ-ing more compelling to write or to read—is craftsmanship.

There's beauty in an instruction manual that explains how to as-semble a barbecue grill with precision and clarity. A research assign-ment about a topic that seems uninteresting can become elegant when we imagine it as an opportunity to learn a particular style or a genre shared by a community of scholars, a way of making sense of the world that we would not have otherwise known.

Successful writers never stop collecting and perfecting their tool kit of writing skills and knowledge. You can grow as a writer throughout your life through continued practice.

- Always *read as a writer*, mining everything you read for new argumentative moves, organizational patterns, sentence structures and stylistic techniques, and vocabulary and punctuation.
- Always *write as a reader*, considering how your intended audience will respond. Take every opportunity for others to read your work and help you to improve its effect.

So What?

Style is part of the message, and it's central to how we connect with audiences. Although many of the components of style are "local" concerns, their impact can be just as powerful as an argument's organization or support. Improving writing style is a lifelong pursuit, one that you can continue developing by experimenting, practicing, and exposing yourself to new genres and audiences.

What's Next
....

Take what you've learned in this chapter and respond to the following prompts.

1. **Magazine profile.** Investigate the style of a magazine that you like to read, and then compose a report that describes and analyzes the stylistic conventions of this magazine. To write your report, scrutinize the magazine overall and read a few sample articles. Consider the magazine's purpose and audience, along with the following features:
   a. Tone
   b. Voice

c. Use of intentional stylistic improvisations
d. Level of detail and vividness
e. Figures of speech
f. Visual design

You might also compare the print version of the magazine with its online version, if available. Then, compose a two-page report that informs your classmates how to vary their style in order to write for this magazine.

2. **Style makeover.** Select some writing that you want to dramatically alter in style. Use many of the strategies we describe in this chapter to edit the punctuation, voice, language, sentence structure, figures of speech, and other stylistic elements. To help you focus, you might begin by changing your purpose or audience.

3. **Sentence variation.** For this exercise, rewrite the sentence "This assignment is challenging" in at least 30 different ways, keeping similar meaning but changing the style at least 50% each time. Try using several of the sentence variation techniques we described in this chapter. Then, share your work with several classmates, compare your results, and discuss how you varied each sentence.

READINGS

"A Wandering Mind Is an Unhappy Mind"
by Matthew A. Killingsworth and Daniel T. Gilbert

> **Matthew A. Killingsworth** is a research fellow at the University of California, Berkeley. As a doctoral student in psychology, he developed a smartphone app to study happiness (http://www.trackyourhappiness.org/). Killingsworth coauthored this article with his Harvard professor, **Daniel T. Gilbert**, who has published extensively on emotions, beliefs, and perceptions. Gilbert has also hosted or appeared in documentaries on PBS, NatGeo, CNN, and elsewhere. This brief article, which examines the correlation between our thoughts and emotions, appeared in 2010 in *Science*, a prestigious journal published by the American Association for the Advancement of Science.

Unlike other animals, human beings spend a lot of time thinking about what is not going on around them, contemplating events that happened in the past, might happen in the future, or will never happen at all. Indeed, "stimulus-independent thought" or "mind wandering" appears to be the brain's default mode of operation.[1-3] Although this ability is a remarkable evolutionary achievement that allows people to learn, reason, and plan, it may have an emotional cost. Many philosophical and religious traditions teach that happiness is to be found by living in the moment, and practitioners are trained to resist mind wandering and "to be here now." These traditions suggest that a wandering mind is an unhappy mind. Are they right?

Laboratory experiments have revealed a great deal about the cognitive and neural bases of mind wandering,[3-7] but little about its emotional consequences in everyday life. The most reliable method for investigating real-world emotion is experience sampling, which involves contacting people as they engage in their everyday activities and asking them to report their thoughts, feelings, and actions at that moment. Unfortunately, collecting real-time reports from large numbers of people as they go about their daily lives is so cumbersome and expensive that experience sampling has rarely been used to investigate the relationship between mind wandering and happiness and has always been limited to very small samples.[8,9]

We solved this problem by developing a Web application for the iPhone (Apple Incorporated, Cupertino, California), which we used to create an unusually large database of real-time reports of thoughts, feelings, and actions of a broad range of people as they went about their daily activities. The application contacts participants through their iPhones at random moments during their waking hours, presents them with questions, and records their answers to a database at www.trackyourhappiness.org. The database currently contains nearly a quarter of a million samples from about 5,000 people from 83 different countries who range in age from 18 to 88 and who collectively represent every one of 86 major occupational categories.

To find out how often people's minds wander, what topics they wander to, and how those wanderings affect their happiness, we analyzed samples from 2,250 adults (58.8% male, 73.9% residing in the United States, mean age of 34 years) who were randomly assigned to answer a happiness question ("How are you feeling right now?") answered on a continuous sliding scale from very bad (0) to very good (100), an activity question ("What are you doing right now?") answered by endorsing one or more of 22 activities adapted from the day reconstruction method[10,11] and a mind-wandering question ("Are you thinking about something other than what you're currently doing?") answered with one of four options: no; yes, something pleasant; yes, something neutral; or yes, something unpleasant. Our analyses revealed three facts.

First, people's minds wandered frequently, regardless of what they were doing. Mind wandering occurred in 46.9% of the samples and in at least 30% of the samples taken during every activity except making love. The frequency of mind wandering in our real-world sample was

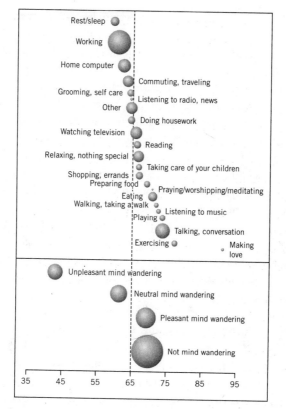

Figure 1

Mean happiness reported during each activity (top) and while mind wandering to unpleasant topics, neutral topics, pleasant topics or not mind wandering (bottom). Dashed line indicates mean of happiness across all samples. Bubble area indicates the frequency of occurrence. The largest bubble ("not mind wandering") corresponds to 53.1% of the samples, and the smallest bubble ("praying/worshipping/meditating") corresponds to 0.1% of the samples.

considerably higher than is typically seen in laboratory experiments. Surprisingly, the nature of people's activities had only a modest impact on whether their minds wandered and had almost no impact on the pleasantness of the topics to which their minds wandered.[12]

Second, multilevel regression revealed that people were less happy when their minds were wandering than when they were not [slope (b) = −8.79, $P < 0.001$], and this was true during all activities, including the least enjoyable. Although people's minds were more likely to wander to pleasant topics (42.5% of samples) than to unpleasant topics (26.5% of samples) or neutral topics (31% of samples), people were no happier when thinking about pleasant topics than about their current activity ($b = -0.52$, not significant) and were considerably unhappier when thinking about neutral topics ($b = -7.2, P < 0.001$) or unpleasant topics ($b = -23.9, P < 0.001$) than about their current activity (Figure 1, bottom). Although negative moods are known to cause mind wandering,[13] time-lag analyses strongly suggested that mind wandering in our sample was generally the cause, and not merely the consequence, of unhappiness.[14]

Third, what people were thinking was a better predictor of their happiness than was what they were doing. The nature of people's activities explained 4.6% of the within-person variance in happiness and 3.2% of the between-person variance in happiness, but mind wandering explained 10.8% of within-person variance in happiness and 17.7% of between-person variance in happiness. The variance explained by mind wandering was largely independent of the variance explained by the nature of activities, suggesting that the two were independent influences on happiness.

In conclusion, a human mind is a wandering mind, and a wandering mind is an unhappy mind. The ability to think about what is not happening is a cognitive achievement that comes at an emotional cost.

References and Notes

1. M. E. Raichle *et al.*, A default mode of brain function. *Proc. Natl. Acad. Sci. U.S.A.* 98, 676 (2001).

2. K. Christoff, A. M. Gordon, J. Smallwood, R. Smith, J. W. Schooler, Experience sampling during fMRI reveals default network and executive system contributions to mind wandering. *Proc. Natl. Acad. Sci. U.S.A.* 106, 8719 (2009).

3. R. L. Buckner, J. R. Andrews-Hanna, D. L. Schacte, The brain's default network: Anatomy, function, and relevance to disease. *Ann. N. Y. Acad. Sci.* 1124, 1 (2008).

4. J. Smallwood, J. W. Schooler, The restless mind. *Psychol. Bull.* 132 946 (2006).

5. M. F. Mason *et al.*, Wandering minds: The default network and stimulus-independent thought. Science 315, 393 (2007).

6. J. Smallwood, E. Beach, J. W. Schooler, T. C. Handy Going AWOL in the brain: Mind wandering reduces cortical analysis of external events. *J. Cogn. Neurosci.* 20, 458 (2008).

7. R. L. Buckner, D. C. Carroll, Self-projection and the brain. *Trends Cogn. Sci.* 11, 49 (2007).

8. J. C. McVay, M. J. Kane, T. R. Kwapil, Tracking the train of thought from the laboratory into everyday life: An experience-sampling study of mind wandering across controlled and ecological contexts. *Psychon. Bull. Rev.* 16, 857 (2009).

9. M. J. Kane *et al.*, For whom the mind wanders, and when: An experience-sampling study of working memory and executive control in daily life. *Psychol. Sci.* 18, 614 (2007).

10. D. Kahneman, A. B. Krueger, D. A. Schkade, N. Schwarz, A. A. Stone, A survey method for characterizing daily life experience: The day reconstruction method. *Science* 306, 1776 (2004).

11. A. B. Krueger, D. A. Schkade, The reliability of subjective well-being measures. *J. Public Econ.* 92, 1833 (2008).

12. Materials and methods are available as supporting material on *Science* Online.

13. J. Smallwood, A. Fitzgerald, L. K. Miles, L. H. Phillips, Shifting moods, wandering minds: Negative moods lead the mind to wander. *Emotion* 9, 271 (2009).

14. We thank V. Pitiyanuvath for engineering www.trackyourhappiness.org and R. Hackman, A. Jenkins, W. Mendes, A. Oswald, and T. Wilson for helpful comments.

For Analysis

1. Identify this article's inspiration, thesis, support, rationales, and implications. For additional guidance, review the Guided Analysis of a Scholarly Argument (pp. 106–113).
2. Compare this article with Killingsworth's video TED Talk, using the WHAT'S NEXT (Question 2) on p. 121.
3. Read the online supplementary material at http://www.sciencemag .org/content/suppl/2010/11/09/330.6006.932.DC1/Killingsworth .SOM.pdf. What kinds of additional support do these materials provide? Does this information make their argument more persuasive for you as a reader? Would it persuade a different audience?

For Writing

Trace the scholarly "genealogy" of this article using the TRY THIS activity on p. 68.

"With Liberty and Justice for Some"
by Emanuel Grant

> **Emanuel Grant** wrote this argument in his first-year writing class at James Madison University. His essay examines the tension between liberty and distribution of wealth, proposing a "maximum wage" for corporate executives.

As Americans, we are in love with the concept of justice. Freedom and fairness are as integral to our identity as hot apple pie and cookouts on a summer's day. I feel downright lucky to be here—in a land of opportunity where the hardworking are rewarded. In my readings of the works of the greats of economic commentary (Milton Friedman, Steven Levitt, and Stephen Dubner to name a few), it has become quite clear that our nation's success is formally attributed to our warm embrace of democratic and capitalistic ideals. We are described as the world's wealthiest country in terms of GDP (Gross Domestic Product), yet what does that wealth mean? Who owns it?

In terms of financial wealth—described by UCSC professor G. William Domhoff as "total net worth minus the value of one's home"—in 2007, 42.7% of our nation's wealth is owned by the top 1% of our population and another 50.3% is owned by the next 19% in the economic ladder. With some simple number crunching, a shocking, unnerving statistic unfolds: the wealthiest 20% in our society own a whopping 93% of our nation's wealth. That leaves a paltry 7% of wealth to the bottom 80% of Americans. Maybe these discrepancies are a good thing. Maybe they prove that if you work hard in life, you're going to be living large. To me, however, these statistics spin a tale much different than that of the American dream. They bastardize any notions of equality, justice, and social responsibility that I once identified as truly American. Though no economic system is perfect, it seems the structure of the one present leaves the poor grasping for straws as the rich enjoy the fruits of their labor.

Unless you are in this top 1% bracket (in which case go ahead and burn my paper now; you won't find comfort here) or *at least* within the remaining 19% of wage earners, you should be furious! Why should a select few Americans live in the lap of luxury while the others are forced to live paycheck to paycheck? I'm no socialist nut; I agree that people should be rewarded for their hard efforts. But, there must be a way to narrow the gap, to spread the wealth a little more. 7% of our nation's wealth for 80% of its people just doesn't *sound* right. With this in mind, I plan to target the highest echelons of our society and find an alternative to the farce of economic justice that pervades our economic system.

A fun little riddle before we delve deeper: try naming one thing NBA, National Rugby League (NSWRL) and MLB players all have in common. If you can't think of an answer besides that they all are athletic and have ridiculous amounts of money, you're probably not alone. In the sports world, the commonality is known as a salary cap—there's a literal limit that a league sets on how much LeBron can make for a year of excellence on the court; in the real world, the same phenomenon has been called a wage ceiling or a maximum wage—a government set standard on how much an earner can take home. I believe the introduction of maximum wage policies is a solution for the income inequality we see in our nation. Yes, I said it; cue the USSR anthem and call up the retired McCarthyites to put me away for good. I think there's a maximum amount of money you should be legally allowed to make. Try your best to palate my words. Remain skeptical; don't trust me yet. But, I beg you to keep an open mind. Remember, I am no politician; I'm not trying to trick you with some underhanded rhetoric. I have a bona fide, genuine concern for the majority of Americans (i.e. the 80%) who are fighting an uphill battle in their "pursuit of happiness," and I will use the principles of Macroeconomics to fortify my argument and fight for you—the little guy.

Though I am arguing for ceilings on wage, I bet you didn't know that the government already built a structural roof on your earnings. You just

Figure 1
Bill's Taco Stand

happen to be standing on it. It's called a minimum wage. We all accept it. Whether you're serving up burgers at your local McDonald's or ripping up ticket stubs at the premier of Tarantino's next violent thriller, the government has already stepped in and said that there's a minimum amount you are allowed to earn for that job. While we generally accept this ideal, there are formidable consequences on the economy at large. These consequences make up the roof of which I previously spoke. To see these consequences, we first need to see how wages are decided.

British economist Alfred Marshall was the first person to depict a complete picture for the determinant of price—what the market decides as a fair amount for a good or service—in his creation of the laws of Supply and Demand (Frank and Bernanke 65). Put simply, there is a market for *anything*. On one side, there's a group of producers that creates a product (the supply) and wants to get as much money as possible for it. On the other, there's a group of consumers that want a product for as low as a price as possible (the demand). These motives are opposing; where the forces meet is the point at which a price is determined. Take a look at Figure 1 for a fictional example of how much our friend Bill will get for his tacos sold at his taco stand. The light gray line denotes the demand. At eight dollars, Bill would like to sell 400 tacos, but his customers are only willing to buy 100 at that price. If he refused to sell below that price, there would be an excess supply of 300 tacos (400 − 100)—the difference between the points of intersection of the horizontal line between the Supply and Demand curves. In a free market, this process goes back and forth until the lines intersect, at what is called an equilibrium price, where Bill's production of tacos meets his demand.

These same principles carry over to labor markets. The only thing that really changes is the label on the axes. What was once the price of a good or service is now the wage of a worker. What was once quantity now becomes employment, the number of jobs available. Again, there is a supply side and a demand side. In this case, employers are the supply while people looking for work make up the demand. A true free market economy would use this model to determine wage, and an equilibrium price (wage in this example) would be reached—this is how much a worker would be paid. However, this supposedly ideal scenario does not reflect reality; the government in an effort to help the lower class has instituted a minimum wage. Reflected in Figure 2, a serious problem emerges. Though the government may have altruistic motives, the minimum wage intrinsically expands unemployment. Companies can't afford to pay workers more than that equilibrium price a free market economy would set for wage, so what they do is simply higher less workers—this time, an excess supply of job seekers (and, thus, more unemployment) ensues.

Suffering an influx of unemployment, a minimum wage economy operates inefficiently; this economy is not utilizing its resource of labor to its full potential, since people that could otherwise be working are not (Frank and Bernanke 177). Regardless, it still seems necessary and just for workers to have some sort of minimum so that we don't have Americans bringing home just a couple of dollars a day, no matter how menial the labor. It becomes a necessary evil. America is not the only country that faces this dilemma. In Australia, there has been heated debate on this same issue. As previous chairman of the Australian Fair Pay Commission, Ian Harper posits that it is equally inefficient to pursue the abolishment of a minimum wage as it is to keep it, for it would evaporate the "safety net" on wage that these laws create (4). In his opinion, all that is necessary is the maintenance of some sort of minimum, anywhere below the equilibrium levels. I would challenge Mr. Harper to think outside the box; the solution

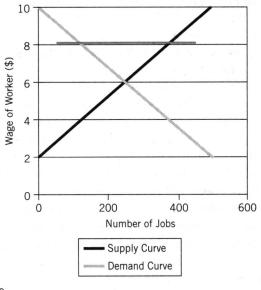

Figure 2
Labor Markets

that we both seek—one "economically efficient" as well as socially acceptable for wage redistributions—may lie in the additional adoption of a maximum wage, the exact opposite policy (5).

The target market for the implementation of this kind of law is American CEOs. They make the most. If the wealth distribution in America got you a little frustrated, go ahead and grab yourself a couple aspirins to calm down that heart of yours before we continue; the magnitude of CEO salaries might just put you in a stretcher. Venkat Venkatasubramanian in a longitudinal analysis of wage distributions for Purdue University magnifies the following statistic in his research: while in the 70s CEOs made about 50 times as much as minimum wage workers, as of 2007 they now make on average 866 (that's right; *eight-hundred-and-sixty-six*) times as much (766). To put that into perspective, for every eight dollars a person makes in an hour, a CEO makes close to 7,000 dollars. If you're working an eight hour day, a minimum wage earner brings home about 64 dollars, while a CEO working that same amount of time brings home 56,000 dollars—more than that worker would make in two years working full time. These are just averages, many CEOs make much more than that. Do CEOs really work 866 times harder than their lowest employees? Emphatically, I answer "of course not!" Sure they have highly stressful jobs, but a free market approach to their salaries makes up a double standard (767). Why do we set wage laws for the lower classes that have proved to increase unemployment while simultaneously ignoring the opposite side of the spectrum? Let's turn the minimum wage graph on its head and show what a wage ceiling will do for our economy; look now to Figure 3. As we can see, a possible benefit occurs in the divergence away from equilibrium; there is now an excess supply of CEO job openings available but not enough CEOs willing to take the wage.

In an interview with James Madison University Economics professor Dr. Vipul Bhatt, I went over this theoretical framework for a maximum wage. Though he lauded the model in theory for what I was

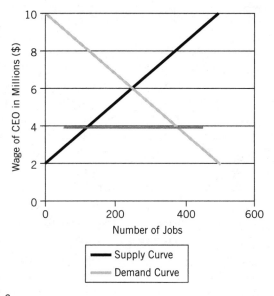

Figure 3
Proposed CEO Labor Market

setting out to solve, he coerced me away from what I now see as naivety and explained what would happen in reality. "There will be a shortage of CEOs in your model," he said. Even if the government did put a cap on CEO wages, "they will always find a way to get money outside of their salary in the form of bonuses and stock options." On top of this, if they are not getting paid in full, their performance will decrease and more poor decisions will be made, and government "does not want to interfere with performance." Fine. But if a maximum wage isn't realistic, then what is?

As we can see, a chasm exists between economic theory and its practice. As Dr. Maureen Ramsay of the University of Leeds expressed in her "A Modest Proposal: The Case for a Maximum Wage," "it seems implausible that it is necessary to make some individuals hundreds of time richer than others in order to retain incentives" (207). But, we somehow continue to operate under that principle. If a flat out ceiling won't work, what else is there? I kept my nose to the grindstone, and the answer hit me in the face while reading Venkat's work: the greater the fairness of a company, the greater the entropy (capability for work) in that company (777). While he posited the idea of pay scales, why not simply tie the salary of the CEO to a set ratio of that earned by the lowest paid worker for the company, fusing the ideals behind a maximum wage with real world practicality (776)? Two enormously successful companies have been built upon such a principle. Praised in *Time Magazine*, Ben & Jerry's ice cream and Whole Foods supermarkets, from their inceptions, tied the top of management to the bottom tier of workers (Fonda 63). Though Ben & Jerry's had to abandon the practice in the mid-90s to hire a new CEO, Whole Foods still operates on a maximum of a 14:1 ratio (63). Their CEO is only taking home 14 times more than the person that's bagging the groceries they sell (sounds much better than 866 times, right?). With this idea in practice, the bosses are still rewarded handsomely for their efforts, but the bottom tier workers do not feel alienated from their executives—growth in salary is still possible. You can have your cake and eat it too. As an added bonus, this practice would inherently boost productivity across the spectrum once implemented; anyone who works in the company, no matter what their rank, has the extra incentive to do their best at all times because any increase in the profitability of the company is shared directly with the worker. The *incentive* to do well serves as a catalyst for both the growth of the company and of personal salary.

Increased incentives for workers, no matter how important, lead to economic growth (Bhatt). While the flat salary caps remain regrettably implausible, the adoption of ratio driven salaries for corporate America has unlimited potential. I'll set a bar, middle of the road, in comparison to today's standards. If we required CEOs to be paid a maximum of 100 times what their lowest workers are getting, that's still a difference in a factor of 766 times what it is today. Think how much more wealth could be shared! Unfortunately, the biggest problem the implementation of a ratio-wage policy faces is founded in the culture of American greed that got us here in the first place: the wretched bedfellow of the free market. However, if our nation is the wealthiest on this planet, why should only a select few enjoy it? Possibly, there may be a need for a call for change—a change in the distribution of wealth in our society. The wealth of our nation should be our greatest benefit as Americans, holistically. That wealth cannot and should not be contained all within the grasp of an elite echelon of the top wage earners. I'm not here to spark a Marxist revolution in America, but I very well want to level the playing field—and expand social justice with economic policy, reframing what it means to be an American and to be free. At the end of the day, if both you and your boss can stand to benefit, what is there to lose?

Works Cited

Bhatt, Vipul. Personal Interview. 3 Nov. 2010.

Domhoff, G. William. "Who Rules America: Wealth, Income, and Power." *Power in America*. UC Santa Cruz, n.d. Web. 8 Nov. 2010.

Fonda, Daren, et al. "The Rumble Over Executive Pay." *Time* 163.22 (2004): 62–64. *Academic Search Complete*. Web. 8 Nov. 2010.

Frank, Robert H., and Ben Bernanke. *Principles of Macroeconomics*. 4th ed. Boston: McGraw-Hill Irwin, 2009. Print.

Harper, Ian. "Why Would an Economic Liberal Set Minimum Wages?" *Policy* 25.4 (2009): 3–7. *Academic Search Complete*. Web. 8 Nov. 2010.

Ramsay, Maureen. "A Modest Proposal: The Case for a Maximum Wage." *Contemporary Politics* 11.4 (2005): 201–215. *Academic Search Complete*. Web. 8 Nov. 2010.

Venkatasubramanian, Venkat. "What is Fair Pay for Executives? An Information Theoretic Analysis of Wage Distributions." *Entropy* 11.4 (2009): 766–781. *Academic Search Complete*. Web. 8 Nov. 2010.

"Crass Frat Boys at Old Dominion"
by Conor Friedersdorf

We have annotated the following article with some comments and questions to model the kinds of notations that apprentice scholars might make while reading any argument and especially when conducting a rhetorical analysis.

Conor Friedersdorf is a journalist who writes about politics and national affairs. He is also the founding editor of *The Best of Journalism* and a staff writer at *The Atlantic*, which published this commentary on August 25, 2015.

The crudely suggestive banners hung to greet first-year students were in poor taste, but the condemnations lacked all sense of proportion.

At Old Dominion University in Norfolk, Virginia, someone at an off-campus fraternity house hung crass, homemade banners from the balcony for incoming freshmen to see while being dropped off by their parents. One banner said, "Rowdy and Fun, Hope Your Baby Girl Is Ready for a Good Time." Another said "Freshman Daughter Drop Off" and featured an arrow pointing to the front door of the house. A third sign said, "Go Ahead and Drop Off Mom Too."

The banners were crude and distasteful. Even at 18, I wouldn't have hung them. If I were a professor there, I'd have told the kids that they have a First Amendment right to display the signs even as I tried to shame them into taking them down. If my kid put up those banners—not that I'd ever pay for a kid to live in a frat house—I'd tell him to take them down or never ask for my help with tuition again.

> He begins by acknowledging how inappropriate the banners were. He probably wants to make it clear from the beginning that he doesn't condone such crude behavior.

> Interesting ways to establish credibility. First he acknowledges that he doesn't really support fraternities, and then he says how harshly he'd deal with the situation if it involved his own son. Doing so makes him seem more sincere/objective when he defends fraternities and their actions – or at least argues against such harsh attacks against them.

Even so, it staggers me that this is an international news story covered by scores of outlets. How did we reach a place where Local Frat Makes Crude Joke causes staffers at the BBC, CNN, *The Washington Post* and *USA Today* to spring into action?

> Interesting question. So, is that his main controversy question – one of cause/consequence? Or is he going to examine how we should respond to the incident (question of policy/procedure)? What other controversy categories will he try to answer?

The answer begins with one interpretation of the banners. For some observers, they aren't just vulgar, rude, suggestive, bawdy, ribald, derogatory, or uncouth—they're an example of "rape culture." As Old Dominion's President John Broderick put it, "While we constantly educate students, faculty and staff about sexual assault and sexual harassment, this incident confirms our collective efforts are still failing to register with some." Nearly every press outlet that has covered the controversy connected it to ongoing efforts to reduce the number of rapes that occur on campus.

> He summarizes one side's views on this issue. People in this camp believe that this incident is exemplary of "rape culture." What's "rape culture"? Is this an issue of definition?

One Old Dominion student told *Jezebel*, "I feel very strongly about how the attitude towards sexual assault on campuses is met with a slap on the wrist . . . As a woman, it's frustrating to see the media bring awareness to the issue and then witness something related in your own community/school and see that nothing is changing."

> The quotations from the student and President Broderick express one way of interpreting the incident (verifications).

> What's *Jezebel*? Is this a credible source for supporting his argument? Would *Atlantic*'s readers be familiar with this publication and trust its credibility?

To other observers, those reactions make little sense.

> Nice transition. This short paragraph functions as a pivot point for his essay.

As they see it, a college's sexual-assault problem is best gauged by the number of sexual assaults. They regard the banners as an obvious joke. And they insist that the humor is rooted in confronting parents, who like to guard the virginity of their daughters, with the trope that they go off to college and have sex with frat guys. In this telling, nothing about the trope implies a non-consensual encounter. And regardless of the joke's meaning, they believe it irrational to operate as if a sophomoric prank that seems like something a couple 19-year-olds cooked up in a few hours reveals their attitudes toward rape; the likelihood that they would rape someone; campus attitudes toward rape; or the success of campus anti-rape efforts.

> Who is this "they" (or "other observers")? He can keep describing "their" perspective for a while, but soon I'll want him to provide a specific reference.

> Then, he summarizes a different view of the issue. People in this camp interpret the incident as "an obvious joke."

> What's a trope? I doubt many people know this term, which might indicate something about who reads *The Atlantic*.

"I'm usually in the position of defending extremely offensive speech on the grounds that it is protected by the First Amendment,"

Robby Soave wrote at *Reason.* "In this case, I struggle to grasp what was even so monstrous about the banners. *Hope your baby is ready for a good time, oh, mom too!* is certainly crude and in bad taste. But no specific person is being maligned, threatened, or disparaged. And some frat brothers are eager to have sex with girls—is this surprising?"

> What's *Reason*? Is this a credible source for supporting his argument?
>
> Okay, so now he's providing a specific example of one of the "other observers" who support his perspective. But wait, he only includes this one example. . . .

He added that, "associating the banners with sexual assault, as Broderick did, is a considerable exaggeration. Sigma Nu members certainly didn't threaten anyone with sexual assault; putting up some mildly suggestive signs does not constitute an act of violence. The banners don't even clear the sexual harassment bar. They aren't severe, pervasive, objectively offensive, or directed at anyone in particular."

Where do I come down? It's lamentable that some women arrived on their college campus only to be greeted by signs treating them as sexual objects. These immature 19-year-olds displayed bad judgment, but so do the adults who are reacting as if they were stockpiling GHB. Pop culture is filled with material far more vulgar and offensive, including content that actually does transgress against the value placed on consent.

> Here is where the author will present his viewpoint (argument).
>
> By summarizing two opposing sides and then presenting his own view, the author shows that he understands the debate and what opposing sides believe. He demonstrates that he's listened to both sides, like a judge listening to both a prosecutor and defense attorney before making his decision. This makes him seem well informed. It also helps him demonstrate that both sides are too extreme in their responses, whereas his perspective is more levelheaded.

> What's GHB?

Debates like this are polarizing because a false choice is often presented: defend the transgression that is generating outrage or join in condemning the perpetrators. But

> This is an "either/or" fallacy or false binary.

there is a third way. It requires circumspection and a sense of proportion.

> He is proposing a third interpretation that takes more of a middle ground. This makes the author seem reasonable and fair.

The banners do deserve criticism.

Sigma Nu, the national fraternity, is within its rights to complain about the way this chapter is representing it; on Monday, it suspended the chapter pending the outcome of an investigation.

> Again, style points for this pithy pivot paragraph.

Should someone at Old Dominion explain to those kids the offensive assumptions implicit in their signs? Yes. Did they do something so awful that it warrants overnight CNN alerts, a BBC headline, and a university investigation into what happened?

No. Of course not.

Should the university president have made a statement? Sure. He could have said, "I've been getting inquiries about crude signs hung by some of our students from their off-campus house, as is their right under the First Amendment. I encourage those students to exercise their rights more thoughtfully in the future, to treat women respectfully, and to take this opportunity to learn from a youthful mistake. We've all made them. And I hope members of the media will recall instances when they showed poor judgment at 18, 19, or 20, as they cover this story."

Instead he showed no sense of proportion.

> This is the problem that the author has with people's responses to the incident.

In a nation where the First Amendment guarantees the rights of Nazis to march through the streets of a Jewish community, the president of a public university declared of clearly protected speech: "Messages like the ones displayed yesterday by a few students on the balcony of their private residence are not and will not be tolerated."

And he asserted that one or two undergrads with bed sheets and black markers "undermine the countless efforts at Old Dominion University to prevent sexual assault." If that isn't hyperbole, he should try a different approach to preventing sexual assault.

Meanwhile, Sharon Grigsby writes in *The Dallas Morning News* that if you think the frat's banners were an obvious joke, as many students at the college reportedly concluded, "You've got to be kidding. Anyone who believes that is part of the problem." In fact, believing that they made a tasteless joke rather than an apology for rape culture does not make someone "part of the problem" of sexual assault. ←———————

> Why not? I'd like to hear him defend this claim. I find myself agreeing with him, but I'd be more convinced if he elaborated more and explained exactly why Grigsby is off base.

Ultimately, this story lays bare a divide.

It is not a divide between people who care about reducing the rate of sexual assault and those who don't; rather, the divide concerns how best to achieve that common goal. Insofar as I can tell, one theory holds that what's best, in this case, is to hold up whoever made those banners as possible-rapist pariahs; to pursue disciplinary charges against them; to suspend their frat; and to condemn them as if they've consigned more women to rape by undermining their college's efforts to prevent it.

I have a different view.

It would be convenient for Old Dominion if harshly denouncing and punishing these boys would be taken as the prime measure of how seriously the school takes sexual assault. ◄

> I had to read this sentence a few times to understand it. Seems like he's making a good point, but I'd prefer not to have to work so hard to get it.

It's easy to grandstand against frat boys with crass signs.

But reducing sexual assaults requires sounder metrics of success. Controversies like this are a distraction; they distract from what's really required to make college campuses safer for women; and they alienate a portion of the public that tires of exaggerated outrage. ◄

> So, according to the author, this is the larger significance of the problem that he's identified. If authorities overreact and fixate on the wrong things, they won't be able to put their energies where they should to address the heart of the issue.

Focusing on the core problem of rape (rather than seizing on offensive comments from obscure undergrads as if they bear meaningful responsibility for that problem) also makes it easier to avoid getting trolled by provocateur 19-year-olds. Words they thoughtlessly scrawl on bed sheets do not belong at the center of our discourse. ◄

> Interesting. This section seems like his thesis statement, but it appears at the end of his essay. Is this how an evolving thesis is supposed to work?

For Analysis

1. How well does Friedersdorf treat both "sides" of this issue? Does he represent them fairly, or does he oversimplify any issues?
2. Friedersdorf advocates a "third way." How might advocating for a middle ground affect readers? How could this approach help build his credibility?
3. How effective is Friedersdorf's writing style? What features stand out, and how do these elements enhance or diminish his argument?

For Writing

Friedersdorf advocates "focusing on the core problem of rape," but he doesn't elaborate on what exactly this would entail. Write a 1,000-word proposal argument that describes specific policy changes or a course of action that you think would help reduce the number of sexual assaults on college campuses.

Sample Rhetorical Analysis

To demonstrate a typical rhetorical analysis assignment, we've included the professor's instructions, a sample draft with marginal peer review comments, a note from the writer to the peer reviewer, and comments from the peer reviewer about the draft.

Professor's Assignment Guidelines: Write a rhetorical analysis of Conor Friedersdorf's article "Crass Frat Boys at Old Dominion" from the August 25, 2015 online issue of *The Atlantic*. Aim for about 1,000 words.

In your analysis, describe the argument's rhetorical situation and evaluate the author's choices. Your goal is to describe *how* Friedersdorf makes his argument. Since you can't analyze all of the rhetorical elements (author, audience, purpose, inspiration, support, rationales, genre, style, controversy categories, and implications), develop a thesis that focuses on a few significant elements of the argument.

After you compose a draft of your essay, write a note to your peer reviewer that identifies what kind of feedback you would like to receive on your draft.

[Student's Name]
[Professor's Name]
[Course]
[Date]

Verbal Assault or Fraternity Pranks?
Stories about campus sexual harassment and assault seem to be everywhere these days in the news and social media. In the August 24, 2015 issue of *The Atlantic* magazine, Conor Friedersdorf argues for a more reasonable response to sexually charged incidents.

> I like that your title introduces your topic, catches the reader's attention, and hints at the main idea of Friedersdorf's article. I'm glad that you didn't just title this "Rhetorical Analysis," but you may want to indicate somewhere in the title or introduction that that's what you're doing.

Referring to a recent event at Old Dominion University (ODU) where members of a fraternity displayed banners with offensive statements aimed at freshmen females, Friedersdorf summarizes the extreme reactions from the University administration and the public to assert that people are responding to such incidents in unhelpful ways. Friedersdorf's argument is effective because the topic is timely and significant, he develops good credibility, his writing style is engaging, and his message is reasonable and thoughtful.

> Good attempt to summarize the article in such a short space. However, this is a lot to pack into one sentence. Maybe break this into two sentences to make it easier to digest?
>
> Also, would readers consider "freshmen" to be a sexist term? Is there an alternative?

A quick review of article titles on *The Atlantic*'s website indicates that the magazine covers a variety of current events involving business, technology, education, politics, culture, and health. Friedersdorf uses the incident at ODU to make a larger point about the problems we face in combatting sexual violence on college campuses. Connecting his commentary to recent events that people care about makes his overall argument seems more relevant. This move also lends a sense of urgency to his case. He takes the opportunity to join a conversation that is already going on, which is evident by the amount of passionate comments that follow the article online.

> This paragraph seems to mostly be about context, but it also touches on the audience, genre, and the author's purpose. That's a lot to do in one paragraph. Would it be better to separate these elements and examine them in more detail?
>
> Also, you haven't really explained everything enough. For example, your first sentence lists the kinds of topics that *The Atlantic* publishes. That seems like support for a claim that you haven't yet written.

Although Friedersdorf taps into a controversial, "hot" topic that many people are currently discussing, he makes his perspective sound reasonable, levelheaded, and informed. By highlighting the extreme responses that people in opposing camps are taking, Friedersdorf underscores the harm of such polarized reactions based in either/or reasoning. The argument's organization reinforces his message. He presents each side from the extreme and then offers his perspective, which he signals in a one-sentence paragraph: "I have a different view" (p. 265). This is effective because his argument emphasizes a "third way" (p. 263) or a middle ground that sounds much more sensible and moderate. By arguing for a more reasonable response, he projects a trustworthy and rationale credibility. Also, by summarizing two opposing sides and then presenting his own view, the author shows that he understands the debate and what opposing sides believe. He demonstrates that he has listened carefully to both sides, like a judge listening to both a prosecutor and defense attorney before making his decision. This makes him seem well informed and judicious. One move that really builds his credibility is when he makes clear upfront that he does not condone or support the young men's actions or the banners' messages. Clarifying this position up front is important because he does not want to alienate readers who are offended by the fraternity's banners. He also does not want to align himself with the fraternity's actions, which would hurt his credibility. ◄

> In this sequence of sentences, I like how you offer an observation (support), then interpretation (make a claim about what it means). Seems almost scientific.

> Again, there seems to be a lot going on in this paragraph. You've got some great ideas, but I think your main point could be clearer. This paragraph seems pretty long, too. Maybe you could break it into two paragraphs?

Friedersdorf's writing style is engaging, conversational, and straight to the point. Throughout the essay, he avoids using dense or overly formal language that would make the essay difficult and boring to read. Instead, he uses the first person, short sentences, and interesting diction and metaphors, such as phrases like "spring into action" (p. 260), "a sophomoric prank that seems like something a couple 19-year-olds cooked up in a few hours" (p. 261), and "so do the adults who are reacting as if they were stockpiling GHB" (p. 262). These engaging metaphors and lively phrasing make the writing style a pleasure to read. His one-to two-sentence paragraphs also assert his message strongly and memorably. By balancing longer paragraphs with one-liners like "No. Of course not" (p. 263) and "Ultimately, this story lays bare a divide" (p. 264), Friedersdorf makes his points quite clear. He has to be careful, though, not to overuse this technique because it may irritate some readers. Even more potentially annoying is his use of frequent questions and answers. He frequently asks a question and then answers it, such as in the following examples: "Should someone at Old Dominion explain to those kids the offensive assumptions implicit in their signs? Yes" (p. 263) and "Should the university president have made a statement? Sure" (p. 263). These short questions and answers have a conversational feel that

> Okay, so here you make the main topic of the paragraph very clear, and you're on your way to making a good claim about that topic. I anticipate that you'll be discussing whether you think style was effective for his audience and purpose, right?

may work for some readers, but others could claim he overdoes it. The danger of employing such a conversational style is he may sound overly informal and risk sounding insincere, lighthearted, or flippant about the issue.

> Who are these readers, specifically? Who is his intended audience?
>
> Is there something about these stylistic moves that might be especially effective for his purpose?

Overall, his argument makes sense and it gets at the heart of the issue. By summarizing the two common reactions as either "defend the transgression that is generating outrage or join in condemning the perpetrators" (p. 262), Friedersdorf shows that neither of these responses will actually prevent sexual assaults—which is the goal everyone shares. His "third way" sounds like a better solution because it promises to focus everyone's energies on "what's really required to make college campuses safer for women" (p. 265). That makes sense. However, I wish that Friedersdorf would describe exactly what these required steps are. He criticizes the public's extreme reactions, but he does not outline how administrators can actually protect students from harm. He advocates "focusing on the core problem of rape" (p. 265), but what exactly does that mean? Without articulating a specific course of action, his argument leaves the reader hanging. He is guilty of leaving holes in other pockets of his argument as well. For instance, he asserts that Sharon Grigsby's response is way out of proportion. Grigsby, according to Friedersdorf, states that "anyone who believes that [the fraternity members were joking] is part of the problem" (p. 264). From Friedersdorf's perspective, that response is hyperbolic. He writes, "In fact, believing that they made a tasteless joke rather than an apology for rape culture does not make someone 'part of the problem' of sexual assault" (p. 264). However, Friedersdorf does not explain why he thinks this way. He makes this claim but does not explain or defend it. Although I find myself agreeing with Friedersdorf, I would be more fully persuaded if he elaborated and explained why Grigsby is off base. While I appreciate his tight, concise argument, claims like these leave me with questions. Overall, I would be more persuaded if he had developed some of these points more fully and specifically.

Work Cited

Friedersdorf, Conor. "Crass Frat Boys at Old Dominion." *The Atlantic* 25 Aug. 2015. Web. Rpt. in *So What? The Writer's Argument*. 2nd ed. Kurt Schick and Laura Schubert. New York: Oxford UP, 2017. 259–265. Print.

Note to Peer Reviewer

Dear [peer reviewer],
I'm worried that my focus is too broad and not sufficiently supported. Can you point out places that seem unfocused or unclear? Also, I don't know if I've organized the essay well, so I'd like some feedback

on that. Finally, I'd like some general feedback about your reading experience: Does the essay make sense? What's most interesting? What am I missing?

Peer Review Comments

Dear [writer],

Good job on this assignment so far! You've included some good analysis and supports from the article. A few bigger questions and comments:

Focus & content: You cover lots of rhetorical elements, like context, style, organization, and reasoning. Why did you choose these elements to focus on? Are there others that are as or more important to discuss? (For example, I notice that you don't talk about the controversy categories.) As a reader, I'd like to hear more about the audience and the author's purpose for writing the article. That seems like a key element for answering whether this argument was effective.

Organization: Some paragraphs seem really long, and sometimes there seems to be more than one idea in a paragraph – or maybe I just can't figure out what your main idea really is. I would suggest trying to reverse outline this draft and then consider adding some clear topic sentences for your paragraphs.

So what? You seem to be heading toward a conclusion (thesis) along the lines of "This article was mostly effective but also had some weaknesses." Is there something more about this argument that you find compelling or significant? Does the author make any argumentative "moves" that really stand out? (I thought the last idea in the third paragraph was really interesting. Maybe run with that?)

Appendix A

How to Benefit from Peer Review and Collaboration

THE ABILITY TO give and receive effective feedback is among the most valuable skills you can learn in life. You probably have a friend or relative who gives great advice, a person whom you and others trust, who listens carefully and provides help when needed. Employers and co-workers also value a person who can identify exactly what is and isn't working and give useful suggestions for improvement. Such sharp critical thinking skills can benefit everyone and make you a sought-after colleague. Peer review is an excellent way to develop and practice these skills.

However, your experiences with peer review may be mixed. Think back on times when you've given or received feedback on writing. What worked, what didn't, and why? Compare those occasions with a time when you received excellent advice about something important other than writing. How was that advice given? What made the experience valuable for you? Now, consider what would be needed for peer review to be effective and for students to take it seriously.

The Advantages of Peer Review

In the following sections, we'll describe the benefits of peer review to you as a writer, a reader, and a collaborator; and we'll give you some suggestions for insightful questions and comments to offer during peer review.

How to Benefit as a Reader

Becoming a strong, critical reader takes careful practice, and peer review can help you cultivate keen analytical skills that you can put to use right away in other classes. In college, you'll be expected to critically review (that is, read and analyze) a considerable amount of scholarly writing. Peer review gives you a chance to do that with essays that are typically more accessible than the professional scholarly writing you'll also encounter. Use peer review to strengthen your reading skills.

How to Benefit as a Writer

Peer review lets you investigate other writers' styles, strategies, and pitfalls. You see approaches you might want to borrow and ones you definitely want to avoid. For example, reading your peer's vivid conclusion might inspire you to try a similar technique. Reading other students' work can also show you different ways to interpret an assignment, and such insight can give you a fuller understanding of the task at hand. If your peers' interpretations conflict, it's a great opportunity to identify potential questions, to talk with your instructor about her expectations, and to clarify the best ways to tackle the assignment.

The most difficult part of writing is imagining how an audience will interpret and respond to your writing. Participating in peer review gives you a glimpse into this perspective by showing you the effect of your writing on readers. Without that perspective, you can only guess whether your ideas are working.

Experienced writers take advantage of every available opportunity to have someone—either their real audience or someone who can play substitute—read and respond to their work in progress. To publish their writing, scholars submit their manuscripts to editors for feedback. Every once in a while, a scholarly journal will accept an article for publication with little revision, but much more often, editors respond with substantial feedback on how to improve the draft and a recommendation to "revise and resubmit." A demanding reader helps you better imagine your audience and then revise your essay to meet their needs.

An Unforeseen Benefit: Practice Collaborating

Practicing peer review will also strengthen your collaboration skills. You'll get to practice the interpersonal skills and social gestures essential for teamwork. For instance, when helping another writer find a better way to communicate a controversial idea or organize an elaborate proposal, you might have to soften your criticism with polite suggestions. Or you might have to help a writer avoid feeling embarrassed about a silly mistake or find a tactful way of saying that his thesis seems clichéd. Such honest communication is not easy. Tactfulness requires sophisticated conversation skills that must be learned through practice. Collaborating on writing is also tricky because you can't just rewrite portions of the paper for the writer. Instead, you have to help a writer help himself, meaning you give assistance but cannot write the paper for him. Examples include asking stimulating questions, highlighting problem areas for the writer to solve, or giving several options and allowing him to choose.

Providing Helpful Feedback

Right about now, you might be wondering, "How can I be expected to provide high-quality response if I'm not an expert writer who has read or written much scholarly writing?"

Indeed, many students find themselves saying things such as "Nice job," or "I don't have much to add," or maybe "I think there's something fishy here but I'm not sure what," simply because they don't know what else to say. We understand that many students have had bad experiences with peer review and that you may feel unprepared to give assistance, so we're offering you a model of questioning and commenting that can facilitate productive peer review. These questions are ones that you can ask each other and ask *yourself*, whenever you are writing.

Keep in mind that peer review shouldn't look the same during every stage of the writing process. In fact, you'll probably want to adapt the review process, just like the writing process and the reading process, depending on what you're trying to accomplish.

Prewriting Feedback

During the discovery (or prewriting) stage of the writing process, it's helpful to have a conversation with your peers: talk about your ideas, pose and answer questions, serve as "devil's advocates" for each other, and identify possible plans for your papers. In this stage, you'll want to ask each other questions such as:

- What interests you most about this assignment? What's your inspiration?
- How does this assignment connect to concepts you're studying in other classes, your personal experience, or other ideas you've thought about?
- What makes your topic controversial?
- Why would this topic matter to your reader? What are the implications?
- Who would care most about this topic? Who are other stakeholders?

Feedback on Drafts

Once you have a first draft, your instructor might ask you to review each other's drafts ahead of time and come to class prepared with questions and comments. Before you give your draft to someone for review, try to develop some specific questions or concerns for your reviewers to address. (See the sample note that the student wrote to his reviewer on page 553). Identifying specific issues will help reviewers customize their feedback to meet your needs as they read.

You might also spend time in class reading your drafts aloud and sharing feedback. A very successful technique that doesn't require much expertise but yields great results is for the writer to read her paper aloud, pausing every paragraph or two for the listener to summarize. This checks clarity, helps the writer better imagine her audience, and gives the reader practice summarizing. Reading your writing aloud or hearing someone else read it may be unnerving at first, but it can be a tremendously helpful way to detect confusing sentences, grammatical errors, or just an awkward tone. We hope you'll keep an open mind about such a useful exercise and be willing to try new strategies throughout the writing process.

When reviewing a draft, a smart place to start is simply to share your perspective as the reader. Writers need to know how their ideas are coming across, whether their points make sense, where their argument falls apart, and what the reader is confused about. Often the best thing you can do is to serve as an "ignorant" reader. You can point out questions that writers didn't consider, identify gaps in their reasoning, challenge their assumptions, and help them see where a reader might stumble. Essentially, you can give them a peek inside the mind of their audience so that they realize why readers might cringe over an insensitive comment, laugh at a lame example, or think of something they overlooked.

You might have noticed that we haven't yet said anything about helping with grammar. You might be tempted to pick the proverbial low-hanging fruit of misspellings, punctuation problems, and grammar errors, but remember, these are later order concerns that you'll want to save for editing. **Early on in the process, try to concentrate on global or higher order concerns that will help the writer revise.**

In fact, one of the best things you can do for a writer, rather than nitpick or criticize, is to talk about what you *appreciate* about a paper, what you think is really working well. Again, dig deeper than saying things like "nice job." Tell the writer *why* you think something works well for her intended audience and purpose, and suggest ways for her to build on that success.

Responding as a reader helps to adjust your expectations, both as a writer and as a reviewer, for how useful peer review will be. As an ignorant but curious reader, you really can't say something wrong or do harm (unless you're being downright mean, of course). You are the reader, and the writer needs to hear what you think and how you experience the text. To see examples of reader response comments, consult the peer review sample in Appendix C.

Responding with Questions

It's particularly useful to ask writers stimulating questions that help them discover what is and isn't working in a draft.

What is your purpose? Ask the writer what he is trying to achieve, and tell him what you perceive as his main points (You can say something like "I think what you're getting at is _____. Is that what you're trying to say, or am I missing something?"). This summary can help the writer see whether his message is coming across as intended.

Who is your intended audience? Talk to the writer about the audience he has in mind and why this audience is a good fit. Think about the background of these potential readers—their values, their experience, their knowledge—and talk about how they might respond to the writer's message. You can ask the writer why he thinks his writing style, analysis, examples, and so forth will work for this particular audience. Often, a writer forgets to think about his audience's perspective, so you can help him imagine that reader.

What questions do you have for me about the ideas presented? Tell the writer how you understand his arguments, saying something such as "So, what I hear you saying is . . ." or "Overall, I'm left with the impression that _____. Is that right?"

Discuss any questions you have about the overall message, share your opinion on the issues presented, suggest other examples that might fit, and help the writer think more carefully about his ideas.

Is the organization working? Ask the writer why he organized his points in this way, and identify any places where you became confused, sidetracked, or lost. To help the writer transition between his ideas more smoothly, you can ask "What is the connection between these two points? How are they related? What do they have in common?"

What is significant about this issue? Ask the writer why his argument matters, why his readers should care. Sometimes, writers assume that the importance of an issue is obvious, but readers wonder, *so what?* You can help a writer identify the significance of his position by raising questions such as "What are the broader implications of this idea?" or "Why do readers need to think about this topic?" or "What other concepts does this controversy relate to?"

Responding with Helpful Comments

All in all, you want to facilitate a *conversation* with the writer, not just search for grammatical errors. Remember, during this stage, your purpose is to critique and to help, not to edit. Be careful, though, not to overwhelm writers by giving them too much feedback. Instead, focus and prioritize your comments. Here are additional examples of helpful comments that offer a reader's perspective:

- "This section of the paper confused me because . . . It is not clear what you mean by . . ."
- "This argument may have more impact if you first start with your own experience, and then incorporate research and statistics."
- "I completely agree with your argument. The issues you raised related to _____ are important because . . ."
- "I see what you're saying about _____, but what kinds of evidence do you have to support that claim?"

- "I'm having a hard time seeing the significance of what you're saying. Can you tell me more about why this is important?"

Feedback during Editing

The kind of response that's needed while drafting and revising is usually quite different from what writers need when editing. Reader response is a good place to start and will remain useful throughout the writing process, but it keeps the reviewer in the driver's seat. As you develop as a writer—and especially as you gain more control with and become more deliberate about adapting your writing process—take the wheel by asking your reader for particular kinds of response. During the editing stage, you can ask your reviewers questions such as:

- How does the writing "sound"? Is the tone appropriate?
- Are there any sentences that are confusing, awkward, or otherwise unclear?
- Are there any word choices that are vague, confusing, or overly technical?
- Where can the writing be more concise? Where can I reduce unnecessary wordiness?
- Where should I combine or divide sentences?
- Where can I add more personality, through humor or vividness or other stylistic devices?
- Where do you see mistakes, such as missing commas, subject-verb agreement problems, or misspellings?

Accepting and Rejecting Advice

As we've said, the right kind of feedback can help you develop your writing expertise. But responding to criticism is not easy. Sometimes you will hear conflicting advice from different readers. At other times, you will disagree with a reader's suggestions. In both cases, you have to make decisions about how to revise. When deciding how to implement changes based on feedback, you should keep in mind that **scholarly writing is public writing**. Unlike writing that you may do simply to express your feelings or to record experiences for yourself, scholarly writing prioritizes the readers' needs, reactions, and preferences over your own. As they say in retail, "The customer is always right." If several reviewers give you similar feedback, then they're probably right—even if you disagree. Keep in mind that it's more important for your readers to understand and be moved by your message than it is for you to keep a potentially unclear sentence, example, or style that you love.

Different cultures place different values on complex, ambiguous expression—the kind you might find in poetry or fiction. Unless you're writing literature, scholars and professionals in the US typically expect writers to express themselves clearly so readers can expend less effort to interpret intended meaning. In some other cultures, writers expect readers to do much more work: to draw subtle linkages, to fill in gaps, to think of examples, to know the source of famous quotations, and so forth. But, in Western writing, you'll typically have to do these things for your readers. This is why you need to add explanations or explicitly state your meaning when readers miss the point, even if the meaning seems obvious to you.

However, that isn't to say that you should just blindly take every piece of advice you're given. In cases of conflicting or questionable suggestions, for example, you should consider the source. Think carefully about the reliability and skill level of the reader and the impact or cost of making recommended changes. You might even want to get a second opinion from a trained writing tutor or your instructor. The most important thing is to be thoughtful and strategic about revision—just as you should be during every stage of the writing process, knowing that good writing is all about good choices.

Collaborating Effectively

Collaboration skills have become essential in nearly every workplace. As a scholarly apprentice, you can learn effective strategies for group brainstorming by participating actively in class discussions or by visiting with your instructor during office hours. By using the techniques for peer review that we've discussed, you can also learn how scholars give and receive feedback on drafts.

Perhaps the most daunting kind of collaboration involves writing with others. At its best, group writing can help you create projects that you could not possibly write by yourself. But if you've ever done group work before, you probably know how frustrating it can be when things go wrong.

Here are some strategies to ensure a more successful and less stressful experience when writing with others:

1. **Plan ahead.** As soon as you get your assignment, meet with your group to develop a detailed, written plan for how you want to accomplish the project. Think carefully about how you will organize your time to give adequate attention to discovery, drafting, revision, and editing. Create a timeline with milestones to mark your progress, and allow extra time in case something goes wrong, like a group member getting sick.

2. **Decide on roles for your group members.** Most groups either write together, delegate tasks, or use some combination of methods. If it's convenient for members of the group to meet, either physically or online, then writing together can be a good technique, especially during the planning stage when many heads can be smarter than one. Drafting and revising can be accomplished together by using online tools, such as wikispaces or shared online documents. Many writers find it easier to take turns when drafting together to avoid tripping over each other in the same document. If you can find a time and place to meet together with a big screen or projector, group editing can be lively and help to achieve a consistent style.

Another common technique is delegated collaboration, which assigns different tasks to team members, usually based on their expertise and interests. One approach is to break the project into chunks; members each investigate and draft a portion that interests them the most.

Alternatively, you can assign someone who's good at research to take a leadership role for that portion of the assignment and let those who are best at drafting and editing lead those efforts. You should also consider assigning a project leader to manage communications and deadlines and generally keep everyone on track.

Delegated collaboration can be more efficient than writing together, but this technique sometimes misses the opportunity for *synergy*—when collaborators create something better than the sum of their efforts. (This book, for example, is immeasurably better because we wrote most of it together.)

However you decide to collaborate, it's a good idea to begin by discussing goals for what each participant wants to get out of the experience: A good grade? Better understanding of course content? More experience with leadership, editing, or organizing a group project? Fun? Not everyone approaches assignments the same way, and you can help boost motivation and trust by trying to help each other achieve your goals—even when they're different for everyone on the team.

3. **Establish rules and expectations for your group.** Most collaboration horror stories result from disagreements among members or group members acting inappropriately. Collaboration is complicated. You cannot completely avoid problems, but you can minimize their negative effects by agreeing up front to some rules and expectations for how you will work together. Here's a checklist of questions to consider before you begin writing:

- How will the group make decisions when circumstances change (as they inevitably will)?

- How will the group handle missed deadlines or substandard work?
- How will you deal with a group member who doesn't pull her weight?
- How will the group respond to a member who's too bossy?

Another issue that's worth settling in advance is project evaluation. Many students cringe at the idea that their grade might be affected by other students' performance. If this is a problem for your group, ask your instructor if he wants—or will accept—separate evaluations for each member of the group. If so, then you could devise a system to document each member's contributions. Settle on criteria in advance (for example, level of effort, quality of work, collaboration performance). When the project is complete, everyone should complete a self-evaluation and peer evaluations for each group member. Realize, though, that it's difficult to weigh collaborative contributions accurately and that everyone will inevitably contribute at different levels.

Any time and effort that you devote to thinking about "what ifs" before you start writing will help you to avoid problems later. We recommend writing down your group's answers to the questions above, along with any others you can think of, in a shared document. You can begin the group conversation by asking each other: What strategies have you used in the past to make group projects work well? What problems or difficulties did you have?

Appendix B
Templates for Organizing Arguments

Research Article

The research article, also known as a scholarly paper, is somewhat different from the research papers you may have done before, when you used library sources or the Internet to learn about a topic. You'll write some of those papers in college, too, especially as an apprentice, but as you develop as a scholar you may begin to conduct research like scholars do, to enlighten the community of scholars. You might, for example, research a medieval poet or battle that no one else has studied before. Or you may investigate a very specific environmental or genetic cause of Parkinson's disease. In either case, you will likely report the results of your research to other scholars in a recognizable genre containing the following elements, along with a title page:

1. **Abstract**, which summarizes the investigation so that readers can quickly preview the article. When reviewing previous research, scholars often sift through stacks of sources by scanning article abstracts.
2. **Introduction**, which engages the reader, establishes the significance of the research (why it's needed), and states the problem or research question.
3. **Research (or "literature") review**, which synthesizes what other scholars have already said about the topic so that readers understand the subject's history and its theoretical foundation. Along

with the introduction, the research review establishes the *so what?* for the research question.

4. **Methods**, which explains the process used to answer a research question or to study a problem (for example, methods used to collect and analyze data). Typically, authors aim to provide enough information so that readers see their methods as valid and reliable.

5. **Results**, which reports and tabulates the data and results gathered through investigation. This section often uses figures and charts to report data. (Sometimes scholars report large quantities of data in a separate *Appendix* at the end of an article.)

6. **Analysis/Discussion**, which presents and makes sense of the findings. Although not necessarily the longest, this section is usually the most meaty—full of analysis, interpretations, and applications—and therefore often the most important part of the research paper. When readers trust the methods and results, they often skim ahead to the analysis and discussion—like peeking ahead to find out how the story ends.

7. **Conclusion**, which synthesizes the discussion, identifies the larger significance and implications of the findings, and/or raises questions for further research.

8. **Bibliography**, which gives credit to other authors and directs readers to other relevant sources. Sometimes called a References or Works Cited page, this section identifies the sources that informed and validated the author's work.

The research article is an appropriate structure for most research papers, especially for papers that showcase *primary source* data (collected through experiments, interviews, surveys, etc.). This format also works well for assignments that ask for portions of a research paper but don't require the whole kit and caboodle. The general structure of the research article can be adapted to fit different assignments and rhetorical situations.

A Research (or "Literature") Review

This genre typically contains four main sections: Introduction, Research Review, Conclusion, and Bibliography. Professors assign research reviews when they want students to summarize, analyze, and synthesize prominent research on a topic. Research reviews help scholars understand and analyze what others have already said about a subject and then identify a research area, topic, or question that has not been fully explored.

A Research Proposal

This genre typically contains an Introduction, Research Review, Methods, and Bibliography. Scholars write research proposals to pitch research projects that they have designed. They describe the experiments or research plans they would conduct to collect data and answer a research question. Often, the purpose of the proposal is to secure funding, support, or approval for a project, so scholars give readers an overview of their plans. A research proposal is a specific kind of *proposal argument* that offers or presents plans to solve an unanswered question or problem.

Proposal Argument

1. **Problem**

   a. Describe the problem.
   b. Explain why it deserves our attention.

2. **Potential solution(s)**

   a. Present one or multiple solutions, along with the costs and benefits of each.
   b. Remember that doing nothing about the problem is also an option.

3. **Justification**

    a. Explain how and why your proposed solution will work.

    b. Describe why the advantages will outweigh the costs or drawbacks.

    c. Convince readers that your solution is better than alternative fixes.

    d. Reference previous similar solutions that suggest similar positive outcomes.

index